Justice In Communist China

Justice in Communist China:

A Survey of the Judicial System of the
Chinese People's Republic

Shao-chuan Leng

Professor of Government and Foreign Affairs
University of Virginia

1967
Oceana Publications, Inc.
Dobbs Ferry, New York

To
Alice and David

CONTENTS

Foreword

It is an honor to present Dr. Leng's book, *Justice in Communist China,* which is the first overall survey of the judicial system of the Chinese People's Republic.

The appearance of the book is timely indeed. Profound changes in official policies toward Communist China are in the air, and, although no one knows just when these changes will come, one thing is beyond debate: the more knowledge we can acquire about this huge land and numerous people the better. And no field of knowledge is more relevant than the legal, for in a country's judicial system are distilled and crystallized many of its most significant attitudes, values, and beliefs touching the goals of society, the place of the individual, and his relation to the state.

It is hoped and believed that this volume will be found useful not only by lawyers and legal scholars, but also by government officials, students of political systems, and indeed all persons who share the conviction that achieving a sound basis for relations with Communist China is one of the most urgent tasks ahead, and that the beginning point must be accurate knowledge of the kind this book has been designed to supply.

Arthur Larson
Rule of Law Research Center
Duke University

September 1966

Introduction

The emergence of the People's Republic of China as a dynamic and totalitarian state has had a powerful impact on world politics. To understand how seven hundred and fifty million Chinese are ruled by the Communist regime is a matter of crucial importance. We cannot expect to have an adequate understanding of the monolithic system in China without some knowledge of the Chinese legal structure, one of the instruments utilized by the Communists to wield total control over the population and to facilitate a sweeping transformation of the socio-economic order.

This book is intended to be an introductory survey of the development, organization, and functioning of the judicial system in the Chinese People's Republic. Its focus is on the judicial pattern rather than on the law. It discusses not only formal institutions and rules but also such extra-judicial organs and methods as are relevant. Substantive laws are treated only within the context of the administration of justice.

The volume is divided into two major parts. The first part deals with the historical evolution of "people's justice" from the late 1920's to the present. The second part covers the machinery and procedures by which justice is administered and disputes are resolved on mainland China. The "people's courts," the procuracy, the police, the lawyers, and other participants in the judicial process are all examined.

In order to have a clear perspective of Communist China's judicial system, it is necessary to set our discussion in proper historical and ideological frames of reference. As a point of departure, we shall outline the concepts of law and justice in Communist theory and Chinese heritage.

Communist Ideology Communist jurisprudence which provides the philosophical foundation of "people's justice" in China stresses the class nature of law and its subordination to political dictates. As viewed by Marx and Engels, legal institutions are parts of the superstructure on an economic base; they are tools of class rule, designed to promote the interest of the ruling class.[1] Lenin also said: "Law is a

---

[1] Karl Marx & Frederick Engels, *Selected Works*, Moscow, 1958, Vol. I, pp. 49, 362, 623-625; Vol. II, pp. 493-495.

political instrument. It is politics."[2] In his official interpretation of Soviet legality, Andrei Y. Vishinsky defined law as the totality of the rule of conduct, reflecting the will of the dominant class and enforced by the coercive power of the state to secure and develop social relations and social orders desirable and advantageous to the dominant class. Socialist law, he asserted, "is entirely and completely directed against exploitation and exploiters. . . . It is invoked to meet the problems of the struggle with foes of socialism and the cause of building a socialist society."[3]

True to Marxist-Leninist dogmas, Mao Tse-tung and other Chinese Communist spokesmen have made similar comments on legal questions. According to Mao, the courts, the police, and the army are instruments with which one class oppresses another, and such state apparatus must be strengthened to consolidate the People's Democratic Dictatorship in China.[4] In the words of Chou Hsin-min, a prominent Chinese jurist, the socialist law of China is "a sharp weapon for carrying out class struggle in the hands of the broad masses of laboring people led by the proletariat." Its primary task is to suppress the enemy, protect the revolutionary order, and insure the success of socialist construction.[5]

One significant point which should not be overlooked in our analysis of the ideological base of the Chinese Communist juridical structure is Mao Tse-tung's emphasis on the unity of theory and practice. In an essay on practice written 1937, Mao had this to say:

> What Marxist philosophy regards as the most important problem does not lie in understanding the laws of the objective world and thereby becoming capable of explaining it, but in actively changing the world by applying the knowledge of its objective laws. . . . Knowledge starts with practice, reaches the theoretical plane via practice, and then has to return to practice. . . . The knowledge which enables us to grasp the laws of the world must be redirected to the practice of changing the world, that is, it must again be applied in the

---

[2] John N. Hazard, "The Soviet Legal Pattern Spreads Abroad," *University of Illinois Law Forum*, Spring 1964, pp. 278-279.

[3] Andrei Y. Vyshinsky, *The Law of the Soviet State* (trans. Hugh W. Babb), New York, 1948, p. 50. For scholarly discussion of Soviet law, see Harold J. Berman, *Justice in the U.S.S.R.*, New York, 1963; John N. Hazard, *Law and Social Change in the U.S.S.R.*, London, 1953; George C. Guins, *Soviet Law and Soviet Society*, The Hague, 1954; "Law and Legality in the USSR," *Problems of Communism*, Vol. 14, No. 2, March-April 1965.

[4] Mao Tse-tung, *On People's Democratic Dictatorship*, Peking, 1951, pp. 16-17.

[5] "Law Is a Sharp Weapon of Class Struggle," *Jen-min jih-pao* (People's Daily), Peking, October 28, 1964.

practice of production, in the practice of the revolutionary class struggle and revolutionary national srtuggle, as well as in the practice of scentific experimentation. This is the process of testing and developing theory, the continuation of the whole process of knowledge.[6]

On the basis of this line of thinking, Mao and his followers have maintained that the theory of Marxism-Leninism must be integrated with the practice of the Chinese revolution, i.e., to apply and develop Marxism-Leninism in accordance with China's specific circumstances.[7] The Maoist principle of integrating theory and practice is reflected in the Chinese Communists' approach toward law and justice. As described by former President Tung Pi-wu of the Supreme People's Court, the "people's democratic legal system" is a product of many years' practical experience gained through application of Communist doctrine and the Soviet model to the concrete conditions of China.[8]

Chinese Heritage   In his book, *Justice in the U.S.S.R.*, Professor Berman points out that Soviet law is not merely socialist law, but also Russian law and must therefore be analyzed in the context of Russian history.[9] The same can be said of the Chinese Communist legal system. To view it in a better perspective, we, too, must examine the distinct features of China's own legal heritage.

Traditionally, *Fa* (positive law) played only a supplementary role to *Li* (moral code or customary law) in Confucian China as a regulator of human behavior and social order. Although Confucius and his disciples recognized the utility of law, they insisted that the role of *Li* through moral example and persuasion was superior to the rule of *Fa* through rigid codes and severe punishment. This view is well illustrated by one of Confucius' statements: "If the people are guided by laws and regulated by punishment, they will try to avoid the punishment but have no sense of shame; if they are guided by virtue and regulated by *Li*, they will have the sense of shame and also become good."[10]

To be sure, a number of impressive and detailed codes were promulgated by the imperial dynasties of China, the most notable ones being

---

[6] "On Practice," Mao Tse-tung, *Selected Works*, New York, 1954, Vol. I, pp. 292-293.

[7] For instance, see "The Role of the Chinese Communist Party in the National War," *ibid.*, Vol. II, p. 260; Teng Hsiao-p'ing, *The Great Unity of the Chinese People and the Great Unity of the World*, Peking, 1959, pp. 8-9.

[8] Tung Pi-wu, "The Legal System of China," *New China News Agency*, Peking, September 20, 1956.

[9] Berman, pp. 171; 174.

[10] *The Analects*, Book 2, Chapter 3.

the T'ang and Ch'ing codes. They were, however, the embodiment of the ethical norms of Confucianism and were invoked only when moral persuasion and social sanction failed. Primarily penal and administrative in nature, the codified law of traditional China was less concerned with the defense of individual interests than with the protection of the social and political order.[11]

As far as the judicial system is concerned, there were in China a rather well-prescribed procedure and a hierarchical structure of institutions for administering justice. An elaborate system of appeals also existed to allow the review of sentences by higher authorities, including sometimes the emperor himself. On the other hand, adjudication and common administration were vested in the same hands on the lower administrative levels. The *hsien* magistrate, for instance, had to perform the duties of judge, prosecutor, and police chief in addition to his other functions as the head of the local government. Since the chief objective of Chinese justice was to assert the power of the state and to punish those who violated the rules of order and good conduct, the imperial judicial practice contained certain features that put the individual at a definite disadvantage. These included the presumption of the guilt of the accused, the nonexistence of defense attorneys, the use of torture for extracting confession, the analogous application of penal provisions, and the enforcement of group responsibility and group punishment.[12]

For obvious reasons, the Chinese traditionally preferred to stay away from the courts of law and considered litigation as strictly a last resort. It was customary for large areas of offenses and disputes to be handled by extrajudicial organs and procedures.[13] The clan, the guild, the village council, and other local groups usually did much to maintain peace and order by settling conflicts and imposing disciplinary

---

[11] For a comprehensive treatment of law in traditional China, consult Derk Bodde, "Basic Concepts of Chinese Law: The Genesis and Evolution of Legal Thought in Traditional China," *Proceedings of the American Philosophical Society*, Vol. 107, No. 5, 1963, pp. 375-398; Ch'ü T'ung-tsu, *Law and Society in Traditional China*, The Hague, 1961; Jean Escarra, *Le Droit Chinois*, Peking, 1936; Sybille van der Sprenkel, *Legal Institutions in Manchu China*, London, 1962.

[12] For some interesting discussion of Chinese judicial practice, see van der Sprenkel, Chapters 5-6; R. H. van Gulik, *T'ang-yin-pi-shih* "Parallel Cases from under the Pear-Tree," Leiden, 1956, pp. 52-63; Ch'ü T'ung-tsu, *Local Government in China under the Ch'ing*, Cambridge, 1962, Chapter 7.

[13] The extrajudicial organs and procedures are examined in van der Sprenkel, Chapters 7-9; Hsiao Kung-chuan, *Rural China; Imperial Control in the Nineteenth Century*, Seattle, 1960.

sanctions. In line with the spirit of social harmony and compromise, the informal means of mediation and conciliation rather than the regular legal process became the prevailing forms of dispute resolution in old China. The following words of Confucius typify the time-honored Chinese attitude: "In presiding lawsuits, I am as good as any man. But the important thing is to cause lawsuits to cease in the future."[14]

During the modern period the Chinese Nationalist government made a special effort to institute a legal system on the Western model. It promulgated in the early 1930's a complete set of new laws of the Continental type, known as the Six Codes (Organic Law, Commercial Law, Civil Code, Criminal Code, Civil Code of Procedure, and Criminal Code of Procedure).[15] It also established an independent judicial hierarchy composed of the district courts, the high courts, and the Supreme Court.

Nevertheless, there was a considerable discrepancy between juridical niceties and their actual application. For one thing, many Nationalists continued to be influenced by the Confucian heritage. Whenever certain legal provisions came into clash with traditional norms, the tendency was to disregard *Fa* in favor of *Li*.[16] For another, the Kuomintang government had merely a nominal rule of the whole country and did not exercise effective control over a large part of China. Much of its effort to implement legal modernization was foiled by warlordism, civil strife, and the Sino-Japanese war.[17] Consequently, in theory mainland China under the Nationalists had an excellent Western-oriented legal structure, but in practice she had a long way to go before the rule of law was accepted as a way of life.

Just how much is the system of "people's justice" linked to the past? To what extent is it influenced by the Marxist-Leninist ideology and the Soviet model? What is the Maoist "creative development" of socialist legality? These and other relevant questions will be discussed in this volume.

---

[14] *The Analects*, Book 12, Chapter 13.

[15] English translation of the Six Codes is available in *Laws of the Republic of China*, Taipei, 1961.

[16] For instance, a high Kuomintang official said that he would not let his wife claim a share of her deceased father's property under the Inheritance Law for fear of public disapproval. Escarra, p. 20.

[17] Even in the Nationalist-controlled area, bandits or robbers were often arrested and executed without going through formal court procedure. Franz Michael, "The Role of Law in Traditional, Nationalist and Communist China," *The China Quarterly*, No. 9, January-March 1962, p. 134.

Source Materials and Acknowledgements

In preparing this book, I have relied principally on documents, newspapers, journals, and books published in mainland China, although these materials have been checked against, and supplemented by, other sources including some eyewitnesses' accounts and personal interviews.* Admittedly, the constant changes in the Chinese experiment, the unavailability of certain relevant data, and the inaccessibleness of the mainland for on-the-spot observations are the common problems confronting me as well as many others engaged in research on contemporary China.

On the other hand, sufficient source materials are available for one to describe after careful analysis the general features of the Communist Chinese judicial system. By no means definitive, my findings and interpretations may nevertheless stimulate future studies to fill the gaps in the present volume.

It gives me much pleasure here to express my sincere gratitude to the Joint Committee on Contemporary China of the Social Science Research Council and the American Council of Learned Societies, the Rule of Law Research Center at Duke University, and the Wilson Gee Institute for Research in the Social Sciences of the University of Virginia for their generous support of my research for this book. I am also grateful to the East Asian Research Center at Harvard University and the Union Research Institute in Hong Kong for the facilities and cooperation extended to me.

Many thanks are due to Dr. Tao-tai Hsia of the Library of Congress and Mr. Anderson Shih of the Union Research Institute, who gave me invaluable assistance in gathering various materials. I am deeply indebted to a number of other friends and scholars, who read the manuscript in whole or in part and gave me the benefit of their comments. Among them are Professor Percy Corbett of Princeton, Professor Luke Lee of Duke, Professor Wallace McClure of Duke, and Professor Quincy Wright of Virginia. In particular I am indebted to Professor Jerome Cohen of Harvard Law School for his valuable suggestions and helpful criticisms. I wish also to express my special gratitude to Professor Arthur Larson, Director of the Rule of Law Research Center at Duke, through whose encouragement and sympathetic aid the publication of this book has been made possible.

* Besides a number of my interviews with former residents of Communist China, I have consulted the findings of intensive personal interviews conducted by others, particularly those by Jerome Cohen.

Part I. Historical Evolution of People's Justice

Chapter 1

Pre-1949 Development of the Communist Chinese System of Justice

Before the People's Republic of China came into being in 1949, the Chinese Communists had instituted through the years revolutionary laws and courts in areas under their control. Many features of "socialist legality" in Communist China today have their roots back in the early years of the revolution. In this chapter we shall attempt to examine the pre-1949 development of the system of "people's justice" through the following three stages: (1) the Soviet period, 1927-1934, (2) the Yenan period, 1935-1945, and (3) the post-war period, 1945-1949.

The Soviet Period, 1927-1934

As early as 1926-1927, "people's justice" began to make its appearance in Hunan province where a revolutionary peasant movement was developed by the Chinese Communists. The peasant associations of Hunan adopted during these years a series of measures to enforce land reform, reduce interest rates, abolish exorbitant levies, advance women's rights, prohibit gambling and opium-smoking, and eradicate corrupt officials and landlords.[1] In a resolution on the judicial problem passed in late 1926, the First Peasant Congress of Hunan Province called for the elimination of illegal and oppressive acts of judicial personnel and the complete revision of civil and criminal laws.[2]

As the sole authority in the countryside, the peasant associations undertook the responsibilities of exterminating banditry, maintaining peace and order, and settling internal disputes among

---

[1] *Ti-i-tz'u kuo-nei ko-ming chan-cheng shih-ch'i ti nung-min yün-tung* (The Peasant Movement in the Period of the First Revolutionary Civil War), Peking, 1953, pp. 309-380; Mao Tse-tung, "Report of an Investigation into the Peasant Movement in Hunan," *Selected Works*, New York, 1954, Vol. I, pp. 33-59.

[2] *Ti-i-tz'u kuo-nei ko-ming chan-cheng shih-ch'i ti nung-min yün-tung,* pp. 355-356.

the peasants.[3] Special tribunals at various levels were set up to try "local bullies, bad gentry, and unlawful landlords." Decisions of these tribunals were final; no appeal was allowed.[4] Methods used against the counterrevolutionary elements included humiliating parades (the accused in tall paper-hats), struggle meetings, imprisonment, and executions.[5] So ruthlessly were the landlords dealt with that a wave of terror was created in Hunan.[6] Mao Tse-tung's justification for these excesses reflected the basic spirit of the Communists' revolutionary justice in the early years:

> . . . a revolution is not the same as inviting people to dinner, or writing an essay, or painting a picture, or doing fancy needlework. . . . A revolution is an uprising, an act of violence whereby one class overthrows another. A rural revolution is a revolution by which the peasantry overthrows the authority of the feudal landlord class. . . . To put it bluntly, it was necessary to bring about a brief reign of terror in every rural area; otherwise one could never suppress the activities of the counter-revolutionaries in the countryside or overthrow the authority of the gentry. To right a wrong it is necessary to exceed the proper limits and the wrong cannot be righted without the proper limits being exceeded.[7]

Violence and radicalism also characterized the Hai-lu-feng* Soviet of 1927-1928. During the course of the uprisings in 1927, the Communists allowed the peasants to maltreat and execute the counterrevolutionaries at will.[8] In November 1927 the Hai-feng Soviet Government was formed and it committed itself to the policies of "confiscation of land," "improvement of workers' life," and "extermination of local bullies and bad gentry."[9] Under the Soviet system, governments at all three levels, *hsien* (county), *ch'ü* (district), and *hsiang* (township) had judicial committees or officials to handle litigation and to try the counterrevolutionaries.[10]

---

[3] Mao Tse-tung, pp. 23, 44, 54-55.

[4] Yang Ch'i, "A Preliminary Discussion of the Development of the People's Criminal Law during the New Democratic Stage, "*Fa-hsüeh* (Jurisprudence), Shanghai, No. 3, 1957, p. 40.

[5] *Ibid.;* Mao Tse-tung, pp. 35-39.

[6] Mao Tse-tung, p. 26.

[7] *Ibid.,* p. 27.

* A district of Kwangtung province.

[8] Shinkichi Eto, "Hai-lu-feng—The First Chinese Soviet Government (Part 2)," *The China Quarterly,* No. 9, January-March 1962, pp. 166, 169.

[9] Chung I-mou, *Hai-lu-feng nung-min yün-tung* (The Peasant Movement in Hai-lu-feng), Canton, 1957, pp. 82-84.

[10] The Hai-feng Soviet government had a judicial committee of nine men; each ch'ü government had a judicial committee of five men; each hsiang

According to a Communist source, some 1,822 landlords were executed within a few months.[11] At the anti-counterrevolutionary meetings, even women were aroused to kill the condemned landlords with spears before the applauding masses.[12]

Following the establishment of a revolutionary base by Mao Tse-tung in Chingkangshan in October 1927, Soviets were formed in Kiangsi, Hunan, Fukien and other provinces. With slogans of "down with the local bullies" and "redistribution of land," the Communists carried out a violent rural revolution throughout the Soviet areas.[13] In the early years of the Soviets, there was no central authority nor any stable legal order. Terror and excesses against the landlords and counterrevolutionaries became a marked feature of the revolutionary justice. The Central Executive Committee of the Chinese Soviet Republic later admitted, in its instruction No. 6 of December, 1931, that Soviet authorities at various levels had committed quite a few mistakes in the past in their suppression of counterrevolutionaires.[14] Among these mistakes were arbitrary arrest without sufficient evidence, corporal punishment at trials, and forced confessions through torture. The local Soviets were urged by the CEC to establish quickly a revolutionary order to give the lives and rights of the toiling masses "full protection."

The formation of the Chinese Soviet Republic in November, 1931, united the red areas under one central government and subsequently brought into being a number of Soviet laws and a system of "people's courts." The Constitution, adopted on November 7, 1931, by the First National Soviet Congress, designated the Soviet Republic as a "democratic dictatorship of the proletariat and peasantry"; and set for her the goals of establishing this dictatorship throughout China, destroying all remnants of feudalism, freeing the country from the yoke of imperialism, improving the living conditions of the workers and peasants, guaranteeing the

---

government had a judge. *Hai-lu-feng Ch'ih-huo-chi* (A Record of Red Calamities in Hai-lu-feng), Canton, 1932, pp. 76-77.

[11] Chung I-mou, p. 93.

[12] *Ibid.*, p. 102.

[13] See Wang Po-yen, *Ti-erh-tz'u kuo-nei ko-ming chan-cheng shih-ch'i ti nung-ts'un ko-ming ken-chü-ti* (The Rural Revolutionary Bases in the Period of the Second Revolutionary Civil War), Shanghai, 1956, chap. 2.

[14] Text of the Instruction is in *Ch'ih-fei fan-tung wen-chien hui-pien* (A Collection of Red Bandit Reactionary Documents), compiled under the sponsorship of General Ch'en Ch'eng, 1935, Vol. 5, pp. 1609-1612.

emancipation of women, and abolishing all burdensome taxation and miscellaneous levies.[15] In accordance with these goals, some basic laws were enacted between 1931 and 1934, i.e., Land Law (1931), Labor Law (1931), Marriage Regulations (1931), Marriage Law (1934), and Regulations for Punishing Counterrevolutionaires (1934).[16]

A provisional judicial system for the Soviet Republic was established by the Central Executive Committee's Instruction No. 6 of 1931 and Temporary Regulations on the Organization and Procedure of Judicial Departments of 1932. It was further regularized later by the Organic Law of Local Soviets of 1933 and the Organic Law of Central Soviet of 1934.[17] At the top of the judicial hierarchy stood two organs, both under the jurisdiction of the Central Executive Committee. One was the Supreme Court; the other was the People's Commissariat of Justice within the Council of People's Commissars. The Supreme Court was composed of a president, two vice-presidents, a chief procurator, a deputy chief procurator, and a number of judges and procurators. It had three separate chambers, criminal, civil, and military, each headed by a chief.

At the various local levels, there were judicial departments (ts'ai-p'an pu) under the provincial, county, district, and municipal executive committees. The provincial judicial departments were subordinate to the Central people's Commissariat of Justice in works regarding administration and to the Supreme Court in matters pertaining to investigations and trials. Judicial departments of all levels set up criminal courts, civil courts, and, if necessary, circuit courts to adjudicate cases. They also had within their structure judicial committees to discuss and study problems of administrative or judicial nature. Each judicial department was composed of a director, one or two deputy directors, and several judges and procurators. The primary function of the procurators was to investigate and prosecute criminal cases.

In addition to the judiciary organs mentioned above, the Chinese

---

[15] English text in Victor A. Yakhontoff, *The Chinese Soviets,* New York, 1934, pp. 217-221, checked against the Chinese text in *Hung-chi chou-pao* (Red Flag Weekly), No. 25, December 4?, 1931, pp. 2-7.

[16] Chinese texts in *Ch'ih-fei fan-tung wen-chien hui-pien,* Vol. 3, pp. 922-927; Vol. 5, pp. 1342-1356, 1594-1602, 1629-1635. Translations of the Land and Labor Laws are available in Yakhontoff, pp. 221-235.

[17] For the texts of these two Organic Laws, see *Ch'ih-fei fan-tung wen-chien hui-pien,* Vol. 3, pp. 682-691, 725-793.

Soviet Republic had certain special courts and quasi-judicial institutions. The Military Courts, whose own hierarchy culminated in the central judiciary, were established in the Red Army to try its personnel as well as inhabitants in war zones. The Labor Courts, formed by the municipal judicial departments, handled cases involving violation of labor laws and regulations. The Comrades' Adjudication Committees and the Mass Adjudication Meetings, organized by the Workers' and Peasants' Inspectorates for individual cases, performed educational functions and enforced discipline in various enterprises and organizations. Finally, there was the powerful State Political Security Bureau directly under the supervision of the Council of People's Commissars. This Bureau, together with its subbureaus or representatives in local governments and military units, was charged with the responsibility of detecting and suppressing the organization and activities of the counterrevolutionaries.

As prescribed by the Central Executive Committee's Instruction No. 6 of 1931, Organs of the State Political Security Bureau had the power to make arrests, conduct preliminary hearings, and initiate legal proceedings in counterrevolutionary cases but it was still the Judiciary that held the sole authority of trying and deciding all cases. Except under extraordinary conditions, a death sentence must be approved by a superior judicial organ and arrest could be made only with the consent of an organ of the State Political Security Bureau.[18]

Apparently in response to the increasing threat of the Kuomintang, the Judicial Procedure of the Chinese Soviet Republic, which was promulgated in April 1934, made several important changes[19] Local judicial departments and counterrevolutionary-suppression committees were now given the right to arrest, try, sentence, and even execute all types of criminals. Organs of the State Political Security Bureau, besides retaining the authority of arrest and preliminary hearing, were permitted to take whatever emergency measures were needed against enemy agents and counterrevolutionaries in border areas or on the front. The new Judicial Procedure also established the two-trial system. All cases

---

[18] Articles 1-5. At the time of uprisings, the revolutionary masses would have the right to take direct action against the local bullies, landlords, and others. Article 6.

[19] Text of this Procedure is available in *Ch'ih-fei fan-tung wen-chien hui-pien*, Vol. 5, pp. 1613-1616.

could be appealed only once; the decision of the court of second instance was final. A third trial might be held, however, if a procurator protested the judgment after two trials.

The primary task of the Soviet judiciary, needless to say, was to protect the "socialist" order against class enemies and counter-revolutionaires. A constant struggle was waged against the landlords, Nationalist agents, Reorganizationists, Social Democrats, Troskyites, and members of the A-B League.[20] On April 8, 1934, the Central Executive Committee promulgated the Regulations for Punishing Counterrevolutionaries.[21] The list of offences in these Regulations covered a wide range of crimes against Soviet rule or the Soviet political and economic structure. The principle of analogy was incorporated in Article 38: "All the counterrevolutionary crimes not included in these Regulations shall be punished according to similar crimes specified in these Regulations."

One serious problem in judicial work was the shortage of qualified personnel in the Soviet areas. By the People's Commissariat of Justice's own admission, directorship of many a judicial department at the district level was concurrently assumed by the head of another department and the provincial and county judicial departments were often too understaffed to exercise effective supervision over the work of the lower levels.[22] Related to this problem was the failure of certain judicial organs to observe Soviet laws and regulations. In some cases, corporal punishment and torture were still used by the judiciary. In others, trials were not held in public but in private offices of judicial directors.[23]

Among the measures employed by the Soviet authorities to cope with these problems and irregularities was the organization of "short training classes" to train judicial cadres. For a period of two weeks or ten days each, these classes were conducted by the central and provincial governments respectively.[24] Their curriculum included study of the laws and courts, discussion of judicial experience and techniques, and analysis of current political and

---

[20] For instance, Mao Tse-tung described this struggle in his report before the Second National Soviet Congress in 1934. Yakhontoff, p. 261.

[21] Text of this Regulation is available in *Ch'ih-fei fan-tung wen-chien hui-pien*, Vol. 5, pp. 1629-1635, also in *Shih-sou Collection* (General Ch'en Ch'eng's private collection of Chinese Communist documents relative to the Kiangsi Soviet period), 008.542/2837.

[22] The People's Commissariat of Justice, *Directive on the Work of Judicial Organs*, June 1, 1933, pp. 8-9, *Shih-sou Collection*, 008.548/3449.

[23] *Ibid.*, pp. 7, 9.

[24] The People's Commissariat of Justice, *The Work Plan for 5 Months (August-December)*, July 20, 1933, p. 4, *Shih-sou Collection*, 008.548/1027.

economic issues.[25] Another step taken by the Communist regime was to instruct judicial officials repeatedly that they should investigate and study each case carefully and do their best to collect relevant evidence. They were by orders prohibited from using torture or corporal punishment.[26] This ban of the "feudalistic and barbarous" practice, boasted Mao Tse-tung in 1934, constituted a move of historical importance on the part of the Soviet courts.[27] A few other features and practices of the system of "people's justice" are described in the following paragraphs.

Class justice The Chinese Soviet government frequently made it plain that "people's justice" must be administered from a class viewpoint. According to the Central Executive Committee's Instruction No. 6 in 1931, distinction should be made in the class elements and between the principal offenders and accomplices when dealing with the counterrevolutionaries. In other words, all the counterrevolutionary elements from landlord-gentry, rich peasant, and capitalist backgrounds as well as the principal instigators must be punished severely (including death penalty), while all those from the ranks of workers, peasants, and the toiling masses as well as the accomplices must be treated with leniency (Art. 7). A similar provision was contained in Article 11 of the Organic Regulations of the State Political Security Bureau (1931), which declared the class line as the criterion for the punitive policy of the Workers' and Peasants' Regime.[28] In the Regulations for Punishing Counterrevolutionaries (1934), lighter penalties were also provided for crimes committed by workers, peasants, or individuals who had performed useful service for the Soviets (Arts. 34 & 35). Illustrative were the Provisional Supreme Court's written judgments Nos. 1-3 in 1932. Not only was the social origin of the accused specifically described but the sentences were passed on the basis of the class elements and the principal-accomplice relationship. Persons of the "exploiting classes" therefore received severe punishment. So hid the principals and those who persisted in falsification without repentance.[29]

---

[25] A list of courses offered in the training class of the Kiangsi Provincial Judicial Department is in *Ts'ai-p'an hui-k'an* (Judicial Magazine), No. 2 (July 9, 1933), p. 2, *Shih-sou Collection*, 008.54105/1732.

[26] The Central Executive Committee's Instruction No. 6 of December 1931 and the People's Commissariat of Justice's Directive of June 1, 1933, both cited before, contained such orders.

[27] In his report to the Soviet Congress, Yakhontoff, p. 262.

[28] *Ch'ih-fei fan-tung wen-chien hui-pien*, Vol. 5, p. 1620.

[29] *Ibid.*, pp. 1656-1667.

Kung-shen (Mass trials) One of the important judicial practices to develop during the Soviet period was mass trials. Conducted by circuit courts as a rule, these trials were designed not so much for the administration of justice as for political education and indoctrination. Circuit courts became widely used only after the Land Investigation Movement was launched in 1933, when their value as a means of securing mass participation in the judicial process received greater attention.[30] Time and again in the years of 1933-1934, the Soviet authorities instructed the local judicial departments that in cases of political and educational significance circuit courts must be organized to hold mass trials in the villages of the accused for the purpose of implementing the mass line and arousing class hatred against the counterrevolutionaries.[31]

Such a trial was usually well prepared and organized. Before the trial, the court was specifically arranged to give it an air of dignity, and the case was fully publicized to attract the attendance of masses of people.[32] At the trial, anyone present could make accusations against the alleged criminal, and the latter or any others could also, at least theoretically, speak in his defense. Members of the court and people's representatives invariably took the opportunity to make political and inflammatory speeches. In the end a swift sentence was often passed and immediate execution carried out in the presence of the stimulated crowd.[33]

A couple of concrete cases may well be cited here. In July 1933 the judicial department of Ch'en-pei district (of Kiangsi) organized a circuit court to conduct mass trial of eleven "local bullies," landlords, and rich peasants who failed in their attempt to escape during the Land Investigation Movement. The masses were agitated beforehand by extensive propaganda and demanded at the

---

[30] "Circuit Courts organized by Various County Judicial Departments," *Chiang-hsi-shen ts'ai-p'an pu pan-yüeh-k'an* (The Kiangsi Provincial Judicial Department Fortnightly), No. 7 (October 1933), p. 2, *Shih-sou Collection,* 008.54105/1732.

[31] The Kiangsi Provincial Judicial Department's Directive (June 28, 1933) in *Ts'ai-p'an hui-k'an,* No. 2, p. 1; Conclusions of the Conference on the Land Investigation Drive (June 1933) in *Guide on the Land Investigation Drive, Shih-sou Collection,* 008.743/4063-3 c. 1; The Resolution of the Second Congress of Chinese Soviets (1934) in L. M. Gudoshnikov, *Legal Organs of the People's Republic,* (Trans. from Russian) JPRS (Joint Publication Research Service), No. 1698-N, 1959, pp. 8-9.

[32] *Judicial Work as Planned by the Hsin-kuo County Judicial Department,* Dec. 31, 1933, pp. 4-5, *Shih-sou Collection,* 008.548/7767.

[33] Consult the sources cited in note 31.

trial the death penalty for the accused. Amid the crowd's cries and shouts for "kill," all the eleven persons were sentenced to death and executed on the spot.[34] Also during the Land Investigation Drive of 1933, the people of Jen-t'ien district were mobilized to combat "feudalistic remnants." Within fifty-five days they uncovered 300-odd landlord and rich peasant families and executed twelve so-called "Big Tigers." In the process they organized three circuit courts and held ten mass trials.[35]

People's assessors, conciliation, and others The System of "people's assessors" was introduced to the Chinese Soviet judicial proceedings as a part of the mass line. Serving on a rotation basis, lay assessors were elected from trade unions and unions of farm laborers for the ordinary courts and from Red army soldiers for the military tribunals.[36] The principle of public trial (*Kung-k'ai shen-p'an*) was established for all soviet courts, with the exception of cases involving state or military secrets. In all cases the court decision had to be announced publicly.[37] During the Soviet period the Chinese Communists also started to use conciliation as a means to settle civil and minor criminal cases.[38] Distinctly in line with Chinese tradition, this method was later developed into one of the standard practices of "people's justice." Labor reform institutions, too, appeared under the Chinese Soviet penal system. These institutions, according to Mao Tse-tung, performed the functions of training prisoners in the Communist spirit and with labor discipline.[39] At the same time they secured income from products manufactured by prisoners.[40]

---

[34] *Ts'ai-p'an hui-k'an,* No. 2, p. 3.

[35] Mao Tse-tung, "Conclusion of the First Phase of the Land Investigation Movement," *Hung-chi* (Red Flag), No. 61 (Oct. 30, 1933), pp. 46-48.

[36] As provided in the Temporary Regulations on the Organization and Procedure of Judicial Departments in 1932, V. Ye. Chugunov, *Criminal Court Proceedings in the Chinese People's Republic,* JPRS, No. 4595, 1961, p. 2; and the Temporary Regulations on the Organization of Soviet Military Tribunals (Arts. 12-13), *C'ih-fei fan-tung wen-chien hui-pien,* Vol. 5, p. 1625.

[37] Provided by the Regulations cited above. Chugunov, pp. 2-3 and *Ch'ih-fei fan-tung wen-chien hui-pien,* Vol. 5, p. 1626.

[38] Ma Hsi-wu, "The People's Judicial Work in the Shensi-Kansu-Nignhsia Border Region during the State of the New Democratic Revolution," *Cheng-fa yen-chiu* (Studies in Political Science and Law), Peking, No. 1, 1955, p. 13.

[39] In his report to the Second Soviet Congress, Yakhontoff, p. 262.

[40] The People's Commissariat of Justice, *Directive on the Work of Judicial Organs* (cited note 22), p. 13.

The above discussion has shown that the Chinese Communists initiated a system of "people's justice" during the Soviet period by instituting legal organs and procedures with strong Russian influence. Unstable and irregular as some of its features were, the Communist judicial system reflected genuine efforts on the part of the Chinese Soviets to establish a revolutionary legal order in place of the old one. Bitter accusations and propaganda notwithstanding, even the Kuomintang authorities admitted that respect for the law and relative freedom from corruption were among the strong points of the "red bandits" of the Kiangsi Soviet.[41]

On the other hand, the Chinese Soviet period can well be described as a period of "War Communism."[42] Not only did the Chinese Communists have to wage war against counterrevolution from within but they had to resist the Kuomintang's "annihilation campaigns" from without. Under the circumstances, normal judicial procedures were often subject to overriding imperatives of security; terror and excesses became a "natural" response to revolutionary emergency and necessities. In the late spring of 1934, for instance, when the KMT's fifth campaign was posing a serious threat to the Central Soviet area, Chang Wei-t'ien called for ruthless measures in an editorial written for *Hung-se Chung-hua* (Red China). Entitled "Only Hatred and No Forgiveness toward Our Class Enemy," the editorial said:

> "The greater is the enemy pressure on the Soviet area, and the more intensive is the war, the more active the alien class elements and counterrevolutionaries become. . . . The Red Terror is our only answer to the counterrevolutionary elements. In war zones and border areas in particular, we must take the most swift action against any counterrevolutionary activity."[43]

The Yenan Period, 1935-1945

After moving their base to northern Shensi in 1935, the Chinese Communists began to modify their radical policy. This strategic shift was climaxed in the formation of a United Front with the

---

[41] *Ch'ih-fei fan-tung wen-chien hui-pien,* Vol. 3, p. 794.

[42] The period of War Communism usually refers to the years of 1917-1921 in the Bolshevik Revolution. For discussion of Soviet law in those years, see Harold J. Berman, *Justice in the U.S.S.R.*, New York, 1963, pp. 29-33 and George C. Guins, *Soviet Law and Soviet Society*, The Hague, 1954, pp. 62-64.

[43] *Hung-se Chung-hua,* No. 193 (May 5, 1934), *Shih-sou Collection,* 008.1052/2125, V7.

Nationalists in 1937. The Yenan period which lasted until the end of World War II was marked by the development of the New Democracy—moderate reforms and cooperation with all anti-Japanese forces, including the Kuomintang.

According to the terms of the United Front, the Chinese Soviet government was replaced by the Border Regions' authorities under the Nationalist regime; the legal system of these Regions was also supposed to fall within the framework of the laws and courts of the Republic of China. On some occasions, the Chinese Communists simply adopted and implemented the Nationalist laws, such as those against opium, banditry, and treason.[44] More frequently, they promulgated their own laws and regulations, which were by and large either moderate in nature or based on the principles and spirit of Nationalist codes. Among these were the Shensi-Kansu-Ninghsia Border Region Government's land Regulations (1939), Regulations on Land Ownership (1944), Regulations on the Lease of Land (1944), and Marriage Regulations (1946) as well as the Shansi-Chahar-Hopei Border Region Government's Regulations on Penalties for Corruption (1942), Marriage Regulations (1943), and Regulations on Rent, Debt, and Interest (1943).[45]

The judiciary hierarchy of the Shensi-Kansu-Ninghsia or the Shansi-Chahar-Hopei Border Region consisted of a High Court, its branch courts, and local courts or county justice bureaus.[46] Nominally under the jurisdiction of the Nationalist Supreme Court, the High Court was for all practical purposes the highest judicial organ supervising both judicial administration and trial work in the Border Region. Below the High Court were its branch courts

[44] Shansi-Chahar-Hopei Border Region Administrative Committee, *Hsien-hsing fa-ling hui-chi* (Compendium of Current Laws and Directives), 1945, Vol. I, pp. 207-214, 341-344, 370-372. See also Gunther Stein, *The Challenge of Red China*, New York, 1945, p. 285.

[45] Chinese Academy of Sciences, *Shan-Kan-Ning pien-ch'ü ts'an-i-hui wen-hsien hui-chi* (Compendium of Documents of the People's Political Council of the Shensi-Kansu-Ninghsia Border Region), Peking, 1958, pp. 59-61, 238-246, 332-333; SCH Border Region Administrative Committee, Vol. I, pp. 164-174, 313-315, 219-222.

[46] For the Organic Regulations of the High Court, Its Branch Courts, and County Justice bureaus of the SKN Border Region, see Chinese Academy of Sciences, pp. 61-65, and SKN Border Region Government, *Shan-Kan-Ning pein-ch'ü cheng-ts'e t'iao-li hui-chi* (Compendium of Policies and Regulations of the SKN Border Region), Yenan, 1944, Vol. II, pp. 96-100. For the Organic Regulations of the Courts of the SCH Border Region, see SCH Border Region Administrative Committee, Vol. I, pp. 46-52.

set up in 1943 in the prefectures. At the Bottom of the Hierarchy were local courts or, frequently in their place, justice bureaus (szu-fa ch'u) of the county governments. The Shensi-Kansu-Ninghsia Border Region had, for instance, besides the High Court and its three branch courts, twenty-nine county justice bureaus and only one local court.[47] Attached to the courts of all levels were procurators, whose duty was to conduct investigations, initiate indictment proceedings, and supervise the execution of court decisions.

As integral parts of the governments of corresponding levels, the "people's courts" accepted the leadership of political authorities. The president of the High Court was from the start elected by the People's Political Council of the Border Region, and all other judicial personnel were government appointees. Later on, judges of the justice bureaus in some important counties were also elected by the County People's Political Councils. To correct the "judicial independence" tendency, the Chinese Communists decided in 1943 to make the special commissioner of a prefecture concurrently the head of a branch High court and the county magistrate concurrently the head of a local court (or a county justice bureau).[48] Political control over the judicial work was further provided by judicial committees of the courts. Composed of party, government, and court officials, these committees had the power to discuss and decide cases of high importance.[49]

The primary task of the "people's courts" in the Border Regions, according to Lin Po-ch'ü (Lin Tsu-han), was to punish traitors, bandits, and other criminals who were harmful to the interest of the anti-Japanese United Front and the democratic system.[50] From 1938 to the end of 1943, as stated by President Lei Ching-tien of the Shensi-Kansu-Ninghsia High Court, altogether 769 political offenders were sentenced in the SKN Border Region for activities detrimental to the war, while other sentences during the same period were 370 for the smuggling, sale, and use of opium, and 174 for manslaughter and murder. In the entire period the Courts only passed 104 death sentences concerning incorrigible enemy

[47] Ma Hsi-wu (cited note 38), p. 8.

[48] Chairman Lin Tsu-han's annual report on the work of the SKN Border Region Government, January 6, 1944, in Stuart Gelder, *The Chinese Communists,* London, 1946, p. 137. For the Chinese text of this report, see SKN Border Region Government, Vol. II, pp. 25-27.

[49] Ma Hsi-wu, p. 8.

[50] In his report on the work of the SKN Border Region Government, 1939. See Chinese Academy of Sciences, p. 27.

spies and other traitors, bandits, and murderers and a few cases of embezzlement and opium smuggling.[51]

Toward the counterrevolutionary elements, the Chinese Communists' policy was one of combining repression with magnanimity. There were distinct differences between the Soviet and Yenan periods in this respect. First, during the Soviet period the term "counterrevolutionary" was used to mean all class enemies (such as the landlords and bourgeoisie) as well as anyone who did not sympathize with Communism. Now during the United Front period this term was only applicable to the Japanese aggressors, traitors, and spies. Second, in the Soviet period the Communist policy was weighted heavily on the side of repression while in the Yenan period the accentuation was on the side of magnanimity.[52] This "Yenan spirit" was reflected in Article 7 of the Program of Administration of the Shensi-Kansu-Ninghsia Border Region adopted on May 1, 1941:

> . . . With regard to traitors, except those resolutely unwilling to repent, a policy of magnanimity should be adopted towards them irrespective of their past history. Efforts should be made to convert them and to provide them with a future in politics and in livelihood. They should not be wantonly killed, manhandled, forced to give themselves up, or coerced into writing statements of repentance. With regard to such elements as renegades and anti-Communists who plot wrecking activities in the Border Region, they should be treated similarly.[53]

In dealing with thieves, robbers, and ordinary criminals, the "people's judiciary" relied mainly on the methods of political education and corrective labor. After being exposed to "right ideas and social behavior," the anti-social elements usually had their rights restored and became "useful and law-abiding" citizens. This was reported to have resulted in a sharp decrease of criminal cases. According to a report of the Shansi-Chahar-Hopei Border Region Administrative Committee, the number of ordinary criminal cases in 1940 dropped by 57% as compared with the year of 1938.[54]

---

[51] Stein, p. 287.

[52] Yang Ch'i (cited note 4), p. 43; also a statement made by Chou Hsing, Chief of the State Political Security Bureau, on October 9, 1936 in Edgar Snow, *Random Notes on Red China* (1936-1945), Cambridge, 1957, p. 43.

[53] Chinese Academy of Sciences, p. 104. A Communist writer criticizes this policy as being too lenient towards the traitors and enemy agents. Yang Ch'i, p. 43.

[54] Yang Ch'i, p. 43.

With respect to civil law cases in the Border Regions, most of them were concerned with land and marriage disputes.[55] As will be discussed later, the chief method used by the Communists in the field of civil law was conciliation. This informal method often succeeded in the resolution of disputes without lawsuits.

Among the "democratic" procedures of "people's justice" were such provisions against arbitrary arrest and detention as those contained in the Shensi-Kansu-Ninghsia Border Region's 1942 Regulations on the Protection of Civil and Property Rights.[56] Except judiciary and public security organs, no organizations or military units were allowed the right to arrest, interrogate, and punish any person (Article 7). When making arrest, the judiciary or public security organ was expected to possess sufficient evidence and to act according to legal procedures (Article 8). In case any organization, military unit, or individual other than the judiciary or public security organ arrested a culprit in the act of a crime, he, along with the evidence, should be sent within 24 hours to a procuratorate or a public security organ to be disposed of in accordance with the law. The procuratorate or public security organ which took the culprit should also examine the case within 24 hours (Article 9). Similar safeguards were provided in the Shansi-Chahar-Hopei Border Region's 1943 Decision on the Arrest, Search, Investigation, and Disposition of Ordinary and Special Criminals.[57] According to this document, only the public security organs could make arrests when approved by the appropriate "people's governments." (Article 3). In emergencies such as insurrections or wars, however, these organs were allowed to arrest and punish criminal elements without delay (Articles 4-5, 23-26).

Other "democratic" practices of the Communist judicial system included the informal and uncomplicated nature of legal proceedings, the holding of open trials, the prohibition of corporal punishment and torture, and the emphasis on evidence rather than confession.[58] As in the past, the two-trial system was also established. The county justice bureaus or local courts were courts of first in-

---

[55] Lin Po-ch'ü's statement in his report on the work of the SKN Border Region Government, 1941. Chinese Academy of Sciences, p. 89.

[56] The text is in *ibid.*, pp. 107-108.

[57] The text is in SCH Border Region Administrative Committee, Vol. I, pp. 358-364.

[58] See Lin Po-ch'ü's report in 1939 and the SKN Border Region's Program of Administration in 1941 (Art. 7) in Chinese Academy of Sciences, pp. 27 and 104 respectively.

stance, and the High Court and its branch courts were courts of second (final) instance. All capital sentences must be reviewed by a higher court irrespective of whether or not they were appealed. These sentences could be carried out only after being approved by the chairman of the Border Region Government.[59]

Probably the most prominent feature of "people's justice" developed during the Yenan period was the policy of the mass line. This policy found its expression in various forms:

On the spot trials and circuit trials   Both were designed to bring the courts into direct contact with the masses, to gather first-hand information and evidence, to settle the disputes with the aid of the local people, and to educate the masses through their participation in trial proceedings. In addition, the circuit trials were used by the higher courts to resolve complicated cases of long-standing and to supervise the work of judicial organs at lower levels.[60]

Ma Hsi-wu, the distinguished Communist jurist, gained his fame in the period under discussion for the efficiency and directness with which he used circuit trials to handle civil and criminal cases while serving concurrently as the Special Commissioner and the head of the Branch High Court of Nungtung prefecture. The most illustrative case was the one concerning Chang Po-erh of Huach'ih county. Chang, a poor man, married his sweetheart Fu Peng-erh over the objection of the girl's father. The latter appealed to the local court and had the marriage ruled invalid. The court decision caused so much agitation in the community that Ma Hsi-wu was asked to settle the dispute. After talking with the local officials, neighbors, relatives, and the girl personally, Ma called a public trial attended by the whole community. At the trial a new judgment was rendered, approving Chang's marriage with the girl in accordance with the principle of free choice of partners.[61]

System of people's assessors   First introduced into the judicial procedures of the Kiangsi Soviet, the system of "people's assessors" received a wider use in the Yenan period. It was intended to raise

---

[59] Ma Hsi-wu, p. 10.

[60] *Ibid.*, p. 11; "Decision on the Improvement of Judicial Work," SCH Border Region Administrative Committee, Vol. II, pp. 688-689.

[61] Harrison Forman, *Report from Red China*, New York, 1945, pp. 102-103. Several changes have been made to conform to the standard romanization of Chinese names. A similar case under the name of "Liu Shao-erh's Petition" is recorded in Anna Louise Strong, *The Chinese Conquer China*, New York, 1949, pp. 182-183.

the people's sense of political responsibility, to improve the quality of judicial work with popular supervision, and to broaden the scope of propaganda for laws and policies. There were three methods for selection of "people's assessors": invitation by the judiciary organs; direct election by various organizations; appointment by appropriate institutions, military units, and organizations. The last method was the one most frequently used by the Communist authorities during the war against Japan. To deal with labor discipline cases, for instance, trade unions were usually asked to appoint assessors. By the same token, women's unions would appoint jurors for marriage cases and peasant associations for land disputes.[62]

Kung-shen (mass trials) Dated from the Kiangsi days, *Kung-shen* continued to serve as a useful device for the Communists to educate the masses and to arouse their class consciousness through the people's direct participation in the administration of justice. To insure its effectivness, each mass trial was carefully guided and planned. Before it was held, steps were taken to conduct investigation, gather evidence, and hold consultations with representatives of people's organizations.[63]

There is no question that mass trials played a major role in campaigns against counterrevolutionaries and frequently resulted in on-the-spot executions of flagrant elements. At the same time, these trials were also employed in all other cases of educationanl and social importance. The trial of a witch doctor in a village near Yenan is a case in point. According to the account of President Lei Ching-tien of the Shensi-Kansu- Ninghsia High Court, the "doctor" used superstitious methods to treat a woman patient and killed her as a result. Considering the case of great social significance, the authorities decided to hold a mass trial. The session was attended by two thousand people. Both the accused and a friend of his were allowed to speak in defense. Villagers present then spoke up and reported former cases in which the accused had killed people. The crowd became furious and demanded his execution. But the "jury," composed of representatives of the local government and various people's organizations, decided on manslaughter and the judge pronounced a sentence of five years' imprisonment, the highest term provided in the Criminal code of the Nationalist Government.[64]

---

[62] Ma Hsi-wu, p. 12.
[63] *Ibid.*
[64] Stein, pp. 284-285.

Conciliation It was during the Yenan period that the Communists developed conciliation as an effective means of dispensation of civil and minor criminal cases. Conciliation by the courts and out-of-court conciliation by the people themselves were the two prevailing types used to settle disputes amicably. The latter was regularized by such documents as the Shensi-Kansu-Ninghsia Border Region Government's 1943 Regulations on Conciliation Work and the Shansi-Chahar-Hopei Border Region Government's 1942 Regulations as well as its 1944 Directives on the same subject.[65] The official reasons for reviving the traditional system of conciliation were to strengthen the unity of the people, to reduce the number of lawsuits, and to promote the increase of agricultural production. As a rule, parties in a dispute first called upon neighbors, relatives, or members of mass organizations to mediate for them. If no reconciliation was reached, then they turned to the local governments of various grades for conciliation. In their work to effect a reconciliation, conciliators must function within the frame work of laws and customs. They were expected to study the dispute carefully and to use persuasion rather than compulsion to achieve their objectives.[66]

Ma Hsi-wu once again was a central figure in instituting a mass movement to popularize conciliation throughout the Border Regians. He was affectionately called by the people as the "Blue Sky" *(Ch'ing-tien)* for the clarity and justice of his exemplary reconciliations.[67] The mass movement resulted in steady increase of the use of conciliation during the war years. This may be seen from the number of cases conciliated by the courts in the Shensi-Kansu-Ninghsia Border Region. In 1942 only 18% of all civil cases were settled by conciliation but in 1944 the figure rose to 48%; in 1942 only 0.4% of minor criminal cases were resolved by mediation but in 1944 the figure increased to 12%.[68]

Judging from all this, it seems clear that the Chinese Com-

---

[65] For texts of these documents see SKN Border Region Government, Vol. II, pp. 266-270, and SCH Border Region Administrative Committee, Vol. I, pp. 319-329.

[66] The Border Regions also started to form commissions of arbitration under the county governments to resolve disputes concerning rent and interest. As different from mediators, the commissions of arbitration had compulsory authority and their decisions were binding. See "Directives on the work of the Commissions of Arbitration (1942)," SCH Border Region Administrative Committee, Vol. I, pp. 179-182.

[67] Stein, p. 289. See also Forman, p. 102.

[68] Ma Hsi-wu, p. 13.

munists during the Yenan period made marked progress in developing judicial organs and procedures. The experience gained through those years undoubtedly had long-range significance. Nevertheless, even the Communist authorities were ready then to admit the existence of certain practical problems and unsatisfactory conditions in their judicial system. First of all, the law codes of the Border Regions were quite incomplete. The lack of some rules and clear-cut standards was responsible for the fact that the people's rights and interests were sometimes trespassed against, while the unlawful elements escaped punishment.[69] Secondly, there was a shortage of trained judicial personnel. Many of the Communist judicial cadres had little experience or competence to meet the requirements of their work.[70] Thirdly, there was still a tendency in the Border Regions to give insufficient attention to the administration of justice. Some cases were allowed to drag on and others were just handled carelessly.[71]

To meet the existing problems in the judicial field, a number of steps were proposed or undertaken by the Chinese Communists. 1. One of the most urgent tasks outlined was the drafting of civil and criminal codes as well as codes for legal procedure according to the spirit of the revolutionary *San Min Chu I* and the New Democracy.[72] Also a suggestion was made for selective publication of such Nationalist laws as were suitable to the conditions of the Border Regions.[73] 2. Local courts and justice bureaus were instructed to study concrete cases of the past, sum up trial experience and principles, and send these examples to the High Court for distribution among the various judicial organs.[74] 3. Instructions were given to court officials to clear accumulated cases, eliminate unnecessary litigations, guard against arbitrary arrest and detention, and facilitate the increase of production through corrective labor.[75] 4. Judicial cadres were told to investigate the minute

---

[69] See Lin Po-ch'ü's statements in Chinese Academy of Sciences, p. 89, and Gelder, p. 137.

[70] Hsieh Chüeh-tsai, "Report of the Standing Committee of the People's Political Council of the SKN Border Region," Chinese Academy of Sciences, p. 197.

[71] *Ibid.*

[72] *Ibid.*

[73] Hsieh Chüeh-tsai's statement in Chinese Academy of Sciences, p. 197.

[74] Lin's Statement in Gelder, p. 138; "Instructions on the Improvement of Judicial Work, 1944," SKN Border Region Government, Vol. II, p. 273.

[75] "Circulars on Judicial Work and the Production Movement, 1944," SCH Border Region Administrative Committee, Vol. II, pp. 692-693.

details of all cases, work closely with the people, and make full use of the legal devices of the mass line. Special attention was drawn to Ma Hsi-wu's dictum that "Three old peasants are equal to a local judge."[76] 5. The strengthening of both political and legal education was urged for the cadres in the judicial field. It was also suggested that judges and other judicial officials be selected from those who were faithful to the New Democratic revolution.[77]

The Post-War Period, 1945-1949

The post-war period witnessed the complete breakdown of the United Front and an all-out struggle for power between the Kuomintang and the Communists. At first the Communist leaders seemed to be interested in the idea of a coalition government and talked much about political democracy and the rule of law. In a report to the People's Political Council of the Shensi-Kansu-Ninghsia Border Region in April 1946, Lin Po-ch'ü pointed out that in order to continue the development of democracy it was necessary to see the judiciary try cases independently, subject only to the law, and the procurators prosecute private citizens and civil servants alike for any illegal acts.[78]

However, with the resumption of the large-scale civil war in 1946, the Chinese Communists once again adopted the policy of violent revolution to overthrow the Nationalist government. Support of the revolutionary struggle and punishment of "war criminals," counterrevolutionaries, and enemy agents, accordingly, became major tasks for the organs of "people's justice" during this period. In a declaration issued by the People's Liberation Army on October 10, 1947, General Chu Teh ordered the arrest, trial, and punishment of the "war criminals" headed by Chiang Kai-shek and the confiscation of all their properties and "bureaucratic capital."[79] The proclaimed policy in dealing with the "war criminals" was to "punish the principal offenders, pardon those who were forced to join in counterrevolutionary activities, and reward those who have established merits." No leniency was to be given

---

[76] "Order concerning the Execution of the Resolution for the Improvement of the Judicial System, 1944," *ibid.*, pp. 686-687.

[77] Lin Po-ch'ü's annual report on January 6, 1944, Gelder, p. 139.

[78] Chinese Academy of Sciences, p. 294.

[79] "The Declaration of the Chinese People's Liberation Army," *Mu-ch'ien hsing-shih ho o-men ti jen-wu* (The Current Situation and Our Tasks), edited by Liberation News Agency, Hong Kong, 1949, pp. 9-10.

to the major "war criminals" or to counterrevolutionary elements with "heinous crimes." Every effort would be used to bring them to justice, and there would be no prescription to limit the right of prosecution in such cases.[80]

As a special device to win mass peasant support in the struggle against the Kuomintang, the Chinese Communists in the meantime undertook to renew their original program of land confiscation and redistribution. The Outline of the Land Law of October 10, 1947 formally sanctioned the replacement of the feudal and semi-feudal agrarian system with that of "land to the tillers." (Article 1). It also provided for the confiscation of the landlords' as well as the rich peasants' properties without compensation (Article 8). Village peasants' organizations were designated as the basic executive organs to carry out agrarian reform (Article 5), and "people's tribunals" as the *ad hoc* judicial organs to punish the enemies of the land policy (Article 13).[81] As a result, a ruthless class war was waged in the countryside and even the interests of the middle peasants were infringed upon in what was later labelled "left deviations" committed by local cadres.[82] To correct this extreme tendency, the Communist leaders in 1948 called for a moderate approach and an alliance with the middle peasants; nevertheless, redistribution of land and harsh treatment of the landlords and rich peasants were still continued in many of the "liberated areas."[83]

In the enforcement of land reform and punishment of "despots" and counterrevolutionaries, the class justice as adminiistered by special people's tribunals usually took the forms of mass trials, struggle meetings, and accusation rallies. Carefully planned and skillfully manipulated by party cadres, these revolutionary judicial devices of the Kiangsi days became powerful weapons in the post-war period to mobilize the broad masses against the landlords, "war criminals," and other hostile elements. During the spring of 1946,

---

[80] *Ibid.,* pp. 10-11. The question of prescription is mentioned in "Circulars Concerning Standards for Determining Punishment in Important Cases," North China People's Government, *Fa-ling hui-pien* (Collection of Laws and Directives), Peking, 1949, Vol. 1, pp. 182-183.

[81] The text of this Law is in *Mu-ch'ien hsing-shih ho o-men ti jen-wu,* pp. 14-19.

[82] Liao Kai-lung, *From Yenan to Peking,* Peking, 1954, p. 68.

[83] Chao Kuo-chun, *Agrarian Policy of the Chinese Communist Party,* 1921-1959, Bombay, 1960, pp. 78-80, 86, 90-91. It should be noted that at the end of 1947 the Central Committee reissued the two documents of the Kiangsi Soviet days (1933) on the classification of the status of various rural classes. *Ibid.,* p. 79.

for instance, one district of North Kiangsu alone organized more than 12,000 "anti-traitor" and "anti-despot" meetings with the participation of some two million people.[84] Violence and terror often went hand in hand with such struggle meetings and mass trials. In some cases, the accused were manhandled or even killed by the enraged "victims."[85] In others, they were sentenced to death and executed on the spot.[86] The use of torture and corporal punishment was also reported.[87]

Speaking before the Cadres' Conference of the Shansi-Suiyuan Liberated Area on April 1, 1948, Mao Tse-tung admitted that in the course of the recent fierce land reform campaign not only many landlords and rich peasants had been unnecessarily put to death but even a number of working people had been wrongfully killed by the bad elements of the rural areas who seized the opportunity for personal revenge.[88] In a speech on the problems of the agrarian reform on January 12, 1948, another Communist leader, Jen Pi-shih, also referred to the practice of corporal punishment, indiscriminate killing and beating as matters of serious concern. Continuation of such practices, he warned, might isolate the Party from the masses and adversely affect the productive labor force in the countryside through the loss of many innocent lives.[89]

As the civil war progressed, the Chinese Communists steadily scored victories over the Kuomintang and rapidly expanded their areas of control in China. Along with new administrative machinery, "people's courts" were set up in the "liberated areas" to enforce the revolutionary order. The structure of these courts was regional in nature, and there was no central supreme judicial organ except for the overall control by the Party. As a rule, the "people's courts" were organized into a two-trial and three-level system. The judiciary hierarchy in North China in 1948 was a good example.

---

[84] Lo Pin-sun, *Su-pei chen-hsiang* (The True Picture of North Kiangsu), 1947, p. 150.

[85] Jack Belden, *China Shakes the World,* New York, 1949, pp. 182-185; Pei Yu-ming, *O lai-tzu Tung-pei nu-kung ying* (I Came from the Slave-Labor Camps in the Northeast), Hong Kong, 1954, pp. 47-50.

[86] Anna Louise Strong, *The Chinese Conquer China,* New York, 1949, pp. 185-187; Huang Chiao, *Hsieh-hsing szu-i* (Four Blood-stained Counties), Hong Kong, 1953, pp. 25-29.

[87] Various types of torture used by the Communists are described by a refugee in Ma Ts'un-k'un, *Chung-kuo ch'ih-se nei-mu* (Inside Red China), Taipei, 1950, pp. 40-43.

[88] *Mu-ch'ien hsing-shih ho o-men ti jen-wu,* p. 89.

[89] *Ibid.,* pp. 70-71.

It consisted of three grades of "people's courts": (1) county or municipal courts, (2) provincial or directly-controlled municipal courts, and (3) the North China People's Courts. Each court, as in the past, had a judicial committee composed of judges, administrative officials, and representatives of people's organizations to discuss and examine highly important cases.[90] A similar court structure was also in effect in the Northeast, where "people's courts" began to be organized as early as 1946.[91]

To operate the "people's courts" in the newly "liberated areas," the Communist authorities used a large number of their judicial cadres from the Border Regions.[92] However, neither in quantity nor in quality were these cadres adequate to meet the demands of a huge country that was rapidly falling under Communist control.[93] Confronted with this shortage of trained legal personnel, the Communists found it necessary to retain some judicial officials of the Kuomintang regime, particularly in the cities. At the county level, they usually combined in one person the chairmanship of both the "people's government" and the "people's court."[94] Steps, too, were taken to organize training classes for judicial cadres with a view toward preparing more competent personnel to undertake the new tasks in the legal field.[95]

A corollary to the establishment of new "people's courts" was the liquidation of the laws of the Koumintang by the Communists. In his statement on the current situation on January 14, 1949, Mao Tse-tung listed the abolition of the Nationalist constitution and the old legal system as two of the eight conditions for peace.[96]

---

[90] For the organization of the people's courts in North China, see North China People's Government, *Fa-ling hui-pien*, Vol. I, pp. 11-12, 179-180, 184-185.

[91] Professor Chu An-ping's account of *Kwan-cha* (Observer), as reported in *The China Weekly Review*, January 14, 1950, p. 113.

[92] Ma Hsi-wu, p. 13.

[93] This inadequacy was clearly admitted by the President of the Peking Municipal People's Court in 1949. Secretariat of the Peking Municipal People's Court, *Jen-min szu-fa kung-tso chü-yü* (Illustrative Examples of People's Judicial Work), Peking, 1950, p. 7.

[94] Gudoshnikov, p. 22.

[95] Tung Pi-wu's report on the work of the North China People's Government. See North China People's Government, Vol. I, p. 213.

[96] The text of Mao's statement is in *Chiang ko-ming chin-hsing tao-ti* (Carry out the Revolution to the Successful End), Shanghai, 1949, pp. 18-22. An explanation for the decision to abolish the Kuomintang's legal system was given by the New China News Agency on February 14, 1949. *Ibid.*, pp. 24-28.

In a directive issued in February 1949, the Central Committee of the Chinese Communist Party abrogated the Six Codes of the Kuomintang and prescribed the principles of justice for the "liberated areas." "Work of the people's judiciary," it stated, "should not be based on the Kuomintang's Six Codes but should be based on new people's laws."[97] Following this directive, the People's Government of North China published on April 1, 1949 a detailed instruction to abolish the Nationalist Codes and all reactionary laws. As explained by the instruction, the laws of the Kuomintang were designed to preserve the domination of the feudal landlords, compradors, bureaucratic bourgeoisie and to suppress the resistance of the broad masses of people; consequently, only through the total destruction of the old laws could the new laws be developed successfully.[98]

In performing their judicial functions, the "people's courts" were told to guide themselves by the programs, laws, orders, regulations, and resolutions promulgated by the "people's governments" and the People's Liberation Army as well as by the policy embodied in the New Democracy.[99] While a unified system of law was lacking for the "liberated areas" as a whole, regional administrative authorities did issue directives and provisional regulations to provide some form of legal order. These directives and regulations usually covered wide areas of subjects ranging from policy and organizational matters to public security and judicial work.[100]

It should be noted that with the complete victory in sight and in an apparent move to allay many people's fears, the Chinese Communists took steps in the latter part of the civil war to check the revolutionary excesses and reoriented their policies toward moderation. The directives on agrarian reform issued during 1948-1949 by the Central Committee as well as by the regional Party organs were discernibly mild in nature, safeguarding the interest of the middle peasants and giving special attention to the program of rent and interest reduction.[101] The proclamation of the People's

---

[97] Ma Hsi-wu, p. 14.

[98] For the text of this instruction, see North China People's Government, Vol. I, p. 181.

[99] Stated in both the directive of the Central Committee of the CCP in February 1949 and the instruction of the People's Government of North China on April 1, 1949.

[100] For instance, see laws and regulations contained in North China People's Government, Vol. I and in *Shang-hai chieh-fang i-nien* (One Year after Shanghai's Liberation), Shanghai, 1940, Part III.

[101] See Chao Kuo-chun, pp. 79-89 for same detailed discussion.

Liberation Army signed by Mao Tse-tung and Chu Teh in April 1949 promised protection to the life and property of every individual, except the "war criminals," and to all privately-owned factories, stores, banks, warehouses, vessels, wharves, etc., except those controlled by "bureaucratic capital."[102] A policy directive issued in 1949 by the North China People's Government contained the following provision for the protection of human rights and democratic freedom: "The people shall enjoy without interference freedom of speech, publication, assembly, association, belief, travel, and change of domicile; they shall also have guarantees for the safety and freedom of their person. Except judicial and public security organs carring out their duties according to the law, no other organs, military units, groups, or individuals may arrest, imprison, try, or punish any person."[103]

Along the same line, Communist authorities in the "liberated areas" proceeded to regulate court procedures and to prohibit, at least in principle, corporal punishment and indiscriminate killing. The Shanghai Municipal People's Court, for instance, promulgated on August 11, 1949 the provisional regulations on civil and criminal procedures. Characterized by their brevity, these regulations had provisions for mediation, appeal, public trial, "people's assessors," the right of defense, the withdrawal of judicial officials, the information service of the court, etc. "In rendering judgment," Article 10 of the regulations stipulated, "special attention must be given to the collection of all possible evidence and the combination of investigation and analytic work on the case."[104] Several regulations on judicial procedures and general principles of law were also published by the North China People's Government during the period of 1948-1949. One of them pointed out that the purpose of punishment was to educate and reform criminals and was not to seek revenge nor to humiliate and torture the offenders.[105] Another required that all death sentences passed by

---

[102] The text of the proclamation is in *Chung-kuo jen-min chieh-fang-chün ju-ch'eng cheng-ts'e* (The Chinese People's Liberation Army's policy on Entering Cities), Hsin-hua she, 1949, pp. 44-46. Compare it with "Directive on Protection of Newly-Liberated Cities," (Northeast Bureau, CCP, June 10, 1948), in *ibid.*, pp. 37-43.

[103] North China People's Government, Vol. I, p. 7.

[104] For the text of these regulations, see *Shang-hai chieh-fang i-nien,* Part III, pp. 13-16.

[105] The leading counterrevolutionaries, however, must be punished severely. "Circulars Concerning Standards for Determining Punishment in Important Cases," North China People's Government, Vol. I, p. 182.

lower courts be sent to the North China People's Court for review and to the Chairman of the North China People's Government for final approval.[106]

As during the Yenan period, conciliation was an important procedure of the "people's judicial system" for settling civil disputes and minor criminal cases. In some "liberated areas" of North China, for example, over 70 per cent of the civil cases were reportedly resolved by conciliation.[107] Although recourse to conciliation was not a pre-condition for litigation, the common practice seemed to be that only after efforts to reach an informal settlement failed would a case be brought to court for a decision. Conciliation usually was undertaken either by the disputants' relatives, friends, and neighbors along with local cadres or by the conciliation commissions set up by the village and *ch'ü* governments. If necessary, even a case already brought to a county court could be conciliated in any of the following ways: (1) conciliation by the court itself; (2) out-of-court conciliation by persons trusted by the disputants; (3) conciliation by judicial officials and local people at the place where the dispute occurred.[108]

Conclusion

In contrast with the Bolsheviks, the Chinese Communists had been engaged in the revolutionary struggle for more than twenty years before their seizure of state power. During these years they had been drawing upon both the Soviet experience and, to a lesser extent, the tradition of China to develop legal institutions and procedures in response to the "objective" conditions of the revolution. To be sure, developments thus far were of an experimental nature, and a complete judicial system still lay in the future. On the other hand, the Chinese Communists had undoubtedly accumulated considerable

---

[106] "Circular Order on the Establishment of the System of Review in Criminal Proceedings," *Ibid.,* p. 184. Art. 19 of the judicial procedures of the Shanghai People's Court required the review of all death sentences by the Military Control Committee of Shanghai.

[107] "Decision on the Conciliation of Civil Disputes," North China People's Government, Vol. I, p. 186. In a report made in February 1949, Chairman Tu Pi-wu of the North China People's Government pointed out that marriage disputes contstituted more than 60 per cent of the civil cases in North China. "Report on the Work of the Government," *Ibid.,* p. 213.

[108] "Decision on the Conciliation of Civil Disputes," p. 186.

experience in legal work through the long period of experimentation, and certain basic features of the system of "people's justice" had also taken shape by 1949.

There is little doubt that the Soviet model had been the chief source of inspiration for the Chinese Communist judicial structure. Both in theory and in practice, the latter bore many imprints of Russian influence. It embraced the Marxist-Leninist-Stalinist concepts of law and functioned mainly as a tool to remold the society and to suppress class enemies. At times, "people's justice" was dispensed through the regular process participated in by the courts, the procurators, and "people's assessors." At others, it was done through the summary proceedings of revolutionary tribunals and public security organs. The alternation of procedures was determined not only by the nature of the cases but also by the relative intensity of the revolutionary struggle in a given time.

During the periods of large-scale civil wars between the Chinese Communists and the Kuomintang (1927-1934 & 1945-1949), the accent of the Communist policy was to wage a ruthless class struggle against landlords, counterrevolutionaries, and other hostile elements. In this context violence and terror often became the pattern of "people's justice." During the Yenan period when a united front was formed against Japan, there was a marked shift toward the soft line as exemplified by Mao Tse-tung's New Democracy. In the legal field moderation and "Maoist creativity" had a number of concrete manifestations. These included the stress on "democratic" procedures and guarantees, the adoption of the policy of combining repression with magnanimity toward criminals, the development of "mass line" devices in judicial work, and the wide use of the time-honored method of conciliation for handling civil cases.

All told, considerable efforts had been made by the Chinese Communists to build a socialist judicial system prior to their 1949 victory. Evolving under the unsettled conditions of revolutionary strife, the system in question understandably had many gaps and irregularities. Nevertheless, it provided the foundation for future legal development in the People's Republic and offered significant clues to the basic character of "people's justice." Two major features in particular may be cited here, both reflecting varying degrees of Soviet and traditional influence. One was the use of legal instruments primarily for enforcing the policy of the state rather than protecting the rights of the individual. The other was the special role given to extrajudicial organs and procedures in imposing sanctions and settling disputes.

Chapter 2

People's Justice Under the Common Program

On the eve of the founding of the People's Republic of China in the fall of 1949, the Chinese People's Political Consultative Conference (CPPCC) adopted three basic laws: the Common Program, the Organic Law of the Central People's Government, and the Organic Law of the CPPCC.[1] As a form of provisional constitution, the Common Program provided the fundamental frame of reference, while the two Organic Laws presented detailed blueprints of the formal structure of the new government.

The era of the Common Program, 1949-1954, was one of internal consolidation and reorganization. In many respects it resembled the early years of the Soviet regime in Russia, when the notorious Cheka and revolutionary tribunals enforced the Red terror to smash the hostile classes and to establish the new order. During the Common Program period, a uniform, nation-wide system of "people's courts" was being developed in China. At the same time special "people's tribunals" and public security organs (the police) often carried out massive purges in implementing the Peking regime's Land Reform, Three-Anti, Five-Anti, and Suppression of Counter-revolutionaries Movements.

Development of the Court System

In line with the policy of the Chinese Communist Party, Article 17 of the Common Program declared the complete abolition of the laws and courts of the Nationalist government: "All laws, decrees and judicial systems of the Kuomintang reactionary government oppressing the people are abolished and laws and decrees protecting the people shall be enacted and the people's judicial system shall be set up." Articles 26 and 27 of the Organic Law of the Central People's Government provided the organization of the Supreme People's Court and designated it as the highest judicial

---

[1] Texts of these three documents are in *Chung-yang jen-min cheng-fu fa-ling hui-pien* (Compendium of the Laws and Regulations of the Central People's Government), 1949-50, Vol. 1 (Peking, 1952), pp. 1-12, 16-25.

body, responsible for directing the work of all judicial organs throughout the country.

Following this, the regime proceeded to establish gradually the "people's courts" at various levels on the basis of the experiences accumulated in the old "liberated areas" and the judicial practice of the Soviet Union.[2] The first step was to organize the Supreme Court and its branches as well as the provincial and municipal courts. The second one was the establishment of the "people's courts" at lower levels.[3] In the meantime, the Law Codification Committee of the Central Government had been preparing draft regulations on judicial organization since the spring of 1950. These regulations were discussed at the First National Judicial Conference in the summer of 1950, and were finally adopted in 1951, after "numerous revisions" by the Central People's Government Council, as the "Provisional Organic Regulations of People's Courts in the People's Republic of China."[4]

Under these regulations, a three-level, two-trial system was set up for the "people's judiciary." The three levels were county courts, provincial courts, and the Supreme People's Court (Article 2). The last two levels were also empowered to organize branch courts to meet specific needs (Articles 26 & 32).[5] As a rule, the county courts were courts of first instance, and the provincial courts were courts of second instance. Trial at the court of second instance should be final. Under unusual circumstances, however, the first or third trial might be the final one (Article 4). The occasional suspension of the right of appeal was officially justified as a means to "effectively suppress counterrevolutionary activities and prevent cunning elements from taking advantage of the two-trial system to delay the settlement of a case."[6]

[2] Shen Chun-ju, "Report on the People's Court," *China Weekly Review,* Shanghai, July 8, 1950, p. 107.

[3] L. M. Gudoshnikov, *Legal Organs of the People's Republic of China,* (Trans. from Russian) JPRS (Joint Publication Research Service), No. 1698-N, 1959, pp. 28-34.

[4] Hsu Te-heng, "Explanatory Report on the 'Provisional Organic Regulations of the People's Courts of the People's Republic of China'," *Jen-min jih-pao* (People's Daily), Peking, September 5, 1951. Hsu was the Acting Chairman of the Law Codification Committee.

[5] It should be noted that these articles were concerned with the ordinary courts. To be established separately were such special courts as military courts and "people's tribunals." The text of the Provisional Regulations is in *Chung-yang jen-min cheng-fu fa-ling hui-pien,* 1951, pp. 79-85.

[6] Hsu Te-hsing's report in *Jen-min jih-pao,* September 5, 1951.

According to these regulations, public (open) trials were to be conducted in all cases except those which the law required to be tried secretly (Article 8), and important cases in all courts were to be heard by a collegium of three judges (Articles 15 & 23).[7] Certain practices of the mass line, too, were incorporated into the judicial procedure, i.e. circuit trials, on-the-spot investigations, and on-the-spot trials (Article 7). There was a rather general provision calling for the instituting of the system of "people's assessors" if the "nature of the cases to be tried is appropriate for the system." In such situations the "people's assessors" would have the right to participate in the investigation and consideration of the cases under trial and to make suggestions (Article 6).[8]

The Communist authorities made no pretense of having an independent judiciary free of political control. There were, in fact, frequent references to the subordinate status of the courts. In a report to the First National Committee of the CPPCC in 1951, Shen Chun-ju, the first President of the Supreme People's Courts, declared: "People's governments at various levels must strengthen their leadership over people's courts."[9] Article 10 of the 1951 Provisional Regulations described the "people's courts" of all levels as organic parts of the "people's governments" of the corresponding level. The same article also put the court under a "dual control": vertical control by a higher court and horizontal control by a government council of the same level.

From the standpoint of the Peking regime, the "people's courts" were no more than a useful instrument to implement its policies and enforce its control. In trying criminal and civil cases, said Article 3 of the 1951 Regulations, the courts were to "consolidate the People's Democratic Dictatorship, uphold the New Democratic social order, and safeguard the people's fruit of revolution and all lawful rights and interests." "Our judicial work," in the words of Shen Chun-ju, "must serve political ends actively, and must be brought to bear on current central political tasks and mass movements."[10] Among the "central tasks" for the "people's judi-

---

[7] Hsu specified the number of judges comprising the collegium in his report.

[8] In the same report Hsu pictured the system of "people's assessors" as "essentially similar to the system of people's jury in the courts of the Soviet Union." However, he pointed out that conditions in general are not yet ripe for the universal application of this system in China.

[9] *Jen-min jih-pao*, October 30, 1951.

[10] *Ibid.*

ciary" were the resolute suppression of "all counterrevolutionary activities and the resistance of reactionary classes" and the protection of "the gains of land reform, production, reconstruction, and democratic order."[11]

The role played by the *ad hoc* "people's tribunals" in the Land Reform, Three-Anti, and Five-Anti Movements will be discussed later. It should be noted here that along with other state organs the "people's judiciary" had been instrumental in implementing the Marriage Law and suppressing the counterrevolutionaries during the era of the Common Program. Often referred to as the chief task of the courts, the struggle against the counterrevolution deserves some special attention.[12]

At the very beginning of the new People's Republic, the 1949 Common Program authorized the government to "suppress all counterrevolutionary activities and punish severely all Kuomintang war criminals and other leading incorrigible counterrevolutionary elements who collude with imperialism, betray the fatherland, and oppose the cause of the people's democracy."[13] It was not until the latter part of 1950, after the outbreak of the Korean War, that a large-scale mass movement was launched against the counterrevolutionaries. While the regime continued the policy of "combining repression with magnanimity" toward the counterrevolutionary offenders, the weight was now definitely on the side of punishment. In official directives and newspaper editorials, judicial workers were told to correct the "deviation of boundless magnanimity" and apply severe measures against the counterrevolutionaries.[14]

---

[11] Shen Chun-ju, pp. 107-108.

[12] For documents of the Suppression of Counterrevolutionaries Movement, see *Chien-chüeh chen-ya fan-ke-ming huo-tung* (Resolutely Suppress Counterrevolutionary Activities), Peking, 1951. For detailed discussion of the Movement, consult Gudoshnikov, pp. 92-102; S. B. Thomas, *Government and Administration in Communist China*, New York, 1953, pp. 108-114; Henry Wei, *Courts and Police in Communist China to 1952*, Lackland Air Force Base, Texas, 1955, Chap. IV.

[13] Article 7. *Chung-yang jen-ming cheng-fu fa-ling hui-pien*, 1949-50, Vol. 1, p. 17.

[14] See, for example, "Joint Directive on the Suppression of Counterrevolutionary Activities" issued by the Government Administrative Council and the Supreme People's Court (July 23, 1950)," *Chien-chüeh chen-ya fan-ke-ming huo-tung*, pp. 18-20; "The Government Administrative Council's Directive on the Strengthening of the People's Judicial Work (November 3, 1950)," *ibid.*, pp. 24-26; "Severely Punish Counterrevolutionary Elements," *Jen-min jih-pao*, July 24, 1950; "Thoroughly Correct the Deviation of Misinterpreting the 'Policy of Leniency,'" *ibid.*, December 26, 1950.

The campaign against the counterrevolution reached a high degree of intensity in 1951 and resulted in the promulgation of the Regulations for the Punishment of Counterrevolutionaries. These Regulations listed in detail a large number of counterrevolutionary crimes, punishable by death or life imprisonment for principal offenders and by lesser prison terms in minor cases.[15] Although Article 14 provided for the reduction or remitting of the sentence under extenuating circumstances, it did not do much to mitigate the severity of the other provisions of these Regulations. For instance, Article 18 made the Regulations retroactive to cover even "pre-liberation" activities. Article 16 contained the principle of crime by analogy: "Persons who have committed other crimes with counterrevolutionary intent that are not specified in the law shall be punished according to analogous specified crimes in these Regulations."

The scale and extent of the Suppression of the Counterrevolutionaries Movement can be seen in Shen Chun-ju's report that during the first six months of 1951 the "people's courts" had dealt with over 800,000 criminal and civil cases involving reactionaries.[16] Besides the regular courts, other judicial organs taking part in the campaign were the military courts attached to the Military Control Committees and the special "people's tribunals" operating in the countryside in connection with the land reform. For many counterrevolutionary cases, justice was carried out in the forms of mass trials, accusation rallies, and struggle meetings. Conducted often with fanfare and before huge crowds, these proceedings performed not only a deterrent function against potential opposition but a "propaganda-education" function of arousing the people's "revolutionary consciousness." In the year of 1951 Peking was reported to have held 29,600 mass trials and meetings with the participation of over 3,379,000 people; from March to July 1951 Tientsin was reported to have held 21,400 mass meetings with the participation of some 2,200,000 persons.[17]

---

[15] The text of these Regulations is in *Chien-chüen chen-fa fan-ke-ming huo-tung*, pp. 9–12. In a report to the Central Government Council on February 20, 1951, P'eng Chen, Vice-Chairman of the Committee on Legal and Political Affairs of the Government Administrative Council, pointed out that these Regulations were still based on the policy that "major criminals will be severely punished, those coerced into joining criminal activities will be forgiven, and meritorious conduct will be rewarded." *Ibid.*, p. 17.

[16] *Jen-min jih-pao*, October 30, 1951.

[17] Lo Jui-ching, "The Powerful Movement for the Suppression of Counterrevolutionaries," *Jen-min jih-pao*, October 11, 1951.

One of the irregularities of the legal system of Communist China was the lack of detailed statutes and comprehensive codes. During the period under discussion only a limited number of important laws were adopted, such as the Marriage Law (1950), the Agrarian Reform Law (1950), the Trade Union Law (1950), the Regulations for the Punishment of Counterrevolutionaries, and the Regulations for the Punishment of Corruption (1952). Although as early as 1950 there were discussions of drafting a civil code, a criminal code, a company law, regulations for judicial procedure, and others, none of them were ever promulgated by the regime.[18]

The incompleteness of laws was admitted by P'eng Chen in his report to the Government Council on May 11, 1951. He argued, however, that there should be no hurry to fix "complete and detailed" law codes which were "neither mature nor urgently necessary." In his opinion, laws should proceed gradually from simple to complex, from general rules to detailed articles, and from single statutes to comprehensive codes.[19] As a basis for judicial work, the courts were frequently told to follow the laws, orders, and policies of the government. Article 4 of the 1951 Provisional Regulations on People's Courts, for example, stated: "The adjudication of cases by the people's courts shall be based on the provisions of the Common Program of the Chinese People's Political Consultative Conference and the laws, decrees, decisions, and orders promulgated by the People's Government. Where no specific provisions are applicable, the policy of the Central People's Government shall be followed."

Another problem in the legal field was the shortage of competent and experienced personnel. To meet the needs of a large country like China, the Communists found their judicial cadres seriously inadequate in both quantity and quality. Even the selective retention of former Kuomintang officials failed to mitigate the situation. Vice Premier Tung Pi-wu pointed out in 1950 that the lack of competent cadres had caused judicial work to lag far behind objective needs.[20] Speaking before the National Committee of the CPPCC in October 1951, Shen Chun-ju conceded that the

---

[18] The preparation of those laws was discussed at the First National Congress on Judicial Work in August 1950. *Jen-min jih-pao,* September 8, 1950.

[19] Wei, p. 10.

[20] *New China News Agency,* Peking, October 7, 1950.

qualifications of judicial cadres were still below the requirements of their tasks.[21]

This shortage of qualified personnel inevitably led to the heavy accumulation of cases and maladministration of justice in many places. At the end of February 1950, the municipal court of Shanghai had 10,962 accumulated cases.[22] Before the launching of the Judicial Reform Movement of 1952, the region of East China reported a backlog of more than 155,000 cases.[23] Some judicial cadres in the Peking Municipal People's Court erroneously treated disputes over house rent in the same manner as land disputes in the countryside. Others confused the poor man's viewpoint with the class viewpoint of the proletariat in handling cases of theft and burglary.[24] Corruption, violation of the law, and "subjective judgment" without investgations were among the reported wrong-doings of the judicial officials of the Suchow Municipal People's Court.[25]

In an effort to resolve the shortage of personnel and its related problems, the Peking regime had used short training classes to prepare cadres for legal work and resorted to conciliation and arbitration devices to settle the people's disputes. While more will be discussed in connection with the Judicial Reform Movement of 1952-1953, this attempt at the improvement of judicial administration was specifically underscored by Premier Chou En-lai's directive to judicial officials on November 3, 1950. In this directive Chou stressed the importance of adopting the method of conciliation to mitigate people's disputes and the need to carry out the mass line to facilitate judicial work. For the solution of the per-

21 *Jen-min jih-pao*, October 30, 1951.

22 *Ibid.*, June 21, 1950.

23 *Chieh-fang jih-pao* (Liberation Daily), Shanghai, February 2, 1953.

24 Reported by Wang Fei-jan, President of the Municipal People's Court of Peking. Secretariat of the Peking Municipal People's Court, *Jen-min szu-fa kung-tso chü-yü* (Illustrative Examples of People's Judicial Work), Peking, 1949, pp. 11–12.

25 *Jen-min jih-pao*, August 19, 1952. The regime's concern over the defective administration of justice was reflected in the joint directive issued on October 13, 1950 by the Government Administrative Council and the Supreme People's Court calling on the judicial organs to clear accumulated cases. Item 5 of the Directive pointed out that it was necessary for judicial organs of various levels to establish a strict system of arrest and detention and a solemn concept of rule of law. *Chien-chüeh chen-ya fan-ke-ming huo-tung* (cited note 12), p. 22.

sonnel question, he urged not only the law schools of various universities to improve the content and methods of their teaching; but also the "people's governments," from the provincial level up, to help the judicial organs train new cadres and re-educate the old ones.[26]

Last but not least, it should be noted that justice in Communist China was often dispensed by administrative agencies, particularly by the police. Besides their routine duties of detecting and investigating crimes, the public security organs had the authority to impose as well as administer punishment. They were in charge of "reform through labor" institutions and had the discretionary power to extend the duration of imprisonment beyond original sentences.[26a] They were also vested by law with the power to impose "control" over certain categories of counterrevolutionary elements.[26b]

In practice, the public security organs had even a freer hand in the administration of "people's justice." Not infrequently, they disposed cases of ordinary offenders or those of serious criminals without resort to court. Indiscriminate arrest, arbitrary detention, "fatigue interrogation," corporal punishment, and wanton trial were among those common police abuses reported by both Communist and other sources.[26c] During the years under discussion many counterrevolution-

---

[26] For the text of this Directive on the Strengthening of the People's Judicial Work, see *ibid.*, pp. 24–26.

[26a] Article 62 of the Regulations on Reform through Labor (September 1954) listed conditions under which a prisoner at the end of his term may be kept by the corrective labor camp for use as manpower. *Chung-yang jen-min cheng-fu fa-ling hui-pien*, 1954, p. 40. These Regulations, of course, formalized what had already been in practice for some time.

[26b] Article 11 of the Provisional Measures for the Control of Counter-revolutionaries (June 1952). *Ibid.*, 1952, p. 54.

[26c] For Communist sources, see *Jen-min jih-pao*, August 8, 1950; *Nan-fang jih-pao* (Southern Daily) Canton, September 7, 1951; An Tzu-wen's reports on the cadres' illegal acts in *Jen-min shou-ts'e, 1953* (People's Handbook, 1953), Tientsin, 1953, pp. 178, 235; Mei Tse-jui's reference to police abuses in the early 1950's in *Hsin-hua pan-yüeh-k'an* (New China Semimonthly), Peking, No. 6, 1957, p. 20. For the accounts of refugees, ex-prisoners, and others, see Commission Internationale contre le Régime Concentrationaire, *White Book on Forced Labor in the People's Republic of China*, Paris, 1956, 2 Vols.; Mark Tennien, *No Secret Is Safe*, New York, 1952; Robert Loh, *Escape from Red China*, New York, 1962. One reputable Indian observer made the following statement: "Terror is dictatorship's most effective weapon and Communist China utilizes its power to compel submission. Concentration camps, the disappearance of people in the middle of night, suicides, public trials and public murders are a common feature of daily life." Raja Hutheesing, *The Great Peace*, New York, 1953, p. 190.

aries were obviously tried and sentenced to imprisonment or death in secret proceedings. When there were cases of important propaganda value, the public security organs then usually requested the local or municipal "people's government" to call public meetings to try the alleged counterrevolutionaries. As is well known, these meetings were no more than a form of propaganda machinery designed to inspire fear, obedience, and class hatred and to endorse government decisions against the accused. A facade of legality was provided by the judiciary which unfailingly gave formal approval to the verdicts "demanded" by the masses.

According to a newspaper account, for example, the Peking Municipal People's Government held a huge public meeting for the accusation of counterrevolutionaries on May 20, 1951. Speaking before the aroused crowd, Lo Jui-ching, Minister of Public Security, "suggested" that some 220 criminals be sentenced to death. He was followed by Mayor P'eng Chen who wound up the drama by saying: "What shall we do with such a group of beasts as these vicious despots, bandits, traitors, and special agents?" "Shoot them!" the audience shouted. "Right, they should be shot," the Mayor replied. "Following this meeting we shall hand over the cases to the Military court of the Municipal Military Control Commission for conviction. Tomorrow, conviction; the next day, execution." The crowd responded with wild applause and loud cheers.[26d]

The Role of People's Tribunals

During the Common Program era "people's tribunals" were often organized outside the regular court system to carry out nation-wide movements for social reform and to inflict severe punishment upon the enemy. Different from the permanent "people's courts" (jen-min-fa-yuan), the "people's tribunals" (jen-min fa-t'ing) were ad hoc in nature and only lasted through the duration of a given movement. As one of the major instrumentalities for wielding the power of the state, these tribunals were used extensively in the Agrarian Reform, Three-Anti, and Five-Anti Campaigns. So ruthlessly did they wage war against the "hostile classes," particularly during the Land Reform, that a reign of terror was created to remind people of the revolutionary justice of the Kiangsi days.

The introduction of "people's tribunals" was foreshadowed by

[26d] Ta-kung pao (L'Impartial), Tientsin, May 23, 1951. Detailed description of some of these public "trials" is in Wei (cited note 12), pp. 34-40.

the Agrarian Reform Law promulgated on June 30, 1950. Article 32 of the Law stated:

> In the course of agrarian reform a people's tribunal shall be set up in every county to ensure that it is carried out. The tribunal shall travel to different places, to try and punish, according to law, the hated despotic elements who have committed heinous crimes whom the masses of the people demand to be brought to justice, and all such persons who resist or violate the provisions of the Agrarian Reform Law and decrees. Indiscriminate arrest, beating or killing of people, corporal punishment and the like are strictly forbidden.[27]

On July 20, 1950, less than a month after the promulgation of the Agrarian Reform Law, the Organic Regulations of People's Tribunals were promulgated to set forth in detail the tasks, organization, jurisdiction, and procedure of the "people's tribunals."[28] According to these Regulations, the "people's governments" at the provincial level or above had authority to establish "people's tribunals" in response to practical needs and to dissolve them upon the completion of their tasks. The main duty of such tribunals was "the employment of judicial procedure for the punishment of local despots, bandits, special agents, counterrevolutionaries, and criminals who violate the laws and orders pertaining to agrarian reform . . . so as to consolidate the people's democratic dictatorship." Another task for the "people's tribunals" was "the disposal of cases involving disputes over the demarcation of land lots in the course of agrarian reform, and other matters connected with agrarian reform" (Article 1).

As a rule, the "people's tribunal" was organized with the county (*hsien*) or municipality as the unit. When necessary, branch tribunals were set up for one or more *ch'ü* (sub-county district) (Article 2). Along with its branches, the "people's tribunal" was under the direct leadership of the county or municipal government, and at the same time formed part of the "people's court" of the county or municipality. To avoid any confusion, the *People's Daily* stressed in an editorial the special character of the "people's tribunal" and its difference from the civil and criminal chambers of

---

[27] The text of the Agrarian Reform Law is in *Chung-yang jen-min cheng-fu fa-ling hui-pien*, 1949–50, Vol. 1, pp. 43–49. For its English translation, see *Supplement of People's China*, Peking, Vol. II, No. 2, July 16, 1950, pp. 3–7.

[28] The text of the Organic Regulations is in *Chung-yang jen-min cheng-fu fa-ling hui-pien*, 1949–50, Vol. I, pp. 71–72. Consult the English translation in American Consulate General, Hong Kong, *Current Background*, No. 151, January 10, 1952.

the "people's court." Ordinary civil and criminal cases should not be handled by the tribunal but should continue to be handled by the relevant chambers of the regular court.[29]

Under its Organic Regulations, the "people's tribunal" was empowered to arrest and detain people and to pass sentences of various kinds, including the death penalty. Any sentence exceeding five-year imprisonment required the ratification of the provincial government (Article 7). The presiding judge, deputy judge, and half of the judges of a "people's tribunal" were appointed by the county or municipal government; the others were elected by the local "people's representative conferences" or by mass organizations (Article 4). Judicial personnel selected by this procedure were mainly local active Party members from among the peasants. "Their engagement in the work of the tribunals," observes a Soviet writer, "consolidated the ties between the legal organs and the masses and served as a safe guarantee of the justness and soundness of a legal decision made by a tribunal of such composition."[30] At the same time it provided the regime with an opportunity to select and train judicial cadres to be used by the regular courts in the future. In a "Directive on Strengthening the Work of the People's Tribunals," the Kwangtung Provincial People's Government had this to say: "The leadership of the *hsien* and *ch'ü* levels must select, for work in the people's tribunals, a group of cadres from among the workers and peasants who are determined in their class stand, active in their work, and correct in their working style; so that after the conclusion of agrarian reform, there may be assembled for training a number of elite cadres from the tribunals who are capable of undertaking judicial duties and can be promoted for service in the people's courts."[31]

The intensity of the Agrarian Reform Movement was reflected in the rapid establishment of the "people's tribunals" throughout the country. According to an official report based on incomplete figures, during the winter of 1950 and the spring of 1951 some 977 "people's tribunals" and 3,693 branch tribunals had been set up in the East, Central-South and Southwest Administrative Regions. The same source also revealed the major role played by the "people's tribunals" in crushing the resistance of the landlords and counterrevolutionaries. Between November 1950 and April 1951 the "people's tribunals" in only 120 counties of the

[29] *Jen-min jih-pao,* July 21, 1950.

[30] Gudoshnikov, pp. 88–89.

[31] *Nan-fang jih-pao* (Southern Daily), Canton, August 23, 1952.

Center-South Region were reported to have handled 143,761 cases against the counterrevolutionaries and law-breaking landlords who tried to sabotage agrarian reform.[32]

In enforcing the revolutionary justice, the "people's tribunals" resorted to such "mass line" devices as circuit courts, mass trials, and struggle meetings. It should be noted that there were provisions for the protection of the accused in the Organic Regulations of People's Tribunals. They included the prohibition of corporal punishment (Article 5) and the guarantees of the right of defense (Article 6) and the right of appeal (Article 8). In actuality, these legal niceties were too often disregarded. At the well rehearsed mass trials, the guilt of the accused was for all practical purposes a foregone conclusion.[33] He was given no chance to speak in his own defense. Nor did anyone dare to serve as his defense counsel before the aroused crowd. Despite the legal requirement of approval by higher authorities, death sentences were frequently executed on the spot. No appeal from such sentences was permitted to "bandits, special agents, and counterrevolutionaries."[34] Under the circumstances an atmosphere of fear and terror prevailed in the countryside throughout the Land Reform Campaign. On one occasion the *People's Daily* proudly declared: "The landlords tremble at the mere memory of the people's tribunals."[35]

The system of "people's tribunals" was also instituted in early 1952 in support of the Three-Anti and Five-Anti Movements. The Three-Anti Movement (anti-corruption, -waste, and -bureaucratism) was aimed at cleansing the Party and government agencies; the Five-Anti Movement (anti-bribery, -tax evasion, -fraud, -theft of state property, and -leakage of state economic secrets) was directed against the business and commercial interests. For the former campaign, "people's tribunals" were organized in various administrative organs and military units; for the latter campaign, "people's tribunals" were set up in the cities.[36] Basically similar to their predecessors in the Land Reform, these *ad hoc* tribunals

[32] *New China News Agency,* November 14, 1951.

[33] For discussions of these trials and some concrete cases, see Wei, pp. 23–26 and Chow Ching-wen, *Ten Years of Storm,* New York, 1960, pp. 98–105.

[34] Article 8 of the Organic Regulations of People's Tribunals.

[35] *Jen-min jih-pao,* November 13, 1951.

[36] The Government Administrative Council decided on March 21, 1952 to establish the "people's tribunals" in the Five-Anti Movement and on March 28, 1952 to form the "people's tribunals" in the Three-Anti Movement. Texts of these two decisions are in *Chung-yang jen-min cheng-fu fa-ling hui-pien,* 1952 pp. 18–19, 20–21 respectively.

served as an effective instrument for the regime to mete out punishment to the "law-breaking and reactionary elements" during the two closely related nation-wide drives.

Reviewing the judicial work of Communist China in September 1952, Minister of Justice Shih Liang paid a special tribute to the major role played by the "people's tribunals" in the Agrarian Reform, Three-Anti, and Five-Anti Movements. She noted with great satisfaction the active participation of the masses in the judicial proceedings of these tribunals:

> In their work the people's tribunals, as a rule, first use criminal trials to conduct propaganda on the laws and policies of the government and to mobilize and educate the masses to denounce the reactionaries and law-breakers. Then they rely upon the help of the masses to investigate, hear, and dispose of cases. Reliance is placed on the people both in the struggle against the enemy and in the mediation of the internal disputes among the people. There are many ways in which the people's tribunals may be dependent upon the masses. In response to the needs of the mass movements, the people's tribunals often invite the relevant departments of the government as well as representatives of the interested people's organizations to participate in their work. At the same time the work is reported to the people's representative conferences to get their support. In this way, the criminals are punished and the masses are educated. Meanwhile, large numbers of workers, peasants, and women are trained to become good judicial workers. During the great Agrarian Reform, Three-Anti, and Five-Anti Movements, many excellent judges have emerged from among the workers and peasants. In Shanghai alone, 600 workers, shop clerks, and housewives have joined the work of the people's tribunals during the Five-Anti Movement. . . . The people's tribunals are also a most convenient system for the people, as they will go wherever they are needed, whether to villages, factories or mines, to save time for the laboring people and assure the speedy and correct handling of cases. . . . In uniting the leadership with the broad masses, the people's tribunals have contributed greatly to the success of the various mass movements.[37]

The Judicial Reform

The Judicial Reform Movement, which lasted officially from August 1952 to April 1953, was designed by the Peking regime to insure the political reliability of court personnel and to solidify the foundation for "socialist legality." As mentioned before, the authorities of the new people's Republic abolished the whole legal

---

[37] Shin Liang, "Achievements in the People's Judicial Work during the Past Three Years," *Chieh-fang jih-pao*, September 23, 1952.

system of the Kuomintang from the outset but were compelled to retain many of the old judicial personnel for lack of enough trained cadres to take their place. The loyalty and reliability of these former Kuomintang personnel was of course under suspicion as they tended to keep their traditional judicial concepts and practices when performing duties for the new courts. Another problem confronting the "people's judiciary" was the over-all defects in the administration of justice. As a result of deficiency of laws and judicial personnel, there were many cases of incompetence, graft, and miscarriage of justice in the operation of the "people's courts." In Wuhsiang county of Shansi province, for instance, the judicial organ exacted a confession from Wu P'u-kuei through "third degree" methods and sentenced him to death for an alleged crime he had never committed.[38] In Wen county of P'ingyüan province, two judges of the "people's court" continued a series of illegal activities, including the acceptance of bribes, for three years without being exposed.[39] In the case of the Suchow Municipal People's Court, its judicial officials were reported to have violated twenty-two women along with other wrongdoings.[40]

By the second half of 1952 the serious nature of these problems became increasingly clear to the regime through the revelations in the course of the Three-Anti and Five-Anti Movements. According to Shih Liang's report to the Government Administrative Council on August 13, 1952, the Three-Anti Movement, in particular, had exposed the serious organizational and ideological defects of the "people's courts" at all levels.[41] Out of the twenty-eight thousand judicial cadres in the country, it was estimated, six thousand, or approximately twenty-two per cent, had worked under the Nationalist regime. Most of these old personnel now served as judges in the "people's courts," especially in large and medium-sized cities. With very few exceptions, Shih Liang pointed out, these people had changed little of their "reactionary outlook." Many of them were former members of the Kuomintang, Youth Corps, and Nationalist secret police; while others were "depraved and law-violating elements." They not only abused their power to continue various criminal activities but brought with them the "old judicial concepts and style of work" to the new courts. Some

---

[38] *Kuang-ming jih-pao* (Kuang-ming Daily), Peking, September 18, 1952.
[39] *Jen-min jih-pao*, July 21, 1952.
[40] *Ibid.*, August 19, 1952.
[41] Shih Liang, "Report Concerning the Thorough Reform and Reorganization of the "People's Courts at All Levels," *Ch'ang-chiang jih-pao* (Yantze Daily), Hankow, August 24, 1952.

old Party cadres even fell victim to their "corrupting influence," thus injuring the interests of the people and national construction. In the opinion of Miss Shih Liang, the presence of the old judicial personnel and legal concepts was therefore to blame for the low esteem in which the masses held the "people's courts," and for the latter's failure to "serve actively the central political tasks of the state."[42]

Against such a background, the Chinese Communist government decided to launch an intensive, nation-wide Judicial Reform Movement. This decision was made public by the *People's Daily* on August 17, 1952 in an editorial titled "We Must Thoroughly Reform the Judicial Work." Responses from the press were immediate and enthusiastic, many in the form of signed articles.[43] The proclaimed objective of this Movement was to purge the undesirable judicial personnel, to reform the entire court system, and to liquidate the old legal concepts and styles of work.[44] More than being only concerned with the matters of reform, the Movement was also described as a "fierce political and ideological struggle" conducted on the political-legal front.[45]

To carry out the campaign, the provincial and municipal authorities were ordered to set up Judicial Reform Committees at the various local levels to be composed of representatives of the Party, mass organizations, and government and judicial organs. Under the guidance of these Committees, people of all walks of life were mobilized to join the struggle, and all the familiar procedures of "criticism and self-criticism" and "accusation and redress meetings" were brought into play in this thought-remould-

---

[42] In an effort to blame the old judicial officials for all the troubles of the "people's judiciary," Shih Liang used rather freely a number of "data" to support her argument. She claimed, for instance, that 83 per cent of the old judicial personnel employed in the T'aiyüan Municipal People's Court were former members of reactionary parties and organizations. Also in the "people's courts" of Shanghai, Nanking, Hangchow, and the whole region of South Kiangsu, about 60 per cent of ths corrupt elements were the old judicial officials. *Ibid.*

[43] As examples, see Li Kuang-ts'an & Li Chien-hui, "Liquidate the Anti-People Old Legal Viewpoints," *Kuang-ming jih-pao*, August 22, 1952; Alumni of the Department of Law, Peking University, "Letter in support of the Judicial Reform Movement," *ibid.*, August 25, 1952; Ch'en Ch'uan-kang, "The Anti-People Old Laws are Absolutely Incompatible with the People's Revolutionary Regime," *Jen-min jih-pao*, August 26, 1952.

[44] Shih Liang's report in *Ch'ang-chieng jih-pao* August 24, 1952; editorial of *Jen-min jih-pao* on August 17, 1952.

[45] "Thoroughly Carry out Judicial Reform," *Nan-fang jih-pao*, October 22, 1952.

ing and guilt-exposing mass movement. Among the old legal principles under attack were "separation of law from politics," "independence of the judiciary," and "equality of the people before the law." The official line pictured these "supra-politics" and "supra-class" principles as nothing but lies used by the reactionaries to cheat the people, incompatible with the socialist view that "law is an expression of the will of the ruling class as well as one of its instruments to suppress class enemies." Those who entertained such concepts as "attempted crime," "elapsing of prescription," "nonretroaction of law," and *"nullum crimen, nulla poena sine lege"* were also accused of giving aid and comfort to the landlords and counterrevolutionaires at the expense of public interest. Finally, the old "judicial procedures" and "legal technicalities" were condemned as the products of the Kuomintang "Book of Six Laws" designed to harass the laboring people and to perpetuate "rotten bureaucratism" in judicial work.[46]

During the course of the Judicial Reform Movement, all judicial personnel and their records were subject to public examination at the struggle meetings or mass trials. Offenses of varying degrees were exposed through confessions and accusations. Some were denounced for old legal viewpoints and working styles: others were charged with "gross injustice" and "malicious crimes." Punishments inflicted upon the guilty ones ranged from dismissal to imprisonment and summary execution. While some Communist cadres were punished in the process, it was, however, the former Kuomintang judicial officials who bore the brunt of the attack. Just how many were actually liquidated is a matter of conjecture, but the official admission was that only twenty per cent of the judicial personnel who had worked under the old regime were retained in their posts after the Reform Movement.[47]

---

[46] T'ao Hsi-chin, "On the Judicial Reform," *Cheng-fa Yen-chiu* (Studies of Political Science and Law), Peking, No. 5, 1957, pp. 12–13; "Judicial Reform," *Jen-min shou-ts'e, 1953* (People's Handbook, 1953), Tientsin, 1953, pp. 232–233.

[47] *Kuang-ming jih-pao*, August 31, 1957. Another Communist source claims that some 1,142 old judicial officials were retained for trial work. T'ao Hsi-chin, p. 15. A non-Communist writer, however, thinks that all old judicial personnel were purged in one way or another. He gives a partial list of those whose punishment was officially announced. Ch'en Shu-fang, *Chung-kung ti ssu-fa kai-ko* (The Judicial Reform of the Chinese Communists), Hong Kong, 1953, pp. 40–45. During the Judicial Reform a large number of former practicing lawyers were also purged, but that will be discussed in Chapter 7.

To fill the vacancies left by the purged judicial personnel, the Communist authorities relied upon the following sources: cadres who had served in the "people's tribunals" during the Agrarian Reform, Three-Anti, and Five-Anti Movements, veterans of the revolutionary wars from the Liberation Army, and active elements among the peasants', workers', and women's organizations.[48] Altogether more than 6,500 new personnel were reported in early 1953 to have been brought into judicial work. Of this number, about 27 per cent were women and 70 per cent were members of the Communist Party or the New Democratic League.[49]

In carrying out the Judicial Reform, the Chinese Communists also instituted and used circuit courts and conciliation committees to clear the accumulated cases and to conduct legal propaganda among the masses. Between June 1952 and February 1953, some 165,000 accumulated and new cases were disposed of in the region of East China alone. Approximately 70 per cent of these cases were resolved by conciliation, 45,960 conciliation committees were established or reorganized, and over 302,000 people actively helped the "people's judiciary" in the administration of justice.[50]

Following the conclusion of the Judicial Reform Movement, the Second National Judicial Work Conference was held in Peking in April 1953. This conference not only reviewed the achievements and experiences of the Reform, but also set forth in a resolution the future course of development for the "people's courts." Among other things, it called for the institution of a regular system of "people's assessors," the introduction of special courts to factories, mines, railroads, and waterways, and the establishment of circuit courts, conciliation committees, and people's reception offices throughout the country. To improve the personnel situation, the conference proposed specific programs to be undertaken by the central and regional political-legal cadres' schools and by the provincial and municipal judicial cadres' training classes.[51]

All in all, the Judicial Reform Movement of 1952-1953 must be considered as a land mark in the development of the judicial sys-

---

[48] Shih Liang's report on the Court Reform (cited note 41), *Ch'ang-chiang jih-pao*, August 24, 1952.

[49] New China News Agency, May 12, 1953.

[50] *Chieh-fang jih-pao*, February 1, 1953.

[51] For the text of the resolution adopted by this conference, see *Chung-yang jen-ming cheng-fu fa-ling hui-pien*, 1953, pp. 93–98. The Ministry of Justice issued on August 31, 1953 a directive concerning the implementation of this resolution. The text is in *ibid.*, pp. 99–101.

tem in Communist China. It played an important role in consolidating the Communist dictatorship, removing obstacles to the new order, and preparing the courts for future tasks in the stage of socialist construction. The significance of this Movement is well illustrated by the following statement of Miss Shih Liang:

> Through this Movement, depraved elements given to evil habits and law violations have been purged; elite worker, peasant, and women elements emerging from the various mass movements have been selected to consolidate the judicial organs of all levels: all judicial cadres have been educated to recognize further the harmful nature of the old legal viewpoints and judicial practices of the reactionary Kuomintang and to begin to form a national and legal outlook based on Marxism-Leninism and the thought of Mao Tze-tung. Moreover, the attitude of dedicated service to the people has been strengthened, and the demarcation line between the new and the old legal concepts has been clearly drawn. At the same time, through the Movement, the spirit of people's legality as possessed by the People's Tribunals has been fully demonstrated, and the new system and new working style which attract the people to take part in judicial construction have been established. All this has laid a solid foundation for the consolidation of the People's Democratic Dictatorship and the strengthening of the people's judicial work in New China.[52]

---

[52] *Chieh-fang jih-pao,* September 23, 1952 (cited note 37).

Chapter 3

Post-Constitutional Development
of People's Justice

The adoption of the Constitution in 1954 inaugurated a new period in the People's Republic of China. Having sufficiently consolidated their power, the Communists took a significant step to
launch China into the stage of socialist transformation and construction. Between 1954 and mid-1957 Communist China appeared to
be following the Soviet example toward the establishment of a stable
legal order and a permanent judicial structure. This trend, however,
suffered a serious setback in 1957-1958 when the Anti-Rightist campaign abruptly displaced the policy of liberalization. Since then, in
company with the increasingly bitter Sino-Soviet dispute, Peking has
departed sharply from the legal model of post-Stalin Russia by stress-
ing flexibility rather than predictability in the field of law.

This chapter will examine the fluctuating development of "people's justice" from 1954 to the present. Special attention will be given
to the legal debates carried on between non-Communist jurists and
official spokesmen during the "Hundred Flowers" and Anti-Rightist
Movements.

Move toward Legal Stability, 1954-1957

During the years of 1954-1957 the Peking regime closely mod-
elled its programs of industrialization and institutionalization after
Soviet patterns. For economic development, there was the first Five
Year Plan, started in 1953, to promote rapid industrialization through
concentration on heavy industry. On the legal front, there was a serious move to lead the country in the direction of stability and codification.

In an effort to generate popular support and enthusiasm for the
Constitution, the Communist regime employed an extensive propaganda campaign in 1954 to mobilize the masses to participate in
the discussion of the draft document before its official adoption.[1]

---

[1] For discussions of this campaign by authors of opposing views, see Chou
Hsin-min, "Review of the Development of Legal Science in the New China

Bearing a striking resemblance to the 1936 Constitution of the U.S.S.R., the Chinese Constitution that was promulgated on September 20, 1954 signified a shift from the arbitrary and repressive processes of the "people's tribunals" to a more orderly development in the legal life of the country. A comprehensive bill of rights, for example, was contained in Chapter III of the Constitution.[2] Among other things, it guaranteed equality before the law, freedom of speech, of the press, of association, of demonstration, and of religion, as well as the right to work, to leisure, to education, and to social assistance. Protection against arbitrary arrest was specifically insured by Article 89, which reads: "Freedom of the person of citizens of the People's Republic of China is inviolable. No citizen may be arrested except by decision of a people's court or with the sanction of a people's procuratorate." Based on this article, the Regulations on Arrest and Detention were promulgated in December 1954 to provide further safeguards in the form of concrete and detailed procedures.[3]

The Constitution, along with the Organic Laws of the People's Courts and the People's Procuratorates (September 21, 1954), also gave the judicial system in Communist China a permanent structure. Under the National People's Congress and its Standing Committee, two separate but interlocking hierarchies were established. The "people's courts," headed by the Supreme People's Court, were given the sole authority to administer justice; the "people's procuratorates," culminating in the Supreme People's Procuratorate, were to exercise the supervisory power over the execution of the law. In addition, there were within the State Council certain executive departments, such as the Ministries of Justice, Supervision, Public Security, and Internal Affairs, charged with responsibilities relative to the maintenance of law and order. Until its abolition in 1959, the Ministry of Justice and the judicial departments at local levels han-

---

during the Past Ten Years," *Cheng-fa yen-chiu* (Studies of Political Science and Law), Peking, No. 5, 1959, pp. 44-45 and Wang Hou-sheng, *Chung-kung chin-hsien p'ing-lun* (A Critique of the Making of the Constitution in Communist China), Hong Kong, 1955, pp. 61-113.

[2] Text of the Constitution is in *Chung-hua jen-min kung-ho-kuo fa-kuei hui-pien* (Compendium of Laws and Regulations of the Chinese People's Republic), Peking, Vol. I (1956), pp. 4-31. English Translation is in *Documents of the First session of the First National People's Congress of the People's Republic of China*, Peking, 1955, pp. 131-163.

[3] Text of the Regulations is in *Chung-hua jen-min kung-ho-kuo fa-kuei hui-pien*, Vol. I, pp. 239-242.

Judicial Structure of Communist China

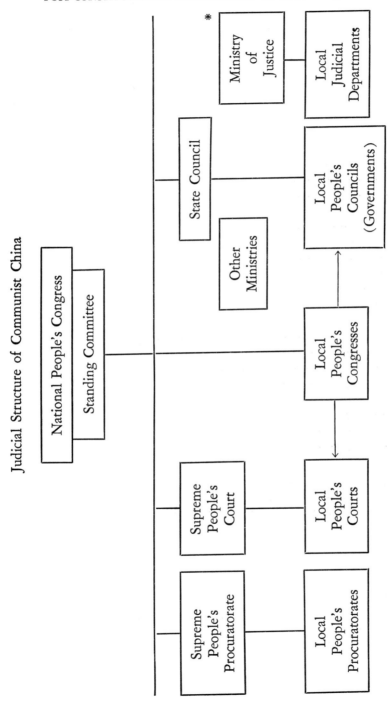

*Abolished in May, 1959.

dled matters pertaining to the staff and internal administration of the courts.[4]

A number of democratic features of the new judicial system were introduced by both the Constitution and the Organic Law of the People's Courts. These included the right of legal defense, the institution of "people's assessors," and the principles of public (open) trials and withdrawal of judges. Probably more significant was the fact that for the first time the Chinese Communists seemed to accept in a limited form the concept of judicial independence. With identical tones, Article 78 of the Constitution and Article 4 of the Organic law stipulated: "In administering justice the people's courts are independent, subject only to the law." Article 80 of the Constitution stated that the courts should be responsible to the "people's congresses" at corresponding levels and should report to them. This was in clear contrast with the previous laws which required the subordination of the courts to the leadership of the "people's governments." In other words, under the new system the courts were granted greater freedom in exercising their authority, with no interference from the local executive organs. To be sure, they were still subject to other types of control and their independence had to be a qualified one. Writing on this subject, Communist spokesmen were quick to point out that in administering justice the "people's courts" not only must obey the law but must follow the guidance of the Party, submit to the control of the people, and accept the supervision of the higher courts and the procuratorates.[5]

Following the promulgation of the Constitution and the Organic Law of the People's Courts, the Communist authorities proceeded to carry out the projected changes in judicial organizations and procedures. At the Judicial seminar of November 1954 and in a joint directive on December 7, 1954, the Supreme People's Court and the Ministry of Justice repeatedly called upon judicial workers throughout the country to study and implement the Organic Law of the courts.[6] During the years between 1954

---

[4] For the functions of the Ministry of Justice, see Articles 14, 35 and 40 of the 1954 Organic Law of the People's Courts. Text of the law is in *ibid.*, pp. 123-132. English text is in *Documents of the First National People's Congress*, pp. 185-199.

[5] Wen Wen-po, "An Understanding of the Fundamental Problems Concerning the Organic Law of the People's Republic of China," *Cheng-fa yen-chiu*, No. 1, 1955, p. 3; Wang Hui-an, "Superiority of Our Judicial System," *Jen-min jih-pao* (People's Daily), Peking, October 16, 1954.

[6] *Jen-min jih-pao*, November 27 and December 11, 1954.

and 1957, steady growth and "democratization" of the judicial system had been reported by Shih Liang, Minister of Justice, and Tung Pi-wu, President of the Supreme Court.[7] As of 1957, there existed in Communist China more than 2,700 "people's courts."[8] The number of "people's assessors" increased from 127,250 in 1955 to 246,500 in 1957.[9] Starting from scratch, the number of "people's lawyers" also reached 2,100 by 1957.[10]

The efforts made by the Peking regime to strengthen the judicial system reflected the importance it attached to the courts as useful instruments for stabilizing the new order and ensuring the socialist transformation of national economy. In their joint directive of December 1954 on the study and implementation of the Organic Law of People's Courts, the Supreme People's Court and the Ministry of Justice clearly defined the major task of the judiciary:

> The enforcement of dictatorship and the protection of democracy are the two inseparable aspects of the basic mission of the people's courts. The work of the judiciary must be made to serve the political mission of the State. During the transitional period, the judiciary's general task is to safeguard the smooth development of socialist construction and the socialist transformation of the State. The people's courts must not only punish people but also educate them. They must carry out their proper functions to serve socialist construction and the central task of the State through the medium of judicial activities.[11]

In view of the above, small wonder that many of the cases handled by the judiciary were those involving economic construction and the counterrevolutionaries. According to incomplete figures, the "people's courts" of all levels dealt with 364,604 cases of such nature between January 1954 and May 1955 alone. Along with the procuratorial and public security organs, the courts were reported to have struck severe blows to the counterrevolutionary and other criminal elements engaged in activities

---

[7] See Shih Liang's speech delivered on July 29, 1955 before the National People's Congress in *Ta-kung pao* (L'Impartial), Tientsin, July 31, 1955; her article, "The Judicial System in New China" in *People's China*, Peking, No. 12, 1957; Tung Pi-wu's speech delivered on July 22, 1955 before the National People's Congress in *Ta-kung pao*, July 23, 1955; his speech before the NPC delivered on June 25, 1956 in *Kung-jen jih-pao* (Daily Worker), Peking, June 27, 1956.

[8] Shih Liang's article in *People's China*, No. 12, 1957, p. 18.

[9] *Ibid.*, p. 17, and Shih Liang's speech in *Ta-king pao*, July 31, 1955.

[10] *Kuang-ming jih-pao* (Kuang-ming Daily), Peking, January 17, 1957.

[11] *Jen-min jih-pao*, December 11, 1954.

harmful to the program of socialist construction and transformation.[12] Just preceding the introduction of agricultural cooperativi-
zation, a new drive was launched by the Chinese Communists in
July, 1955 to liquidate the counterrevolutionaries. On July 30, in
a resolution on the First Five-Year Plan, the Second Session of
the National People's Congress called upon all state organs and
the entire population to "heighten their revolutionary vigilance
in order to uproot all counterrevolutionaries, open or under cover,
and smash all subversive activities."[13] Based on the traditional
policy of "combining punishment with leniency," this new movement was carried out with great vigor and wide publicity.[14] As a
result, numerous counterrevolutionaries were exposed and arrested,
and many others gave themselves up and confessed their guilt.[15]
In the Political Report of the Central Committee of the Chinese
Communist Party on September 15, 1956, Liu Shao-chi praised the
movement as a great success for breaking the back of the counterrevolutionaries. At the same time he urged the continuation of
the fight against internal enemies within the framework of the
law:

> Our public security organs, our procurator's offices and our courts
> must continue to wage a determined struggle against counter-
> revolutionaries and other criminals. But . . . this struggle must be
> conducted with strict observance of the law, and, in accordance with
> the new situation which obtains today, further steps must be taken
> to put the policy of leniency into practice. The Central Committee
> of the Party holds that, with the exception of a handful of criminals
> who have to be condemned to death in response to public indig-
> nation by their atrocious crimes, no offenders should be given the

[12] Shih Liang's speech before the NPC in *Ta-kung pao*, July 31, 1955.
[13] *First Five-Year Plan for Development of the National Economy of China in 1953–1957*, Peking, 1956, p. 4.
[14] A collection of press comments and reports on this movement is in "The Movement for Liquidating All Hidden Counterrevolutionaries," *Jen-min shou-ts'e, 1956*, (People's Handbook), Tientsin, 1956, pp. 342-362.
[15] Tung Pi-wu, "Report on the Liquidation of All Counterrevolutionaries" (delivered on January 31, 1956 before the National Committee of the People's Political Consultative Conference), *Jen-min shou-ts'e, 1957*, pp. 219-222. According to Chou En-lai's estimate in late 1955, more than 76,000 counterrevolutionaries had been arrested and punished since the beginning of the campaign in July 1955. Chow Ching-wen, *Ten Years of Storm*, New York, 1960, pp. 155-156. In his report to the National People's Congress on July 1, 1957, Procurator-General Chang Ting-ch'eng said that more than 190,000 counterrevolutionaries had voluntarily reported and confessed their guilt. *Ta-kung pao*, July 2, 1957.

death penalty, and, while serving their terms of imprisonment, they should be accorded absolutely humane treatment. All cases involving the death penalty should be decided upon or sanctioned by the Supreme People's Court. In this way step by step we shall be able to achieve our aim of completely abolishing the death penalty, and this is all to the good of our socialist construction.[16]

It may be noted here that the question of observing the law was frequently referred to by Communist spokesmen during the years of 1954-1957. This actually reflected two opposite trends. One was the genuine move on the part of the Peking regime to establish socialist legality; the other the persistent tendency of government workers and Party cadres to ignore laws and regulations. Some newspapers, for instance, reported the use by the courts of public notices, judgment-proclaiming meetings, and other propaganda devices to educate the people to obey the law and discipline.[17] Others cited the punishment of law-breaking officials as a reminder that there was no exception to the observance of laws by all citizens.[18] An article in *Hsüeh-hsi* (Study) took the position that the Communist Party members should be required to serve as a model for the Chinese people in obeying the law: "Party members are the vanguard of the proletarian class and have as their responsibilities the liberation of the working people, elimination of the classes, and establishment of a socialist society. As the Party is the leading force of national life, law-abiding has a special meaning for every Party member. . . . Failure to obey the law is to violate the Party constitution and the obligations of Party members. The Party demands all its members to obey the Party discipline and to set an example in observing the law. No exception can be made to anyone."[19]

Probably more revealing were writings and reports by top judicial officials with reference to the observance of the law. In an article for *Cheng-fa yen-shiu* in 1956, Ma Hsi-wu of the Supreme People's Court pointed out that some judicial personnel openly violated the provisions of the Constitution and the Organic

[16] *Eighth National Congress of the Communist Party of China*, Peking, 1956, Vol. 1, pp. 83-84.

[17] *Hsin hu-nan pao* (New Hunan Journal), Changsha, August 31, 1954; *Kuang-ming jih-pao*, August 23, 1955.

[18] *Chieh-fang jih-pao* (Liberation Daily), Shanghai, August 17 and October 17, 1954; *Jen-min jih-pao*, December 6, 1954.

[19] Ch'en Han-pai, "A Discussion of the Law-abiding Spirit," *Hsüeh-hsi* (Study), Peking, No. 7, July 2, 1954.

Law of the Courts by disregarding the legal rights of the accused in court proceedings. They even used illegal methods ranging from threats to corporal punishment to deprive the accused the rights of defense and appeal.[20] In his report to the Eighth National Congress of the Chinese Communist Party on September 19, 1956, Tung Pi-wu admitted as a serious problem the existence in China of a small number of Party members and government functionaries who did not pay attention to the legal system of the State. According to him, cases of violating the law and infringements of the people's democratic rights had been discovered in some places and departments. Accidents had occurred in factories and mines due to violations of the labor protection regulations; disputes had arisen from failure to fulfill contracts on the part of certain economic departments; proper legal procedures had not been fully observed by judicial organs; maltreatment of criminals had taken place in prisons and labor reform units. One major reason for these occurrences, Tung said, was the profound hatred in the Party and among the masses for the old system of law, which tended to breed contempt for all legal systems. It was possible, he added, that this contempt was increased by the mass revolutionary movements that swept the country in the early period after liberation, because such movements did not entirely rely on laws. He also referred to the "petty bourgeois background" of the overwhelming majority of the Chinese people as another reason for the general contempt for the legal system. For the future, however, all such law-breaking tendencies must come to an end, he stressed. As demanded by the Central Committee of the Party,

> all the laws must be strictly observed. No violations of the law should henceforth be permitted. Particularly all the judicial bodies should abide by the law more strictly. . . . We are opposed to all law-breaking practices as represented by doing work not in accordance with the laws. In future any person who deliberately violates the law must be prosecuted even if he is in a high position and has rendered meritorious service to the state. As for those who are ignorant of the laws, we must not only teach them what the laws are but also educate them to abide by the laws. To demand every one to do his work in accordance with the law is one of the chief methods to end the occurrence of violations of the laws of the state.[21]

[20] Ma Hsi-wu, "Several Problems Concerning the Current Trial Work," *Cheng-fa yen-chiu*, No. 1, 1956, p. 6.

[21] For the text of Tung's speech on the legal system of China, see *New China News Agency*, Peking, September 20, 1956.

Closely related to the question of observing the law was that of a complete legal system in Communist China. Although the Communists could boast in the mid-1950's a few important laws and regulations covering marriage, land reform, trade unions, agricultural producers' cooperatives, suppression of counterrevolution, penalties against corruption, etc., they nevertheless had to concede that "people's legality" still left something to be desired. One Chinese writer, for example, pointed out that the laws and decrees promulgated by the state were mainly in the form of provisional programs and were not "well-developed" laws.[22] Two other authors stated that there was much confusion in the Chinese legal system, resulting from the combination of vague terminology, conflicting provisions, and uncertain procedures.[23] Even Tung Pi-wu admitted in his report cited above that China was lacking in some urgently needed basic laws, such as a criminal code, a civil code, a law of procedure, a labor law, and a law of utilization of land. And many existing laws and regulations, he added, had to be revised in the light of changed political and economic conditions. The following passage from Liu Shao-chi's 1956 Political Report provided an official explanation for the absence of comprehensive codes and at the same time underlined the Peking regime's move to build up a complete legal system:

> During the period of revolutionary war and in the early days after the liberation of the country, in order to weed out the remnants of our enemies, to suppress the resistance of all counter-revolutionaries, to destroy the reactionary order and to establish revolutionary order, the only expedient thing to do was to draw up some temporary laws in the nature of general principles in accordance with the policy of the Party and the People's government. During this period, the chief aim of the struggle was to liberate the people from reactionary rule and to free the productive forces of society from the bondage of old relations of production. The principal method of struggle was to lead the masses in direct action. Such laws in the nature of general principles were thus suited to the needs of the time. Now, however, the period of revolutionary storm and stress is past, new relations of production have been set up, and the aim of our struggle is changed into one of safeguarding the successful development of the productive forces of society, a corresponding change in the methods of struggle will

---

[22] Li Ch'i, "Struggle to Strengthen the People's Democratic Legal System of Our Country," *Jen-min jih-pao*, November 6, 1956.

[23] Wen Hung-chün and T'ang tsung-shun, "Strive to Strengthen the Construction of Our Legal System," *Hsin chien-she* (New Construction), Peking, No. 12, 1956, pp. 8-9.

consequently have to follow, and a complete legal system becomes an absolute necessity.[24]

Indeed, there were signs during 1956-1957 that certain fundamental codes were being prepared or ready for adoption. According to *Kuang-ming jih-pao* on November 24, 1956, the Supreme People's Court had for some time taken steps to summarize the civil and criminal procedures of the "people's courts" at all levels. The draft summary had been sent to the Standing Committee of the National People's Congress for reference and to the lower courts for experimental purposes. The same source also reported that the Law Section of the Standing Committee of the NPC was about to complete a draft criminal code of 261 articles. On July 15, 1957 as reported by another source, the People's Congress authorized the Standing Committee to discuss and amend the draft criminal code in consultation with all concerned and then to have it published and put into effect on a trial basis.[25] Writing in the June 1957 issue of *People's China,* Shih Liang also stated that both the civil law and the law of procedure were actively taking shape.[26] All this indicated that until the Anti-Rightist Movement got into full swing in late 1957 there had been noticeable efforts made by the Peking regime to build a more stable and complete legal system despite the obvious gaps existing between juridical niceties and political facts in the Chinese mainland.

The Reversal in 1957

The period of 1956-57 in Communist China was one of relative political freedom and intellectual ferment, characterized by the official policy of "letting one hundred flowers blossom and one hundred schools contend."[27] During this period and especially in the spring of 1957, a good many liberal-minded jurists took ad-

---

[24] *Eighth National Congress of the Communist Party of China,* Vol. I, pp. 81-82.

[25] *New China News Agency,* July 16, 1957.

[26] "The Judicial System in New China," *People's China,* No. 12, 1947, p. 19.

[27] For useful information on this period, consult Roderick MacFarquhar, *The Hundred Flowers Campaign and the Chinese Intellectuals,* New York, 1960; and Theodore H. E. Chen, *Thought Reform of the Chinese Intellectuals,* Hong Kong, 1960, Chapters XIII-XIX.

vantage of the opportunity to criticize the government for the lack of basic laws and the defective administration of justice. Suggestions were made to restore certain legal concepts and judicial procedures of Western tradition.

Alarmed at the strong criticisms evoked by the "Blooming and Contending" Movement, the Peking regime launched an Anti-Rightist Campaign in the summer of 1957 to counter-attack its outspoken critics. On the legal front, this meant a serious setback for the development of a stable system of justice. In the course of the Campaign, those who had criticized the irregularities of "people's legality" were branded as "rightist" and their ideas as "anti-socialist" and "reactionary." Prominent among the "rightist" jurists so exposed were Ch'ien Tuan-sheng (President, Peking College of Political Science and Law), Yü Chung-lu (Advisor, Supreme People's Court), Yang Yü-ch'ing (Assistant Editor-in-Chief, *Cheng-fa yen-chiu*), Wu Ch'uan-yi (Bureau of Legal Affairs, State Council), Chang Ying-nan (Deputy Head, Legal Bureau, the Standing Committee of the NPC), Lou Pang-yen (Deputy Head, Peking Judicial Bureau), Wang T'ieh-yai (Professor, Peking University), Wang Tsao-shih (Professor, Futan University), Yang Chao-lung (Professor, Futan University), and Ch'en T'i-ch'iang (International Relations Research Institute).[28] Also included in this impressive list of names were a member of the Standing Committee of the NPC (Huang Shao-hung), four members of the Supreme People's Courts (Chia Ch'ien and others), and a host of officials in the Ministry of Justice and the local judicial departments and "people's courts."[29]

Probably more important than who were denounced as "rightist" was what ideas were attacked during the campaign. An examination of the major points of contention between the "rightist" jurists and official spokesmen would seem to reveal much of the true nature of socialist legality in Communist China.

"Inadequacy of the legal system" During the "Hundred Flowers" period, the "rightist" lawyers were frank to point out that there was only policy but "no law to rely on." Even the few exist-

---

[28] *Jen-min jih-pao*, September 13, 14, 15, 1957; *Chung-kuo ch'in-nien pao* (Chinese Youth Journal), Peking, September 18, 1957; *China News Analysis*, Hong Kong, No. 203, November 1, 1957.

[29] *New China News Agency*, September 18, 1957; *Jen-min jih-pao*, September 20 and December 12, 1957.

ing enactments, they said, were so full of confusing and conflicting provisions that the people hardly knew which laws to observe.[30] Citing the fact that the Soviet Union and Eastern European countries promulgated their basic law codes within three or five years after the establishment of socialist rule, Yang Chao-lung questioned the Peking regime why the Chinese People's Republic founded eight years ago had failed to do the same.[31] On the question of legislation, Huang Shao-hung also stated that "the country's legislative machinery is not perfect, and lags behind the development of the objective situation. The criminal code, the civil code, police regulations and regulations for the punishment of public functionaries have all not been enacted and promulgated. Economic laws and regulations are especially incomplete. The first five year plan is about to be fulfilled, and yet the country still has not enacted regulations governing weights and measures."[32]

In reply, the Chinese Communists called these complaints unfounded and a bourgeois plot to slander "people's democratic legality," although Liu Shao-chi, Tung Pi-wu and others had in the recent past admitted themselves the existence of significant shortcomings in China's legal system. The official line now insisted that many important laws had been drawn up and put into force since 1949. According to an editorial of *People's Daily* on October 9, 1957, during the eight years of the People's Republic 4,072 different laws and regulations were passed, 3,452 before and 620 after the promulgation of the Constitution in September, 1954. Among them were, before the Constitution, the Regulations for the Punishment of counterrevolutionaries, Trade Union Law, Land Reform Law, and Marriage Law; after the Constitution, the Military Service Law, Model Regulations for Agricultural Producers' Cooperatives, Regulations on Factory Safety and Sanitation, and Regulations for Labor Protection. The delay in enacting complete codes

---

[30] These views were expressed by many participants in the forums held in Peking between May 26 and June 7, 1957 by the Chinese Association for Political Science and Law. Note particularly the statements of Wu Ch'uan-yi, Yü Chung-lu, and Ch'en T'i-ch'iang. *Kuang-ming jih-pao,* May 29, June 1 and 10, 1957; *Jen-min jih-pao,* May 29, June 5, 1957.

[31] "Why Is It That the Promulgation of Our Important Codes Has Long Been Delayed," *Hsin-wen jih-pao* (News Daily), Shanghai, June 6, 1957. Another lawyer, Chi Ch'ing-yi, just could not understand why the criminal code, under preparation for a long time, was still not promulgated. This, he said, was like "only hearing the sound of footsteps on the stairs but seeing no one coming down." *Kuang-ming jih-pao,* June 1, 1957.

[32] *New China News Agency,* May 16, 1957.

of a fundamental nature was explained by the Communists as unavoidable in China where political and economic conditions were changing too rapidly. "For instance," stated Premier Chou En-lai, "it is difficult to draft the civil and criminal codes before the completion in the main of the socialist transformation of the private ownership of the means of production and the full establishment of socialist ownership of the means of production. Under these circumstances, it is necessary and proper for the state to issue provisional regulations, decisions and directives as terms of reference for general observance."[33]

"The class nature of law" Another controversial subject during the period under discussion was the character of law. A number of liberal-minded lawyers criticized the Communist regime for overemphasizing the political and class nature of law to the neglect of its "technical and scientific character." They pictured law as a "special science," understood only by the experts and not to be led by politics.[34] Closely related to this was the continuity of law. Many lawyers regarded the old legal system as a part of historical heritage and maintained that the "successiveness" of law and its "class nature" were not mutually exclusive. Elements of the old law, they said, could and should be selectively adopted, modified, and developed to serve the needs of the new society.[35]

Communist spokesmen, on the other hand, denounced the view on the non-political character of law as an attempt of the "rightist" to take away from the working class the "weapon of dictatorship."

[33] *Ibid.*, June 26, 1957. With a similar argument, a writer named Kao Ming-hsuan refuted Professor Yang Chao-lung's contention that China should have followed the Soviet example of promulgate important codes within three to five years after the establishment of the new government. According to Kao, the Soviet Union did it only after she had basically settled the question of socialist ownership of means of production, while in the case of China, the country was still going through the period of the socialist revolution and could not have possibly drawn up in the past important basic laws suited to long-term needs. *Kuang-ming jih-pao*, October 22, 1957.

[34] As an example, see Yang Chao-lung, "Relations between the Communist and Non-Communist Parties in the Legal Field," *Wen-hui pao* (Wen-hui Journal), Shanghai, May 8, 1957.

[35] "Legal Circles Discuss the Class Nature and Successiveness of Law," *Jen-min jih-pao*, May 22, 1957; Yang Pai-yu, "Is There Any Contradiction between the Successiveness of Law and Its Class Nature," *Kuang-ming jih-pao*, April 1, 1957; Ts'eng Ping-chün, "On the Question of the Successiveness of Law," *Cheng-fa yen-chu*, No. 3, 1957, pp. 34-38; Chang Chin-fan, "Views on the Class Nature and Successiveness of Law," *Ibid.*, pp. 39-42.

According to a writer in a leading legal journal, "law possesses a strong class character. It is the manifestation of the will of the ruling class; it is an instrument used by the ruling class to protect its interest and to repress the opposition of the oppressed classes. . . . As everyone knows, law and politics are inseparable and law must serve politics."[36] From the standpoint of the Communists, the new law in China reflected the "will and interest of the broad masses headed by the working class," while the old law, particularly the Six Codes of the Kuomintang, reflected the "will and interest of the exploiting classes of landlords and bureaucratic capitalists." The two systems of law were irreconcilably opposed to each other and there existed no possibility of continuity between them whatsoever.[37] Consequently, those who advocated the sucession of law, Shih Liang charged, really aimed at the revival of the old legal system. This was like "borrowing the corpse of the rightist element to resurrect the spirit of Chiang Kai-shek."[38]

"Defective administration of justice" With respect to the problems and difficulties in the administration of justice in China, the "rightist" jurists complained specifically about the poor quality of judicial cadres and their arbitrary attitude toward the law. The Judicial Reform of 1952 was blamed for "killing the old judicial workers in one stroke" and creating a serious shortage of trained personnel in the courts. As a result of the sectarianism of the Communist Party, the critics charged, most of the former lawyers had been compelled to work in non-legal fields, some even as coolies, while Party cadres who knew little about law had been given the responsibility of judicial work.[39] The cultural level of these cadres were so low that some of them did not know how to write a decision and others even confused "extradition" (*yin-tu*) with the "ferry" (*lun-tu*) and "necessary" (*pi-hsü*) with "unnecessary" (*pou-hsü*).[40] As observed by Yü chung-lu, many of the judicial personnel were unable to draw "the line of demarcation

---

[36] Yeh Ming, "Beat Back the Attack on the People's Legal System by Rightist Elements," *Fa-hsüeh* (jurisprudence), Shanghai, No. 4, 1957, p. 1.

[37] Wan Shan, "Refute 'the Theory of Inheriting the Legal Heritage of the Fatherland'," *ibid.*, No. 3, 1957, p. 5.

[38] Shih Liang, "Thoroughly Crush the Attack on Judicial Work by Rightist Elements," *Kuang-ming jih-pao*, August 31, 1957.

[39] *Wen-hui pao*, May 18, 1957; *Kuang-ming jih-pao*, May 29 and August 28, 1957.

[40] Yang Chao-lung's article in *Wen-hui pao*, May 8, 1957; *Kuang-ming jih-pao*, August 28, 1957; "Contradictions in Judicial Work Exposed," *Hsin-wen jih-pao*, May 19, 1957.

between crimes and non-crimes" and often passed sentences according to their whims rather than fixed rules.[41] Professor Wu Wen-han of Lanchow University also declared that there were a number of leading cadres who tended to put the Party above the law and regard their own words as "golden rules and jade laws."[42] Under the circumstances, the liberal jurists stated, violation of laws and miscarriage of justice had become a commonplace in the New China. The First Middle People's Court in Shanghai, for example, was said to have wrongfully adjudicated 34 per cent of its cases.[43]

Against the above criticisms, the Chinese Communists first of all defended the 1952 Judicial Reform as a significant movement to purge the courts of "old legal concepts" and the "corrupt and law-violating personnel." Contrary to the charge that the old judicial workers were "killed in one stroke," Shih Liang reported that as a result of the Reform, 20 per cent of the lawyers were still retained in the legal profession, 70 per cent were given employment in other fields, and only 7 per cent were expelled and punished.[44] As for the quality of the new judicial cadres in the "people's courts," it was pointed out that most of them were of worker and peasant origin but were not necessarily Party members.[45] While admitting the low cultural level of a small minority among them, one Communist writer insisted that these cadres as a whole possessed many outstanding qualifications, such as a "firm class stand," "clear and correct viewpoints," "high degrees of activism and efficiency," etc.[46] Just to show the excellent work the judges of worker and peasant background were capable of, Shih

---

[41] *Kuang-ming jih-pao,* June 10, 1957; *Jen-min jih-pao,* September 2, 1957.

[42] *Jen-min jih-pao,* May 29, 1957.

[43] *Hsin-wen jih-pao,* May 19, 1957.

[44] Shih Liang's article in *Kuang-ming jih-pao,* August 31, 1957 (cited note 38). According to the 1953 data for the country, 2,369 old judicial workers were retained in their posts after the Judicial Reform, and of this number 1,142 continued trial work. T'ao Hsi-chin, "On the Judicial Reform," *Cheng-fa yen-chiu,* No. 5, 1957, p. 15.

[45] Shih Liang, *Kuang-ming jih-pao,* August 31, 1957. To refute the complaint that "judicial workers are all communists," Shih Liang pointed out that she herself was not a Party member but had been the Minister of Justice for almost eight years. As another example, she cited the fact that out of 52 judicial workers in the Middle People's Court of Peking, 24 were not Party members.

[46] Hsi Tsu-te, "To Undermine the People's Judicial Organs Is Absolutely Not Allowed," *Wen-hui pao,* July 3, 1957.

Liang said that between January and July 1957, the courts in Shanghai adjudicated correctly more than 96 per cent of some 7,000 cases they dealt with.[47] All in all, according to the official line, the "malicious attacks" on the "people's judicial cadres" and their work were a part of the "rightist conspiracy" to "usurp" from the Party the Leadership over the judiciary and to "restore" the "reactionary, old legal order" throughout the country.[48]

"The suppression of counterrevolutionaries" The legality of the campaign for the suppression of counterrevolutionaries was one of the major issues of dispute between the Peking regime and the intellectuals. As charged by the latter, the arbitrary arrests and mob violence during the mass movement against the counter-revolutionaries infringed upon the people's civil rights and vio-lated the constitutional guarantees.[49] One liberal critic, for in-stance, complained that in the course of the anti-counterrevolu-tionary drive members of the democratic parties were arrested without notifying their families or giving reasons for their ar-rest.[50] Another stated that the campaign against the counterrevolu-tionaries was so oppressive that "the 'red terror' is now the order of the day replacing the 'white terror' of the past."[51] Two others blamed the "rather be leftist than rightist" tendency for putting too many persons to death during the campaign for suppressing counterrevolutionaries and called it unnecessary to continue this struggle "when the world is already in peace."[52] There was a con-sensus among many jurists that the class struggle in China had come to an end and that the current important task of the courts was to handle the contradictions among the people. From their point of view, democracy should now take precedence over dicta-torship, and persons accused of counterrevolutionary offenses should be treated according to democratic principles.[53]

[47] Shih Liang, *Kuan-ming jih-pao,* August 31, 1957.

[48] *Ibid.;* T'ao Hsi-chin, p. 15; Yeh Ming (cited note 36), p. 4.

[49] This type of complaint was made by Ku Chih-chung, a lawyer in Shang-hai, who said that the Constitution of the Chinese People's Republic existed in name only. *Jen-min jih-pao,* June 26, 1957.

[50] A statement by Ch'en Ch'i-yu, chairman of the Chih-kung-tang, in *Kuang-ming jih-pao,* May 10, 1957.

[51] Chin Yung-hsün, "In the Past It Was the White Terror; Now It Is the Red Terror," *Yün-nan jih-pao* (Yünnan Daily), Kunming, July 4, 1957.

[52] See the joint speech made on June 10, 1957 by Chang Po-sheng and Huang Chen-lu of the Mukden Normal College in *Shen-yang jih-pao* (Muk-den Daily), June 11, 1957.

[53] *Jen-min jih-pao,* September 17, 1957; *New China News Agency,* Sep-tember 18, 1957.

In defense of the anti-counterrevolutionary drive, Communist spokesmen pictured it as implementing the provision of Article 19 of the Constitution: "To safeguard the people's democratic system, supress all treasonable and counterrevolutionaries." Criticisms against this drive were called a "wicked scheme" of the "rightists" designed to discredit the "mass line" and Party leadership in political and legal work.[54] While admitting the occurrence of some mistakes in the nation-wide struggle against the counterrevolutionaries, *People's Daily* of July 18, 1957 insisted nevertheless that the achievements of this struggle far outweighed the mistakes. As a result of the 1955 campaign, it pointed out, over 81,000 counterrevolutionaries had been dealt with by law and some 190,000 counterrevolutionaries had given themselves up. Citing the continuous activities of the hidden counterrevolutionaries, Shih Liang said: "The anti-counterrevolutionary campaign is just as absolutely necessary as it was in the past. To deny the necessity and correctness of this campaign is in actuality to deny the people's democratic dictatorship. The Chinese people will never permit this."[55]

"Independence of the judiciary" A group of liberal jurists took a strong stand for the principle of judicial independence during the "Blooming and Contending" stage. Chia Ch'ien (Chief Justice of the Criminal Division of the Supreme People's Court), for instance, was quoted as saying: "The Party realizes its leadership in judicial work through the enactment of laws. Since the law represents the will of the people as well as that of the Party, a judge who obeys the law obeys in effect the leadership of the Party. Hence, all a judge needs to do is to obey the law; there is no need for any more guidance from the Party."[56] In Chia Ch'ien's view, the Party should only exercise its leadership over the judiciary in general policies and directions and should not interfere with the actual trial work of the courts. Otherwise, it would run counter to the provision of Constitution (Article 78) that "in adminis-

---

[54] See Li Shih-wen, "Refute the Rightists' Erroneous View 'Anti-Counterrevolutionary Campaign Has Violated the Law'," *Cheng-fa yen-chiu*, No. 5, 1957, pp. 33-37; Chin Wen-sheng, "Condemn the Rightist Slander against the Suppression of Counterrevolutionaries," *Cheng-chih Hsüeh-hsi* (Political Study), No. 9, September 13, 1957, in American Consulate General, Hong Kong, *Extracts from China Mainland Magazines*, No. 107, November 12, 1957.

[55] *Kuang-ming jih-pao*, August 31, 1957.

[56] Jo Ch'üan and Ho Fang, "No Perversion of the Nature of the People's Courts Is Allowed," *Jen-min jih-pao*, December 24, 1957.

tering justice the people's courts are independent, subject only to the law." He was of the further opinion that "the Party committees do not know the law or the circumstances of individual cases. Their leadership therefore may not be correct."[57]

The stand taken by Chia Ch'ien and others evoked a series of rebuttals from the Communist press and legal journals in the subsequent Anti-Rightist Campaign. One article in *People's Daily* argued that Party leadership should be manifested not only in the process of legislation but also in the administration of justice: "The Party's leadership over the state is expressly set forth in the Preamble and Article 1 of the Constitution. . . . The people's courts, being an instrument of the state, should of course follow the Party's guidance in the administration of justice. This is fully in accord with the constitutional provisions. . . . Facts have shown that the Party's active intervention in the trial work of the people's courts not only breaches no law but can effectively supervise and correct unlawful phenomena that may appear in the judicial process."[58] A writer of *Fa-hsüeh* also stated: "To effect its leadership, the Party must first formulate correct policies and programs. But this alone is not enough. The Party must also supervise and investigate how these policies and programs are carried out by the people's court; it must exercise concrete leadership in the trial work of the courts in order to assure the thorough implementation of its policies."[59] As to the Party Committees' competency for legal matters, an article in *Cheng-fa yen-chiu* had this to say: "Our laws are the manifestation of the will of the people led by the working class. . . . They are enacted and enforced by the people under the leadership of the Party. . . . How can one say, 'The Party Committees do not know law'? . . . Furthermore, the Party Committees have a complete grasp of the entire situation, know the political conditions as a whole, understand the relationship between the enemy and ourselves, and are well acquainted with the feelings and demands of the people. Therefore, they are most qualified to weigh the pros and cons of a case in relation to the situation as a whole and to properly direct the work of all departments. It is only under the leadership of the Party that the people's

---

[57] *Ibid.*

[58] *Ibid.*

[59] Wang Nai-yuan & Ch'en Ch'i-wu, "Our Understanding Regarding 'In Administering Justice the People's Courts Are Independent, Subject Only to the Law'," *Fa-hsüeh*, No. 2, 1958, p. 32.

courts can be assured of their correct administration of justice."[60]

"The benefit of doubt for the accused" Among the major issues of the legal debate were the "benefit of the doubt for the accused" and the "presumption of innocence" advocated by Chia Ch'ien and the other "rightist" jurists. According to their view, "the accused must be presumed innocent until proven guilty in the criminal proceedings, and 'extenuating circumstances' must be considered in cases where the accused are found guilty of serious crimes." Also expounded by them was the related principle of "free conscientious judgment of evidence," under which "a judge is free to use his 'inner convictions' (conscience, justice, moral concepts, etc.) as the yardstick to determine the facts of a case and the validity of the evidence."[61]

Communist spokesmen, however, denounced all these principles as "theories of bourgeois jurisprudence," incompatible with the socialist judicial system. To apply such principles in the administration of justice, they contend, would be putting the interest of the accused above the interest of the people. This in effect would mean "the protection of guilty persons from punishment" and "the restriction of the freedom of the judicial organs and the masses in their fight against counterrevolutionary and other criminal elements." In order to strengthen the "people's democratic dictatorship" and consolidate the Party's guiding role in judicial activities, asserted the official line, resolute efforts must be made to combat and liquidate the "reactionary and dangerous" views of "presumption of innocence," "benefit of the doubt for the accused," and "free conscientious judgment of evidence."[62]

Recent Development, 1958—the Present

While 1957 marked the official reversal of the trend toward legal stabilization along Soviet lines, the years that followed further wit-

---

[60] Feng Jo-ch'üan, "Refute Chia Ch'ien's Anti-Party Erroneous View of 'Judicial Independence'," *Cheng-fa yen-chiu,* No. 1, 1958, pp. 21-22.

[61] Jo Ch'üan and Ho Fang, *Jen-min jih-pao,* December 24, 1957; "Anti-Rightist Struggle in the Supreme People's Court," *New China News Agency,* December 11, 1957.

[62] Jo Ch'üan and Ho Fang, *Jen-min jih-pao,* December 24, 1957; Wu Lu, "Refute the View on the Benefit of Doubt for the Accused," *Cheng-fa yen-chiu,* No. 4, 1958, pp. 59-62; Chang Tzu-p'ei, "Criticize the Bourgeois Principle of 'Free Conscientious Judgment of Evidence'," *ibid.,* No. 2, 1958, pp. 42-48.

nessed the progressive deterioration of Chinese relations with Russia and the frequent use of informal procedures and apparatus to administer justice in the China mainland. During the period between early 1958 and the present, the Peking regime has been preoccupied with the problems of socialist construction ranging from the failures of the Big Leap Forward to the recent efforts for economic recovery. At the same time it has been engaged with vigor in ideological struggles against both the "rightist" and "revisionist" influences at home and on the international scene. In the context of this political climate, most of the new laws and regulations adopted have been mainly concerned with economic matters and the work of the judiciary has been primarily geared toward the repression of opposition and advancement of the interest of socialism.

One noticeable feature of Peking's policy during the period under discussion has been its repeated stress on absolute Party leadership in judicial work. At the Fourth Judicial Work Conference in August 1958, the principle was reaffirmed that "the people's courts should be absolute in its submission to Party leadership, and there could not be the least negligence and vacillation. . . . Only in this way could court work be made to meet the change of situation as well as to implement concretely the lines and policies of the Party under the guidance of the correct line."[63] "Politics must assume command" and "Obey the Party Committees" were also among the conclusions reached by the National Conference of Advanced Public Security, Procuratorial, and Judicial Workers, held in May of 1959.[64] The official line has been frequently expounded by writers in *Cheng-fa yen-chiu*. One group of them, for instance, wrote in 1959: "The policy of the Party is the soul of the people's democratic legal system; the people's democratic legal system is the instrument for implementing the Party policy. This is to say, the Party policy commands legal work and legal work can never be separated from the Party policy. Legal work can only serve as a tool for the Party policy and cannot be above or beyond politics. . . . Without the leadership of the Party there would not be the people's democratic legal system. Therefore, legislative and judicial activities as well as other forms of legal work must all be under the absolute leadership of the Party."[65] Another writer stated in 1960 that the leadership of the

---

[63] *New China News Agency,* August 28, 1958.

[64] *Jen-min jih-pao,* May 23, 1959.

[65] Yin P'ing and others, "Several Problems Relating to Our People's Democratic Legal System," *Cheng-fa yen-chiu,* No. 2, 1959, pp. 7-8.

Party in judicial work should be comprehensive and all-embracing, to be exercised over matters from principles and policies to organization and concrete trial work. The "people's courts," according to him, must obey absolutely not only the leadership of the Central Committee of the Communist Party but also the leadership of the Party Committees at both higher and corresponding levels.[66] Writing in 1962, still another author pointed out that law could never be properly administered to fulfill its functions without the correct leadership of the Party and the guidance of correct ideology and policy.[67]

The pursuit of the mass line in judicial work has, too, been strongly emphasized by the Communist authorities since the beginning of 1958. Several major features of this policy may be noted in the following. (A) Under the direction of the mass line, the courts have been brought directly to the people, judicial procedures have been simplified, and justice has been carried out on the spot. This was particularly evident during the years of the Big Leap, when the "5 goes" (go to factories, go to mines, go to communes, go to streets, and go to markets) and "3 on-the-spots" (investigation on the spot, mediate on the spot, and try and sentence on the spot) became a standard practice for judicial workers to "improve the quality of their work" and to "create closer ties between the people's courts and the masses."[68] In the province of Liaoning the "people's courts" reportedly tried and judged on the spot more than 80 per cent of the total number of cases handled from January to October 1959.[69] Judicial personnel in Hopei province adopted during the Big Leap the slogan: "when cases come up at daytime, they shall be disposed of during the day; when cases come up at night, they shall be dealt with under lamplight; and if they cannot be settled in one day, then work shall be carried on continuously."[70] A 1960 report from Honan province exalted the success of the mass line in elevating the legal outlook of the vast

[66] Ch'i Wen, "We Must Thoroughly Liquidate the Influence of the 'Judicial Independence' Concept of the Bourgeois Class," *ibid.,* No. 2, 1960, p. 55.

[67] Wang Chia-fu, "Certain Problems in the Compiling and Writing of 'The Theory of State and Law'," *ibid.,* No. 1, 1962, p. 37.

[68] See Li Lin, "Several Points in Our Understanding of Judicial Work during the Big Leap," *ibid,* No. 5, 1958, pp. 42-48; Fan Min-hsin, "The Mass Line Is the Basic Line of Our Political and Legal Work," *ibid.,* No. 2, 1959, pp. 13-16.

[69] Liu P'eng, "Work Report of the Higher People's Court in Liaoning Province," *Liao-ning jih-pao* (Liaoning Daily), Mukden, December 22, 1959.

[70] *Ho-pei jih-pao* (Hopei Daily), Tientsin, October 29, 1958.

masses and in improving the quality of trial work. Not only were all kinds of civil and criminal cases handled with speed and accuracy, but some perplexing old cases were settled and the accumulation of cases was cleared up, so it reported.[71]

(B) Another important aspect of the mass line is the integration of judicial work with productive labor. Since the start of the ill-fated Big Leap, judicial cadres have been sent to lower levels for labor training and for productive work in all forms. They have been asked to live, eat, and labor with the masses and to take a direct part in production. The legal personnel of Liaoning, for example, were said to have participated in production 1,685 times during a five-month period.[72] The judges of a city court in Shantung, while working in a commune, reportedly collected 6,200 catties of manure and adjudicated 77 cases all within six months.[73] Justifications for this policy was presented by Communist spokesmen in such publications as *Hung-ch'i* and *Cheng-fa yen-chiu*. According to the official line of reasoning, the integration of judicial work with productive labor would help the judicial cadres to combat the influence of bourgeois ideology, strengthen their class consciousness and mass viewpoints, and solidify their relations with the working people. It was further pointed out that by participating directly in production along with the masses, the judicial workers would learn production skills, raise labor productivity, facilitate the correct implementation of the Party policy, and temper themselves into "red and expert" cadres.[74]

(C) As a part of the mass line style of judicial work, the Communists have put a premium on the use of conciliation for resolving disputes and on the "integration of court trial with mass debate." Specific efforts have been made to encourage the masses to enter into "socialist patriotic pacts" with the professed purposes of promoting voluntary observance of law and social discipline, strengthening internal solidarity among the

---

[71] Wang Kuang-li, "Work Report of the Higher People's Court in Honan Province," *Ho-nan jih-pao* (Honan Daily), Chengchou, March 1, 1960.

[72] *Jen-min jih-pao*, July 27, 1960.

[73] *China News Analysis*, Hong Kong, No. 397, November 17, 1961, p. 2.

[74] See Li Shih-ying, "A Brief Discussion of the Meaning of the Participation of Political and Legal Cadres in Productive Labor," *Cheng-fa yen chiu*, No. 1, 1959, pp. 17-22; "Participation in Collective, Productive Labor by Cadres Is of Fundamental Importance under the Socialist System" (Editorial), *Hung-ch'i* (Red Flag), Peking, Nos. 13-14, July 10, 1963.

people, and maintaining socialist peace and order.[75] Letters and personal visits to the authorities have also become important channels for the masses to make complaints and report wrong-doings. Between January and October of 1961 the number of such letters and visits received in Kansu was estimated to be 29,000, an increase of 70 per cent over the previous year.[76] In 1962 the Kiangsu authorities at the *hsien* level and above were reported to have received 500,000 letters and visits from the people.[77]

The courts being instruments of the People's Democratic Dictatorship, struggle against counterrevolutionaries has also continued to be a focal point of the judicial work during the period under discussion. Such a struggle was waged with special intensity in the 1958 campaigns for the Big Leap Forward and for the communization of agriculture. As told by a newspaper account that year, in Shansi alone 11,352 counterrevolutionaries and 12,898 criminals were uncovered and punished within a six-month period.[78] While claiming a great victory over the counterrevolution, Vice Premier Lo Jui-ch'ing nevertheless said in September 1959: "Our enemies, although greatly weakened, have not been completely wiped out. They will not give up the struggle and are continuing to intensify conspiratorial activities. Recently, our public security organs arrested special agents and spies dispatched by American imperialism and the Chiang Kai-shek gang. At the same time they broke some cases of sabotage involving remnant counterrevolutionaries in our country. All these facts tell us that we must not become self-complacent and belittle the enemy and that we must not relax our vigilance and struggle."[79] Lo's statement was echoed by the Central Committee of the Chinese Communist Party in a passage of its communique on January 20, 1961: "The overwhelming majority, or over 90 per cent, of the urban and rural population in the country support the line and policies of the Party and the People's Government. . . . There is,

---

[75] For discussions of these pacts, see Hsien Chia-lin and others, "The Utility of the Socialist Patriotic Pacts," *Cheng-fa yen-chiu*, No. 1, 1959, pp. 52-53; Wang Kuo-shu, "A Brief Discussion of the Socialist Patriotic Pact," *Ibid.*, No. 1, 1961, pp. 38-40.

[76] *Jen-min jih-pao*, January 9, 1962.

[77] *New China News Agency*, Nanking, February 20, 1963.

[78] *Shan-hsi jih-pao* (Shansi Daily), Taiyuan, December 8, 1958.

[79] Lo Jui-ch'ing, "The Struggle between Revolution and Counterrevolution over the Past Ten Years," *Jen-min jih-pao*, September 20, 1959.

however, an extremely small number of landlord and bourgeois elements, accounting for only a few per cent of the population, who have not yet been sufficiently remoulded and are always attempting to stage a come-back . . .; they have taken advantage of the difficulties caused by natural calamities and of some shortcomings in the work at the primary levels to carry out sabotaging activities."[80]

The continual struggle against counterrevolutionaries has been underscored recently by occasional reports in the Communist press about the trials of saboteurs and secret agaits in mainland China, especially in the southern and coastal regions. On April 27, 1962 the Canton Municipal People's Court held a judgment meeting, at which four persons were accused of being Nationalist agents. One was sentenced to immediate death, another to death with a two-year suspension of the execution, the third to 20 years' imprisonment, and the fourth who gave himself up was exempt from punishment.[81] In January 1963 the courts in Kwangtung tried fifteen persons for the crimes of placing bombs and causing arson. Five of them were executed and the others either received sentences of varying kinds or were acquitted.[82] Between October 1962 and October 1963, 24 groups of saboteurs and enemy agents were put out of action in the coastal provinces of Communist China. In dealing with them, the "people's judicial organs" were said to have always followed the principle of "leniency for those who confess; severity for those who resist; rewards for those who have merit."[83]

To all these reports must be added some new official pronouncements as further illustration of Peking's concern with the problems of counterrevolution and class struggle. The Central Committee of the Chinese Communist Party pointed out in September 1962 that "throughout the historical period of proletarion revolution and proletarian dictatorship, throughout the historical period of transition from capitalism to communism, there is class struggle between the proletariat and the bourgeoisie and struggle between the socialist road and the capitalist road. . . . This struggle is complicated, tortuous, with ups and downs and sometimes it is

[80] "Communique of the Ninth Plenary Session of the Eighth Central Committee of the Communist Party of China," *Peking Review,* January 27, 1961, p. 6.

[81] *Wen-hui pao,* Hong Kong, April 29, 1962.

[82] *Jen-min jih-pao,* January 13, 1963.

[83] *New China News Agency,* November 18, 1963.

very sharp."[84] Premier Chou En-lai also stated in December 1964 that during this historical period "a thoroughgoing socialist revolution must be carried out on the economic, political, ideological, and cultural fronts. Moreover, as long as the world still contains imperialism, capitalism, reaction and modern revisionism, it is inevitable that the sinister winds of capitalism will frequently blow into socialist countries. Consequently, the struggle of which will win out, socialism or capitalism, must take a very long time in a socialist country before it can be finally decided."[85] Along the same line, many newspaper editorials and journal articles have been written to play up the incessant class war during the socialist era. Typically, the Chinese people and various state organs were urged to maintain their vigilance in the face of the combined threat of foreign and domestic enemies. Abroad, they should wage the class struggle against "the imperialists, reactionaries, and modern revisionists of different countries who have raised a hue and cry in the grand anti-Chinese chorus"; at home, against "those landlords, rich peasants, and bourgeois rightists who have not reformed themselves and the remnant counterrevolutionaries who are still seeking the restoration of the feudalist rule in China."[86]

Our discussion of the legal life in the post-1957 China would be incomplete without mentioning the fact that in the last few years the Peking regime has taken occasional steps to soften the prevalent rigidity of "people's justice" and to allow the return of some legal discussions among the juridical circles. One sign of this limited relaxation may be seen in the amnesty granted to the reformed "war criminals" and the removal of the "Rightist hat" from the reformed Rightists.

The first amnesty order was issued by Liu Shao-chi, Chairman of Communist China, on September 17, 1959 in connection with the celebration of the tenth anniversary of the founding of the People's Republic. It granted pardons to "war criminals of the Chiang Kai-shek clique and the puppet Manchukuo," counter-

---

84 "Communique of the Tenth Plenary Session of the Eighth Central Committee of the Communist Party of China," *Peking Review*, September 28, 1962, p. 7.

85 "Report on the Work of the Government," *ibid.*, January 1, 1965, p. 12.

86 For this type of argument, see Editorial of *Jen-min jih-pao*, June 19, 1963; Huang Wen-yü, "There Is Still Class Struggle," *Nan-fang jih-pao* (Southern Daily), Canton, May 28, 1963; Liu Hu-p'ing, "Correctly Recognize the Class Struggle during the Socialist Period," *Cheng-fa yen-chiu*, No. 2, 1963, pp. 18-24; Editorial of *Kuang-Ming jih-pao*, May 8, 1966.

revolutionaries, and common criminals who had, through a certain period of reform through labor, really changed and turned over a new leaf.[87] In accordance with this order the Supreme People's Court released in December 1959, 33 major "war criminals," including P'u Yi, ex-Emperor of Manchukuo, and Tu Yü-ming, former Commander of the Nationalist forces in the Northeast.[88] At the same time the provincial judicial organs set free a large number of counterrevolutionaries and common criminals. In the provinces of Anhwei and Honan, for example, 6,000 and 4,263 persons were granted special pardon and released respectively.[89]

Subsequently, four more orders were issued by Liu Shao-chi granting amnesty to major "war criminals" of the "Chiang-kai-shek clique," the puppet Manchukuo, and the puppet Inner Mongolian Autonomous Government who had genuinely reformed. On the basis of these orders the Supreme People's Court pardoned and released 50 "war criminals" in November 1960, 68 in December 1961, 35 in April 1963, and 53 in December 1964.[90] As a rule, those criminals were given their release at public meetings where they dutifully expressed their boundless gratitude to the Communist regime and voiced their determination to continue remolding their ideology and render their services to the building of socialism in China. For propaganda purposes, many of them were further given publicized interviews in which they usually recounted how they rid themselves of reactionary ideas through political education and learned to appreciate the value of labor as well as had their health improved through participation in production. The interviews were often concluded with an appeal to the people in Formosa for coming to grips with the true light and returning to the arms of the motherland.[91] All in all, the granting of amnesty to "war criminals" was described by official statements as a demonstration

[87] *Jen-min jih-pao,* September 18, 1959.

[88] *Ibid.,* December 5, 1959.

[89] *An-hui jih-pao* (Anhwei Daily), Hofei, December 28, 1959; Wang Kuang-li's report in *Ho-nan jih-pao,* March 1, 1960.

[90] See *Chung-hua jen-min kung-ho-kuo fa-kuei hui-pien* (Compendium of Law and Regulations of the Chinese People's Republic), Peking, Vol. 12 (1962), pp. 67-71; *Jen-min jih-pao,* November 29, 1960, December 26, 1961, April 10, 1963; December 29, 1964.

[91] For some of these interviews, see *Wen-hui pao,* December 13, 1959 (with Wang Yao-wu); *Ta-kung pao,* Hong Kong, December 13, 1959 (with Tu Yü-ming); *Ta-kung pao,* Peking, December 19, 1959 (with P'u Yi; *Ta-kung pao,* Hong Kong, January 27, 1962 (with Liao Yao-hsiang).

of "the prosperity and might of the country, the unprecedented consolidation of the state power of the People's Democratic Dictatorship, and the correctness of the policy of the Chinese Communist Party and the People's Government of combining punishment with leniency and labor reform with ideological education." It also showed that "those who have committed crimes against the people will eventually be pardoned if only they confess their crimes and show signs of having truly changed."[92]

By the same token, the Central Committee of the Communist Party and the State Council made a decision on September 16, 1959 favorable to the reformed Rightists: "Anyone who has changed from evil to good and has shown that he has really changed in both views and activities will no longer be considered a bourgeois rightist from now on, that is, the label of 'rightist' shall be removed from him."[93] In accordance with this decision the central organs of the state and of the democratic parties proceeded to relieve 142 persons of their "Rightist designation" in December 1959, 260 in November 1960, some 370 in December 1961, and more than 100 at the end of 1962. Among those prominent figures so affected were Fei Hsia-t'ung, Huang Shao-hung, Ch'ien Tuan-sheng, Ku Chih-chung, and Ch'en Ming-shu.[94] Local authorities, too, occasionally removed the "Rightist label" from less-known individuals. Throughout the country altogether 26,000 Rightists had their "hats taken off" in 1959.[95]

Another sign of the "sweet" side of Peking's recent policy is the "love the people month" movement. Since early 1959 the Ministry of Public Security has regularly directed its agencies at all levels to launch a "love the people month" during the traditional Spring Festival, with the express purpose of rendering a helpful hand to the production and livelihood of the masses. In February 1959, for example, public security personnel throughout the country "performed over four million good deeds for the masses, leaving behind many touching stories of self-sacrifice for and devotion to the people."[96] In the "love the people month" of 1963, more than 100,000 "good things for the masses" were

---

[92] Same sources as in note 90.
[93] New China News Agency, September 17, 1959.
[94] Jen-min jih-pao, December 5, 1959, November 25, 1960, December 17, 1961; New China News Agency, February 24, 1963.
[95] Jen-min jih-pao, January 4, 1960.
[96] New China News Agency, December 27, 1959.

reportedly done by the "people's police" in 15 provinces and municipalities.[97] Services rendered during the movement usually include distributing commodities, transporting manure, irrigating land, and repairing farm tools. An integral part of the mass line strategy, the "love the people month" movement further indicates Peking's attempt to mitigate the tensions wihin China arising out of political repression and economic failures in recent years.

More illustrative of Peking's limited retreat from the harshness of the Anti-Rightist and Big Leap Campaigns has been the reappearance of legal discussions in juridical circles. In the last few years legal forums have been held and textbooks and journal articles have been written on such subjects as "philosophy of law," "state and legal theories," "history of Chinese law," etc. Reference again has been made to the implementation of the 1956 slogan "let a hundred flowers bloom, let a hundred schools contend." There has been a basic agreement among the jurists that law is the expression of the will of the ruling class and that although always subservient to Party policy, law has a useful role to play during the stage of socialist construction. In the words of a director of the Chinese Association for Political Science and Law, for instance, socialist law is an instrument of class struggle against all reactionary forces, and at the same time it performs important educative functions for the furtherance of the proletarian cause.[98] Divergent opinions, on the other hand, have also been expressed by Chinese lawyers as to what are the other characteristics of law, which organs have the law-making authority, and whether legal coercion applies to all citizens or to the enemy only.[99]

As a result of the Peking-Moscow split, juridical circles in Communist China have understandably begun to show more interest in legal systems other than that of the Soviet Union. This is

---

[97] *Ibid.,* February 19, 1963.

[98] Chou Hsin-min, "Law Is a Sharp Weapon of Class Struggle," *Jen-min jih-pao,* October 24, 1965.

[99] Consult particularly the relevant articles and reports in the 1962 issues of *Cheng-fa yen-chiu.* A good summary on the legal symposiums held in Peking in 1962 (sponsored by the Research Department of the Chinese Association for Political Science and Law, the Editorial Board of the *Studies of Political Science and Law,* and others) is in "Concerning the Questions of Nature and Functions of Law during the Socialist Stage of Our Country," *Cheng-fa yen-chiu,* No. 3, 1962, pp. 23-24, and also in a report in *Kuang-ming jih-pao,* September 7, 1962.

reflected in the new attention given to the legal traditions of China by individual researchers and academic instiutions. Interesting essays, for instance, have been published on the development of criminal legislation and criminal procedure in old China.[100] Major works have been undertaken to edit with annotations the laws of the imperial dynasties in general and the laws of the T'ang dynasty in particular.[101] Law schools at Peking and Kirin Universities have organized scholarly discussions and prepared teaching material on topics like "the T'ang Law," "political philosophy of Han Fei-tzu," and "relations between *li* and *fa.*"[102] The official line has also favored "critical inheritance of the cultural legacy." According to it, one should not cut off history and must understand the past in order to serve the present. Consequently, it is a duty of legal scholars to examine the entire process of development of Chinese law in a scientific, objective, and realistic manner. Only through the use of the Marxist-Leninist method of historical analysis, can one differentiate the elixir from the dregs and decide on what to accept and what to reject in the legal legacy.[103]

In a similar manner the Chinese have shown guarded and yet discernible interest in Western legal theories and institutions during the last few years. As an example, the well-known Commercial Press has recently published a new translation of Montesquieu's *Esprit Des Lois*. A *Cheng-fa yen-chiu* writer points out that since Montesquieu's theory holds an important place in bourgeois jurisprudence his writings should therefore be appropriately introduced.[104] Another author writes with considerable enthusiasm about Rousseau, calling the latter an outstanding liberal of the

---

[100] Fu Wong, "The History of Chinese Criminal Procedure," *Kuang-ming jih-pao*, March 20, 1962; Ch'en Kuang-chung, "A Brief Description of Criminal Legislation in Ancient China," *Cheng-fa yen-chiu*, No. 4, 1963, pp. 28-35.

[101] The Research Institute of Political Science and Law of the Shanghai Academy of Social Sciences has undertaken such a project since 1959. *Jen-min jih-pao*, February 3, 1962. See also *China News Analysis*, No. 467, May 10, 1963.

[102] News items in *Cheng-fa yen-chiu*, No. 1, 1962, p. 48 and No. 2, 1963, p. 42.

[103] See, for example, Hsiao Yun-ch'ing, "Preliminary Discussion of the Study of the History of the Chinese Legal System," *Cheng-fa yen-chiu*, No. 3, 1963, pp. 25-35.

[104] Chou Hsin-ming, "Some Ideas Regarding the Study of Montesquieu's Theory," *ibid.*, No. 2, 1962, p. 41.

18th Century despite his "class and historical limitations."[105] Toward the contemporary jurists of the West, particularly those of the United States, the Communist Chinese attitude has been less sympathetic. Hans Kelsen's "pure theory of law" is described as a bourgeois trick and his concept of international law a tool of American imperialism.[106] Roscoe Pound's "sociological jurisprudence" is also pictured as reactionary and serving only the interest of the monopolistic capitalist class.[107] Even all this, however, must not be viewed as purely negative. The fact that Chinese jurists can go to some length to *describe* the "reactionary" theories of the West is a marked improvement over the total absence of any meaningful legal discussion during the "Anti-Rightist" and "Big Leap" Movements.

Currently, a vigorous "proletarian cultural revolution" is being carried on in China to establish Maoism as a universal philosophy and to eradicate Western and Soviet influences from the Chinese way of life.[108] In many ways it recalls the radicalism of the disastrous "Big Leap" of 1958. The purge of a number of top officials and intellectuals in the current campaign seems to indicate the existence of a rather strong opposition to Mao's rigid policy within the Party and intellectual elite. Indeed, the "great cultural revolution" launched by Mao and his associates may be regarded as a desperate measure to postpone the inevitable: the rise of "modern revisionism" among the Chinese to bring their country back to the mainstream of the twentieth century.

---

[105] Han Yen-lung, "A Brief Discussion of the Political Thought of Rousseau," *ibid.*, No. 3, 1962, pp. 11-16.

[106] See articles by Wu En-yü, Chao Chen-chiang, and Chou Hsin-ming in *Jen-min jih-pao*, February 27, 1962.

[107] Kuo Wei-hsiung, "The Reactionary Pragmatic Legal Thought of Pound," *Cheng-fa yen-chiu*, No. 3, 1963, pp. 43-50.

[108] "Decision of C. P. C. Central Committee Concerning the Great Proletarian Cultural Revolution (adopted on August 9, 1966)," *Peking Review*, August 12, 1966, pp. 6-11; Harrison E. Salisbury, "Mao Effort to Steel Youth Seen Behind Peking Purge," *New York Times*, August 16, 1966.

Part II Structure and Process of People's Justice

Chapter 4

The People's Courts

There are two types of apparatus through which the system of "people's justice" operates in Communist China. One is the formal judiciary structure; the other is the extrajudicial machinery consisting of administrative agencies and social organizations. While the latter handles a large number of disputes and offenses, particularly those of minor or routine nature, the former provides the necessary legal framework for the adjudication of cases of greater importance. Together they serve as useful instruments for the Communist regime to exercise social control, suppress the enemies of the state, and enforce its far-reaching revolutionary programs.

According to the Organic Law of the People's Courts adopted in September 1954, judicial authority in Communist China is vested in the hierarchy of the "people's courts" headed by the Supreme Court (Article 1).[1] The task of the courts is to try criminal and civil cases and to punish criminals and settle civil disputes, in order to safeguard the "people's democratic system," maintain public order, protect public property, safeguard the rights and lawful interests of citizens, and ensure the "successful execution of socialist construction and socialist transformation of the country." In addition, the courts are expected to "educate citizens in loyalty to their country and voluntary observance of law." (Article 3)

The court system established by the Organic Law is composed of the Supreme People's Courts, local "people's courts," and special "people's courts." The local courts are further divided into higher "people's courts," intermediate "people's courts," and basic "people's courts" (Article 1). There are in Communist China approximately 30 higher courts, 200 intermediate courts, and over 2,000 basic

---

[1] Text of the Organic Law is in *Chung-hua jen-min kung-ho-kuo fa-kuei hui-pien* (Compendium of Laws and Regulations of the Chinese People's Republic), Peking, Vol. 1 (1956), pp. 123-132. English text is in *Documents of the First Session of the First National People's Congress of the People's Republic of China*, Peking, 1955, pp. 185-199.

courts.[2] In this chapter we shall examine in some detail the structure and powers of the "people's courts" at all levels.

The Supreme People's Court

The Supreme People's Court is the highest judicial organ of the Chinese People's Republic. Composed of criminal, civil and other divisions, it has a president, vice-presidents, chief judges, associate judges, and judges (Article 29 of the Organic Law).[3] It is accountable to the National People's Congress, and, in the intervals between the sessions of the full Congress, to the Standing Committee of the NPC (Article 14).

Under Articles 28 and 30 of the Organic Law, the Supreme Court is empowered to (1) supervise the judicial work of all "people's courts," (2) try cases of first instance it deems necessary or assigned to its jurisdiction by laws and decrees, (3) hear appeals and protests against judgments of higher courts and special courts, and (4) consider protests lodged by the Supreme People's Procuratorate in accordance with the procedure of judicial supervision. By a resolution of the Standing Committee of the National People's Congress, the judicial committee of the Supreme Court is authorized to rule on questions raised by the concrete applications of laws and decrees in the course of trial, but the power to interpret laws is still reserved to the Standing Committee itself.[3a]

In addition, the Supreme Court has been given other powers by the National People's Congress. On July 15, 1957 the Congress adopted a resolution requiring that all death sentences of the lower

---

[2] Figures given in *Shin Chugoku nenkan, 1962* (New China Yearbook, 1962), Tokyo, 1962, p. 70 are 30 higher courts, 200 intermediate courts, and 2,000 basic courts; figures given in Subhash Chandra Sarkar, "Judiciary in China," *India Quarterly*, New Delhi, 13 (1957), p. 308 are 28; 200; 3,000 respectively. It should be noted here that *Jen-min shou-ts'e, 1957* (People's Handbook, 1957), Peking, 1957, listed 27 higher courts and the names of their presidents and vice-presidents (p. 317), but subsequent publications have omitted this part completely.

[3] Among the other divisions of the Supreme Court are the Military Tribunal and the Railway and Water Transportation Division. However, beginning with the 1961 issue, *Jen-min shou-ts'e* has stopped listing the names of the chief judges and associate chief judges of the divisions of the Supreme Court.

[3a] The resolution was adopted on June 23, 1955. For its text, see *Jen-min shou-ts'e*, 1956, p. 296 and *New China News Agency*, Peking, June 23, 1955.

THE COURT STRUCTURE OF THE PEOPLE'S REPUBLIC OF CHINA

(including the system of selection of court personnel)

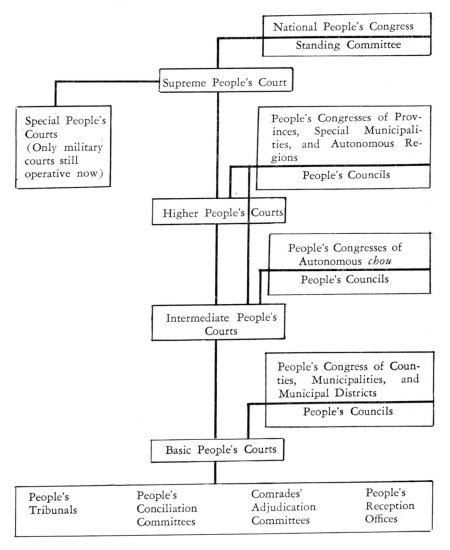

courts be submitted to the Supreme Court for approval.[4] On April 28, 1959, following what the Supreme Soviet of the U.S.S.R. did in May 1956, it passed another resolution abolishing the Ministry of Justice and transferring the judicial administrative work to the Supreme People's Court.[5] Similar actions have been taken at the local levels to close down the judicial departments and assign their duties to the courts. In the opinion of a Chinese legal writer, this decision to integrate the functions of adjudication and judicial administration would simplify the line of leadership, ensure the proper guidance over the courts, and eliminate the inevitable overlap of work between the courts and judicial administrative organs.[6]

Special People's Courts

The Organic Law of the People's Courts lists three types of special courts: Military Courts, Railway-transport Courts, and Water-transport Courts (Article 26). The Standing Committee of the National People's Congress has the authority to prescribe the organization of these courts (Article 27), and the Supreme Court has supervisory power over them.

In actuality Military Courts are the only special courts still operative in Communist China today. To be sure, the Peking regime began to build special transport courts on the soviet model back in July, 1953. By 1955 there were ten Railway-transport Courts in Peking, Tientsin, Shanghai, Taiyuan, Harbin, Kirin, Lanchow, Liuchow, Chinchow, and Chengchow and three Water-transport Courts in Wuchang-Hankow, Tientsin, and Chungking.[7] These courts were charged with the responsibility of handling cases of counterrevolutionary activities, sabotage, corruption, larceny, and negligence of duties in the transportation system, for the purpose of protecting production and serving the economic construction of the country.[8] Mass trial and on-the-spot trial were the frequently-used procedures by these courts to perform their education-propaganda functions.[9] In August

---

[4] *Jen-min jih-pao* (People's Daily), Peking, July 16, 1957.

[5] Text of the resolution is in *Chung-hua jen-min kung-ho-kuo fa-kuei hui-pien*, Vol. 9 (1959), p. 108.

[6] Wu Chien-fan, "The Reform of the Judicial Administrative System of Our Country," *Cheng-fa yen-chiu* (Studies of Political Science and Law), Peking, No. 3, 1959, pp. 50-51.

[7] *Kuang-ming jih-pao* (Kuang-ming Daily), Peking, March 15, 1955.

[8] *New China News Agency*, April 1, 1954.

[9] For reports of mass and on-the-spot trials conducted by these courts, see *ibid.*, and *Jen-min jih-pao*, September 4, 1954.

1957, apparently inspired by the Soviet action a few months earlier, Peking abolished all the special transport courts and transferred the cases previously under their jurisdiction to the jurisdiction of regular courts.[10]

As to the Military Courts, information about their organization and functions has been rather scant. There is a Military Tribunal within the Supreme People's Court, which, for instance, tried in November 1954 thirteen American nationals in two alleged espionage cases.[11] Below the Supreme Court, there is a hierarchy of Military Courts in the People's Liberation Army.[12] The tasks of these Courts would seem to be similar to those of their Soviet counterparts: to combat any criminal encroachments on the security of the state, the fighting capacity of the armed forces, military discipline, and rules of military service.[13]

Local People's Courts

Before 1954 the regular courts at local levels consisted of provincial and county courts. The 1954 Organic Law has added an intermediate level to the local judiciary hierarchy, which is now composed of higher, intermediate and basic courts.

These local courts are essentially organized on an identical basis. Each court is composed of a president, one or more vice-presidents, and a number of judges (Articles 16, 21 & 24). Each of the higher and intermediate courts has a criminal chamber, a civil chamber, and such other chambers as are deemed necessary (Articles 21 & 24). A basic court may also set up a criminal chamber and a civil chamber, if necessary (Article 16). Each chamber is headed by a chief judge and associate chief judges (Articles 16, 21 & 24). The courts are responsible to the local "people's congresses" at corresponding levels and report to them. The judicial work of the lower courts is subject to the supervision of the upper courts as well as to the overall direction of the Supreme Court (Articles 14 & 21).

A. *Higher People's Courts*   The higher "people's courts" consist

---

[10] Text of the State Council's decision to abolish the transport courts (adopted on August 9, 1957) is in *Chung-hua jen-min kung-ho-kuo fa-kuei hui-pien*, Vol. 6 (1957), pp. 297-298.

[11] *Jen-min jih-pao*, November 24, 1954.

[12] L. M. Gudoshnikov, *Legal Organs of the People's Republic of China*, (Trans. from Russian) JPRS (Joint Publication Research Service), No. 1698-N, 1959, p. 50.

[13] A. Denisov and M. Kirichenko, *Soviet State Law*, Moscow, 1960, p. 307.

of those set up for provinces, autonomous regions, and municipalities directly under the central authority (Article 23). These courts take initial jurisdiction over cases assigned to them by laws and cases transferred from the lower courts. They also hear appeals against judgments of the lower courts as well as protests lodged by the procuratorates (Article 25).

B. *Intermediate People's Courts* The Chinese Communists added the intermediate courts to their judicial hierarchy in 1954 to facilitate litigations and relieve the burden of the upper courts.[14] Under Article 20 of the Organic Law, intermediate courts may be established in various areas of a province or autonomous region, in municipalities directly under the central authority and other large municipalities, and in autonomous *chou* (prefectures). Each province thus can have several intermediate courts below its higher court. Kwangtung, for example, has six intermediate courts within its jurisdiction.[15]

The intermediate courts examine cases of first instance either assigned to them by laws or transferred from the basic courts. They also take cognizance of appeals from the basic courts and protests of the procuratorates. Moreover, if an intermediate court considers a case as highly important, it may request the upper court to take jurisdiction of the trial (Article 22).

C. *Basic People's Courts* The basic "people's courts" include the courts of counties, municipalities (undistricted), autonomous counties, and municipal districts (Article 15).[16] They are the courts of first instance for ordinary criminal and civil cases. In the event of important cases, they may ask the upper courts to take over the original jurisdiction (Article 18). Among their other duties are to settle civil disputes and minor criminal cases without a formal trial and to direct the work of the "people's conciliation committees" (Article 19).

In addition, the basic courts are empowered to set up "people's

---

[14] Huang Yuan, *Jen-min fa-yuan chi-pen chi-shih chiang-hua* (Lectures on the Basic Knowledge of the People's Courts), Canton, 1956, p. 14; Ministry of Judicial Administration, *Kung-fei szu-fa hsien-k'uang* (Current Situation in the Judicial System of the Communist Bandits), Taipei, 1960, p. 11.

[15] Huang Yuan, p. 14; Ministry of Judicial Administration, p. 12. It is contemplated that each of the municipalities directly under the central authority, such as Peking and Shanghai, will have several intermediate courts under its higher court. See Gudoshnikov, p. 74.

[16] Amoy, for instance, is an undistricted municipality while Canton is a municipality divided into several districts.

tribunals" according to the conditions of the locality, population, and cases (Article 17). These tribunals, it should be emphasized here, are totally different from the "people's tribunals" that existed during the Common Program era. The latter were essentially *ad hoc* and temporary tribunals, organized to carry out specific campaigns such as the Agrarian Reform, Three-Anti, Five-Anti, and Suppression of the Counterrevolutionary Movements. They disappeared from the scene as soon as the movements were concluded.[17]

The present "people's tribunals," on the other hand, are a part of the regular court system and have as their predecessors the circuit courts. Following the resolution of the Second National Judicial Work Conference held in April 1953, circuit courts were widely organized in rural areas by the basic courts.[18] Moving from one district to another and holding on-the-spot trials, the circuit courts were designed to economize time, facilitate the people's lawsuits, settle cases with high efficiency, and protect and promote agricultural production.[19] By September 1954 3,795 circuit courts reportedly had been established in mainland China.[20] One major shortcoming of the circuit courts, however, was their great mobility which often made it inconvenient for parties seeking access to them. To remedy the situation, the 1954 Organic Law instituted the new "people's tribunals" at fixed localities, to which the people may bring their disputes at any time. Some of the "people's tribunals" have been converted from the circuit courts already in existence, while the others have been set up for the first time in accordance with the need of the masses.[21]

Among the most noteworthy features of the present "people's tribunals" are that they are permanent organs and form component parts of the basic courts and that their judgments and orders are the judgments and orders of the basic courts (Article 17). As their chief responsibilities, they try ordinary civil cases and minor criminal cases,

----

[17] See the section on the "people's tribunals" in Chapter 2.

[18] The resolution proposed a number of steps to be taken to improve judicial work in the People's Republic. Its text is in *Chung-yang jen-min cheng-fu fa-ling hui-pien* (Compendium of the Laws and Regulations of the Central People's Government) 1953 (Peking, 1955), pp. 93-98.

[19] See the editorial of *Jen-min jih-pao*, May 20, 1954. For some detailed discussion of the circuit courts, see Lung Chien-fu, *Chung-kung szu-fa p'ou-shih* (An Analysis of the Chinese Communist Judiciary System), Hong Kong, 1957, pp. 41-46.

[20] Reported in a speech by Shih Liang, Minister of Justice, in *Ta-kung pao* (L'Impartial), Tientsin, July 31, 1955.

[21] *New China News Agency*, April 10, 1955.

conduct propaganda on laws and policies, guide the conciliation committees, handle letters and visits from the people, and take care of matters referred to them by the basic courts. Evidently an important organizational device for carrying out the mass line in judicial work, the "people's tribunals" have developed in the past few years a workstyle of combining mobility with stability through the use of both on-the-spot trials and regular court hearings.[22]

Judicial Committees

The judicial committees of the "people's courts" are important organs through which the Communist principle of "collective leadership" is implemented in trial work. According to Article 10 of the Organic Law, these committees are appointed by the "people's councils" at the corresponding levels upon the recommendation of the presidents of the local courts; the judicial committee of the Supreme People's Court is appointed by the Standing Committee of the National People's Congress upon the recommendation of the President of the Supreme Court. As a rule, members of the judicial committee comprise the president, division chiefs, and judges of the courts.[23] Meetings of the committees are presided over by the court president, and the chief procurator of the corresponding level has the right to participate in the discussions at such meetings.

One of the major functions of the judicial committee is the review of a legally effective judgment. The Organic Law (Article 12) empowers the committee to review a legally effective court decision if some definite error is found. The committee may thus nullify an erroneous judgment and ask the court for retrial or the procuratorate for additional investigation.[24]

Another important task of the committee is the summarization

[22] Ch'en Fou, "A Tentative Discussion of Some Problems of the People's Tribunals," *Cheng-fa yen-chiu*, No. 3, 1964, pp. 22-24, 38.

[23] Members of the committee were listed in Article 15 of the 1952 Provisional Regulations Governing the Organization of the People's Courts of the People's Republic of China. Text of the Regulations is in *Chung-yang jen-min cheng-fu fa-ling hui pien*, 1951, pp. 79-85. Although the Organic Law of the People's Courts now does not prescribe the composition of these committees, the "people's councils" usually appoint the same judicial personnel as committee members. Lung Chien-fu, pp. 21-22.

[24] For the detailed procedure of the judicial committee in reviewing a legally effective judgment, see V. Ye, Chugunov, *Criminal Court Procedures in the Chinese People's Republic* (Trans. from Russian) JPRS, No. 4595, 1961, pp. 200-201.

of judicial experience, a useful technique for coping with some existing problems in China's partial legal vacuum. While this technique
can be traced back to the Yenan period, it did not receive special attention until the 1953 conference called by the Supreme People's
Court to sum up judicial work and practice.[25] It was further regularized
in 1954 when the Organic Law of the People's Courts (Article 10)
specifically entrusted the task of summing up judicial experience to
the judicial committees. An editorial of the *Kuang-ming Daily*
stated on May 22, 1955:

> At present we do not have a comprehensive and detailed legal sys-
> tem to refer to; nor are we able to produce such a thing in a moment.
> Furthermore, many of our judicial personnel are without sufficient
> knowledge about matters pertaining to policy, society, and profes-
> sional duties. In order to make our judicial work capable of meeting
> the demands of objective conditions and expanding activities, the
> people's courts   not only have to study diligently the policy and
> laws of the state, the writings of legal science, and the advanced
> experience of Soviet Russia, but also must summarize conscientiously
> and promptly our past judicial practice.

The summarization of judicial experience takes various forms. One
of them involves a general summation of the overall record. It
reviews judicial practice, examines the past achievements and mistakes, and suggests ways to raise the efficiency and improve the work
of the courts. A good example is the summary of the judicial work
of the Peking Municipal People's Court, published in 1950.[26] Also
illustrative are the 3,753 preliminary draft reports prepared by the
courts of Kweichow province in 1959 to sum up the experience of
judicial work over the past ten years. These reports covered a wide
range of subjects, including the implementation of the Party line, the
work of conciliation committees, and the role of publicity and education in the legal system.[27]

A more specific form of summing up judicial practice is the collection of exemplary cases and court decisions. This process calls for

---

[25] Ma Hsi-wu, "Several Problems Concerning the Present Judicial Work,"
Hsin-hua pan-yueh-k'an (New China Semimonthly), Peking, No. 9, 1956,
p. 19.

[26] Text of the summary is in Secretariat of the Peking Municipal People's
Court, *Jen-min szu-fa kung-tso chu-yu* (Illustrative examples of People's
Judicial Work), Peking, 1950, pp. 9-33.

[27] Yeh Ku-lin, "Report on the Work of the Kweichow Higher People's
Court," American Consulate General, Hong Kong, *Survey of China Mainland Press*, No. 2143, November 25, 1959.

the classification of past cases, selection of model cases from each category, analysis of the causes of crimes and civil disputes, and generalization of uniform standards for determining punishment and rendering judgments. In 1956, for instance, a classified collection of law cases was reported to have been published jointly by the higher courts of Peking, Tientsin, and the provinces of Fukien, Shantung, and Liaoning.[28] Another form of summarizing judicial experience is concerned with trial procedures for both civil and criminal cases. In the early part of 1956, the Judicial Committee of the Supreme People's Court compiled two summaries of the civil and criminal procedures used by the "people's courts" in fourteen cities and then sent them to the lower courts on an experimental basis.[29]

The summarization of judicial practice, in the views of Communist spokesmen, can accomplish several important tasks. First, it can enrich judicial cadres' professional knowledge, improve their workstyle, and raise the efficiency and quality of court trials.[30] Secondly, it can lift the political level of judicial personnel, sharpen the struggle against the class enemy, and insure the correct execution of Party policy by the courts.[31] "As a result of summing up trial experience," said the *People's Daily* on November 1, 1954, "we have strengthened the control of Party committees over legal work at all levels . . . In the past many courts failed to draw up summaries of judicial practice. Consequently, their reports to the Party committees were often fragmentary and vague, and it was difficult for the Party committees to give comprehensive and practical guidance to these courts in their work."

Last but not least, summarized judicial practice can help fill some gaps in the legal system and provide the legislative body with relevant source material for drafting laws.[32] It should be noted here that the courts in Communist China officially do not have the law-creating authority in the form of mandatory judicial precedents. Previous court decisions are not meant for the judges to "copy or transplant" but only for them to use as "references" in dealing with individual

[28] Lu Ming-chien, "New Development in the Work of Summarizing Judicial Experience," *Cheng-fa Yen-chiu*, No. 3, 1956, p. 8.

[29] Kao Ko-lin, "Work of the Supreme People's Court since 1955." *New China News Agency*, April 24, 1959.

[30] Ma Hsi-wu, p. 19; "Overcome Conservative Thought and Expand the Advanced Experience in Judicial Work," *Kuang-ming jih-pao*, January 15, 1956.

[31] Ma Hsi-wu, p. 19; Lu Ming-chien, p. 11.

[32] Ma Hsi-wu, p. 19.

cases.[33] On the other hand, because of the existence of a partial legal vacuum in China and the special emphasis on "practice" by Mao Tse-tung, principles and procedures derived from judicial experience do play a useful role in the development of "people's legality."[34] By way of illustration, the following description of the Chinese legislative process from an official text book is cited:

> Many of our country's laws and decrees . . . were first drafted by the state's directing core, the Communist Party of China, through investigation and study of the practical work, evaluation of the people's experience in struggles, and concentration of the people's revolutionary will. Then, the Party sought opinions from various walks of life and gradually formed these opinions into drafts. Through state organs' discussion and revision, some of these statutes were disseminated in the form of drafts down to *hsien* and *hsiang* for extensive mass discussion. Others were put into trial for a certain period of time, and then became formal laws and decrees after examination and adoption by the state legislative organ.[35]

People's Assessors

Participation of "people's assessors" in judicial work is a manifestation of the "mass line" policy of the Chinese Communist Party. As discussed before, the assessor system has been instituted by the Communists since the early years of their revolution. It was regularized in 1954 by the Constitution and the Organic Law of the People's Courts with a strong resemblance to the system of people's assessors in the U.S.S.R.[36] Article 75 of the Constitution states: "The system

[33] Lu Ming-chien, p. 10; *Kuang-ming jih-pao*, January 15, 1956 (cited note 30). Also consult Wang Yu, "Criticism of the Concept that 'Court Decisions Are Rules of Law' in America's Legal Realism," *Cheng-fa yen-chiu*, No. 2, 1964, pp. 47-52.

[34] Ma Hsi-wu (p. 19) points out that the law must be the summary of the "struggle experience" of the masses and should never be made on the basis of mere imagination and "subjectivism." For Mao's discussion of important relations between theory and practice, see Mao Tse-tung, *On Practice*, Peking, 1958.

[35] *Lectures on the General Principles of Criminal Law in the People's Republic of China*, JPRS, No. 13331, 1962, p. 22. The original text, *Chung-hua jen-min kung-ho-kuo hsing-fa tsung-tse chiang-i*, was published in 1957 by the Institute of Criminal Law Research, Central Political-Judicial Cadres' School, Peking. A similar statement on the law-making process is in K'ang Shu-hua & Chou Hsin-ming, "Crush the Attack of the Rightist Elements on the People's Democratic Legal System," *Hsin chien-she* (New Construction), Peking, No. 9, 1957, p. 19.

[36] For the Soviet system of people's assessors, see Denisov & Kirichenko, pp. 308-310.

of people's assessors applies, in accordance with law, to judicial proceedings in the people's courts."[37] Article 8 of the Organic Law provides that "people's assessors" shall participate in the trial of all cases in the first instance, except in minor civil and criminal matters. In the following paragraphs we shall examine how "people's assessors" are selected, what rights they possess, and what advantages and problems the assessor system has in China.

Selection of People's Assessors   According to the Organic Law, any citizen over 23 years of age who has the right to elect or be elected and has not been deprived of political rights is eligible to be elected a "people's assessor" (Article 35). He or she is expected, of course, to have a good character and a "clear political history."[38] Since the Communists control the selection process, reliability of those chosen is thus insured. A directive issued in July 1956 by the Ministry of Justice has served as a provisional guide on the number, selection, and term of office of "people's assessors."[39] It leaves each "people's court" to determine the number of "people's assessors" on the basis of (1) the number of cases handled, (2) the ratio of two assessors to one judge, and (3) the ten-day term a year for each assessor.

The method of selecting "people's assessors" is given by this directive as follows. In the case of the basic courts, "people's assessors" are elected by local residents directly or by the "people's congresses" of *hsiang*, towns, and municipal districts. In the case of the intermediate courts, "people's assessors" are elected by the "people's Congresses" of *ch'ü* (districts), municipalities, and counties; they may also be chosen from among the workers of institutions, people's organizations, and enterprises at the corresponding level. In the case of the higher courts, "people's assessors" are selected from among the workers of people's organizations and enterprises at the same level. By 1957 some 246,500 assessors were reported to have been elected from all walks of life: workers, peasants, clerks, industrialists, businessmen, and others.[40] According to more recent information from China,

---

[37] Text of the Constitution is in *Chung-hua jen-min kung-ho-kuo fa-kuei hui-pien*, Vol. 1, pp. 4-31. English text is in *Documents of the First National People's Congress* (cited note 1), pp. 131-163.

[38] "Questions Concerning Elections of People's Assessors Answered," *Hei-lung-chiang jih-pao* (Heilungkiang Daily), Harbin, March 25, 1958.

[39] Ministry of Justice, "Directive on the Number, Tenure, and Selection of People's Assessors," *Chung-hua jen-min kung-ho-kuo fa-kuei hui-pien*, Vol. 4 (1957), pp. 239-241.

[40] Shih Liang, "The Judicial System in New China," *People's China*, Peking, No. 2, 1957, p. 17.

there are usually forty to a hundred "people's assessors" elected in each county.[41]

For every elected "people's assessors," the term of office is two years. An assessor is normally required to perform his duties for not more than ten days a year, but the time can be extended if his continued presence is needed to complete the trial of a case.[42] Participation of "people's assessors" in court work is arranged through the combined use of unscheduled individual invitations and a fixed system of rotation. Specific invitations are used by the courts when cases come up which demand "people's assessors" with special and technical knowledge.[43]

Rights of People's Assessors   Under the Organic Law "people's assessors" enjoy theoretically "equal rights" with the judges in the exercise of their functions (Articles 36). They can examine the files of a case, verify all facts and evidence, and question the parties and witnesses at the trial. Along with the judges, they also have the right to decide on a judgment and sign the court decision.[44] While on duty "people's assessors" are entitled to receive wages as usual from their regular place of employment. Assessors who are not wage-earners receive proper compensation from the courts. For those who have to come from a great distance to carry out their work, travel allowances are provided.[45]

Although not specified by the law, it is an established practice that "people's assessors" should not discuss confidential matters pertaining to a case with the parties involved or any other people during the course of the trial.[46] Like the judge, a "people's assessor" may be asked to withdraw by a party to a case if he considers that the assessor has a personal interest in the case or, for any other reason, cannot administer justice impartially. In such a situation the president of the

---

[41] See the statement by Wu Teh-feng (President of the Chinese Political Science and Law Association) in Felix Greene, *Awakened China*, New York, 1961, p. 195.

[42] Articles 3 and 4 in the directive issued by the Ministry of Justice in July 1956 (cited note 21).

[43] Li Pang-ning, "Talk about the System of People's Assessors," *Kuang-ming jih-pao*, May 13, 1957.

[44] *Ibid.*; *Hei-lung-chiang jih-pao*, March 25, 1958 (cited note 38). A court decision is reached through a majority vote. Two assessors can conceivably out-vote the judge. In case of a stalemate in voting, the judicial committee of the court is the final authority to furnish a decision.

[45] See Article 37 of the Organic Law of the People's Courts and *Hei-lung-chiang jih-pao*, March 25, 1958.

[46] Li Pang-ning, *Kung-ming jih-pao*, March 13, 1957.

court has the authority to decide whether or not the assessor would withdraw.[47]

Advantages of the Assessor System   Writers in Communist China have praised the "superiority" of the system of "people's assessors" and listed its three major advantages to support their claim.[48]

1. The system attracts the masses to participate directly in both political and judicial activities. Given a sense of responsibility in national affairs, the broad masses of people are inspired by the system to take an active part in protecting the interest of the state against its enemy and furthering the cause of socialist construction. For instance, after Ai Ch'ing-hai of a pipe and tube foundry in Anshan was elected assessor, the workers of his unit reportedly drew up on their own an emulation pact to take over the work he left behind and fulfilled the production task satisfactorily.[49]

2. The enforcement of the "people's assessor" system improves the quality of court work. Coming from all parts of society, "people's assessors" are most familiar with the life and aspirations of the masses. Thus, their participation in judicial proceedings enables the courts to have a better grasp of thoughts and feelings of the people and to implement more properly the laws and policies of the state. It also can help increase the efficiency of trial work, prevent the miscarriage of justice, and minimize the occurrence of biased and subjective judgments. Take the report concerning the court of Hsi-tan district of Peking as an example. In the past each judge averaged some 20 cases a month. After the introduction of the assessor system, the average of each judge increased to 50 cases a month. During a nine-month period, 27.5% of the appealed judgments of the court in cases where no assessors had been used were either altered or returned for retrial. In the same period, only 22.8% of its appealed judgments in cases where assessors had taken part were not upheld by the upper court.[50]

3. The assessor system facilitates the spread of legal discipline.

---

[47] Concerning this question, Article 13 of the Organic Law of the People's Courts mentions judicial officers in general terms to include both judges and assessors.

[48] Huang Yuan (cited note 14), pp. 28-30; "Fully Develop the Functions of People's Assessors," *Kuang-ming jih-pao* (editorial), January 28, 1956; Tseng Li and T'ung Ko, "The Advantages of the People's Assessor System," *Kung-jen jih-pao* (Daily Worker), Peking, January 18, 1957; Wang Huai-an, "The Superior Quality of the People's Assessor System of Our Country," *Hsin chien-she*, No. 1, 1956, pp. 37-41.

[49] *Kuang-ming jih-pao* (editorial), January 28, 1956.

[50] Wang Huai-an, p. 41.

By participating directly in court activity, "people's assessors" become well acquainted with the laws and policies of the state. When they return to their regular place of work, they are in a position to propagate the concept of socialist legality and to impress upon the masses the importance of observing the laws and maintaining social order. A good many cases have been reported, ranging from one assessor's achievement in settling family quarrels to another's success in revolving disputes and promoting unity between two villages.[51]

Problems of the Assessor System Despite the advantages of the assessor system listed by the Communists, there is, however, official admission that in actual practice a number of problems do exist. For one thing, some judicial officers have a contemptuous attitude toward "people's assessors" and regard their presence as merely hampering the administration of justice.[52] For another, certain administrators of state organs and enterprises have no understanding of the "people's assessor" system and are often reluctant to let their men serve as assessors lest the production work of their units may be adversely affected.[53] Moreover, there are some assessors who look upon their participation in court proceedings as an extra burden. Still others have so little self-confidence that they consider themselves totally subservient to the judges. The negative views of those assessors are frequently reflected by their failure to get to the court on time and to perform their judicial duties conscientiously.[54] All told, it appears obvious that at the present stage "people's assessors" participate in the judicial process often for window-dressing rather than decision-making purposes.

Auxiliary Organs

People's Conciliation Committees Below the basic courts are "people's conciliation committees" charged with the responsibility of settling civil disputes and minor criminal cases through conciliation. Although existent in the Communist-held areas long before 1949, these committees were regularized by the Provisional Rules Governing Organization of People's Conciliation Committees issued by the State Administrative Council in March 1954.[55] Composed of three to eleven elected members each and operating on the village and

[51] *Jen-min jih-pao*, March 14, 1957; Huang Yuan, pp. 30-31.
[52] Li Pang-ning, *King-ming jih-pao*, May 13, 1957; Wang Haui-an, p. 41.
[53] Tso P'ing, "How to Solve the Difficulties of Inviting People's Assessors?" *Kuang-ming, jih-pao*, August 11, 1956.
[54] Tseng Lu and T'ung Ko, *Kung-jen jih-pao*, January 18, 1957.
[55] Text of the Rules is in *Jen-min jih-pao*, March 23, 1955.

precinct levels, the conciliation committees soon became widely established and numbered 157,966 by the middle of 1955.[56]

In response to Mao Tse-tung's famous speech "On the Correct Handling of Contradictions Among the People," greater efforts have been made by the Communists in recent years to expand the role of conciliation work as an instrument for resolving "internal contradictions."[57] The old conciliation committees have been thoroughly reorganized into new ones* Throughout the country the new committees, together with their sub-committees and small teams, have been set up at the various street offices, stores, schools, residents' committees, enterprises, factories, and workshops in the cities; and in the production brigades and production teams of the "people's communes" in the countryside. Compared with the old conciliation committees, the new ones have greater power and wider areas of activities. Their task is through conciliation and "patriotic public pacts" to settle the people's disputes, to strengthen internal solidarity, to preserve social order, to promote production, and to conduct propaganda and education in law and discipline.[58] In order to make sure that neither mediators nor the parties involved in a dispute will miss any productive activity, conciliation work now is advised to be carried out in evenings and on holidays under normal circumstances.[59]

Old or new, the conciliation committees operate in accord with the laws and policies of the state, and under the direction of both the judicial organs and political authorities at basic levels.[60] Members of the committees are residents of the local communities, chosen for their pure political background, good reputation, and enthusiasm for conciliation work.[61] Parties in disputes come before the committees on

[56] Shih Liang's report in *Ta-kung pao*, July 31, 1955.

[57] Mao's speech was made on February 27, 1957. The official English text was published by the Foreign Language Press, Peking, in 1957.

* Even the name has been changed from the conciliation (*t'iao-chieh*) committee to adjustment (*t'iao-ch-u*) committee. Lately, however, the old name is being used again.

[58] Wang Min, "The Significant Meaning of the People's Conciliation Work as Regards the Settlement of the People's Internal Contradictions," *Cheng-fa yen-chiu*, No. 2, 1960, pp. 27-32; Yeh Ku-lin, "Develop Fully the Role of People's Conciliation Work in the Construction of Socialism," *ibid.*, No. 4, 1964, pp. 13-14.

[59] *Ibid.*, p. 16.

[60] See Articles 2 & 6 of the Provisional Rules of 1954; Wang Min, pp. 30 & 32; Yeh Ku-lin, p. 17.

[61] Article 5 of the Provisional Rules of 1954; K. S. Woodsworth, "The Legal System of the Republic of China," *The Canadian Bar Journal*, August 1961, p. 305.

a voluntary basis. The committees cannot compel disputants to appear nor can they apply punishment and make arrests.[62] As a rule, the people feel obligated to attempt conciliation before carrying their disputes to the length of actual lawsuit; consequently, the conciliation committees have managed to settle a large number of grievances which would otherwise be clogging the courts. In Chungking, for instance, fourteen conciliation committees under one street office alone handled 202 civil cases during the period of January-August, 1956.[63] In Tungmen brigade, Kolou commune, Foochow municipality, a woman director of the "people's conciliation committee" had been so successful over the years in converting many neighbors from "enemies" to "friends" and persuading numerous quarreling couples into reconciliation that she was called the "untying-knots person."[64] Commenting on the work of the conciliation committees in China, one Western lawyer said that he was very much impressed with "the judiciousness and the common sense conduct."[65]

Comrades Adjudication Committees   These quasi-judicial institutions were first formed by the Chinese Soviet regime during the Kiangsi days. However, not until early 1953 did the People's Republic of China begin to institute them on an experimental basis.[66] Like the Comrades' Courts of the Soviet Union, the Comrades Adjudication Committees were organized in factories and mines. They were elected by the workers and employees of various industrial units and subject to the general supervision of the "people's courts" as well as the guidance of Party and government functionaries.[67]

Technically, the Comrades Adjudication Committees are not courts of law and have no authority to pronounce sentence. Their function is to deal with industrial accidents, breaches of labor discipline, neglect of duty, and minor thefts committed in a factory or mine. They may criticize and educate offenders; in the event of more serious lapses, they may request the management to impose such penalties as repri-

---

[62] Articles 6 & 7 of the Provisional Rules of 1954; Wang Min, p. 30; Woodsworth, p. 305; Yeh Ku-lin, p. 16.

[63] *Szu-ch'uan jih-pao* (Szechwan Daily), Chengtu, December 7, 1956. For more discussion of the role of conciliation in civil disputes, see Chapter 8.

[64] Li Ch'iang, "The Untying-Knots Person," *Chung-kuo fu-nü* (Chinese Women), Peking, No. 6, 1962, p. 20.

[65] Woodsworth, p. 305.

[66] Shih Liang's report in *Ta-kung pao*, July 31, 1955.

[67] *Jen-min jih-pao*, April 19, 1954; *Kuang-ming jih-pao*, May 30, 1955; Lung Chien-fu (cited note 19), pp. 54-56. For a brief description of the Soviet Comrades' Courts, see Harold J. Berman, *Justice in the U.S.S.R.*, New York, 1963, pp. 288-291.

mands, demotion, dismissal, etc. They also conduct propaganda-education campaigns among the workers to heighten the "revolutionary vigilance" and the respect for the rules and regulations.[68] After two years of operation, for instance, the Comrades Adjudication Committes of the Anshan Steel Works and the Machine Section of the Harbin Railway were reported to have achieved good results. Production in the plants had increased, labor discipline had improved, industrial accidents had shown a general decline, and absenteeism and negligence in work had been substantially stopped.[69] Since 1957, however, little has been heard about the Comrades Adjudication Committees in China, probably because much of their function has been performed by other informal and administrative institutions.[70]

People's Reception Offices　In compliance with the resolution of the Second National Judicial Work Conference of 1953, people's reception offices have been established by the courts at all levels.[71] Originally, these offices had four major functions: (1) to handle letters from the public and receive the people's call; (2) to settle simple cases requiring no extensive investigation; (3) to answer inquiries on matters relating to law and litigation; (4) to prepare petitions and record agreements.[72] Since 1955 most of the last two functions have been performed by the Legal Advisory Offices of the "people's lawyer" system formed in Communist China. However, the people's reception offices have continued to be active in receiving letters and visits from the people, hearing their complaints, and resolving uncomplicated problems.

From the standpoint of the Communist authorities, the people's reception offices are a useful channel through which to contact the masses and to exercise supervision over the "people's courts" of lower

---

[68] *Jen-min jih-pao*, April 19, 1954; Shih Liang's report in *Ta-kung pao*, July 31, 1955.

[69] *Kuang-ming jih-pao*, May 30, 1955.

[70] This seems to be the conclusion drawn by other researchers too. See, for instance, Jerome A. Cohen, "The Criminal Process in the People's Republic of China," *Harvard Law Review*, Vol. 79, No. 3, 1966, p. 531, note 150.

[71] By mid-1954 over 1,200 people's reception offices had been established. "Several Problems Concerning the Work of the People's Reception Offices of the People's Courts," *Jen-min jih-pao*, July 21, 1954.

[72] Ibid.; "The People's Reception Offices of the People's Courts," *Jen-min jih pao*, December 2, 1953.

levels.[73] During the "Big Leap Forward" campaign judicial personnel in the people's reception offices went to factories and streets directly to help industrial workers and local residents settle their problems.[74] In recent years there has been a general tendency on the part of all state and Party organs to encourage letters and personal visits from the people. It was reported, for instance, that the authorities in Kansu province, at the county level or above, received 500,000 such visits and letters during the year of 1962.[75]

Selection and Training of Judicial Personnel

According to the Organic Law, the presidents of the "people's courts" at all levels are elected for a four-year term by the corresponding "people's congresses," which also have the power to remove them from office (Articles 32 & 33). The vice-presidents and judges of the Supreme Court are appointed and removed by the Standing Committee of the National People's Congress while the vice-presidents and other officials of the local courts are appointed and removed by the "people's councils" at the corresponding levels (Article 32). Any citizen over twenty-three years of age and not deprived of political rights to elect and be elected is eligible to be chosen as a member of the courts (Article 31). As is true elsewhere, the actual power of selection and removal rests with the Communist Party. Consequently, only those who are loyal to the socialist cause may be chosen and kept as judges.

It should be noted that some degree of "redness and expertise" is attained at the top of the judiciary hierarchy in China. As revealed through an examination of their background, a number of high judicial officials are persons with considerable legal training and experience, some having practiced law before and others having been engaged in judicial work for a long time. The following names are cases in point. Shen Chün-ju, President of the Supreme People's Court during 1949-1954, and Shih Liang, Minister of Justice, 1949-1957, were both practicing lawyers when China was under the rule

---

[73] See the speech delivered by Tung Pi-wu, President of the Supreme People's Court, before the National People's Congress in *Ta-kung pao*, July 23, 1955. Also consult Chuang Yun-shu, "Discussion of the System of Handling Letters and Receiving Calls from the People," *Cheng-fa yen-chiu*, No. 2, 1962, pp. 27-30.

[74] *Kuang-ming jih-pao*, March 3, 1958.

[75] *Jen-min jih-pao*, February 21, 1963.

of Kuomintang. Tung Pi-wu, President of the SPC during 1954-1959, received his legal education in Japan and is a prominent legal expert in the Communist leadership. Hsieh Chüeh-tsai, President of the SPC during 1959-1964, served as Minister of Justice of the North China People's Government in 1948, and Vice-President of the Central Political-Judicial Cadres' School in 1954. Yang Hsiu-feng, current President of the SPC, has had important posts in education but was also once the Procurator-General of the North China People's Government. Cheng Chih-jang, a Vice-President of the SCP, held a number of legal positions in the Kuomintang era including the judgeship of a high court and deanship of the School of Law of Futan University. Wang Pei-jan, President of the Higher People's Court of Peking, was a leading figure in the Communist court system in North China long before the People's Republic came into being in 1949.[76]

At the lower levels, however, the qualifications of judicial personnel leave much to be desired. It should be recalled that at the outset the People's Republic did retain many old judicial officials of the Kuomintang regime, only to have them purged during the Judicial Reform Movement of 1952-1953.[77] To meet the demand for judicial cadres to run the local "people's courts," the Communist authorities have recruited the "active" elements from among the workers, peasants, intellectuals, and veterans of the Liberation Army. The overriding considerations have been the individuals' political reliability and correct "class stand" rather than legal training and educational background. As a result, the quality of judicial cadres in the New China is relatively low. Violation of law, miscarriage of justice, and even inability to write a decision on the part of judges have been reported.[78]

A few official accounts given in 1957 are quite illustrative. In the fifteen basic courts of Shanghai, there were over seventy judicial cadres who were former workers and store clerks.[79] In the "people's courts" of the Wuhan area, 43.3% of 367 judicial officials were

---

[76] Names of high judicial officials in Communist China can be found in the various issues of *Jen-min shou-ts'e* (People's Handbook). For brief biographies of these officials, consult Ministry of Foreign Affairs, *Gendai Chugoku jinmei jiten* (Biographical Dictionary of Contemporary China), Tokyo, 1957; Union Research Institute, *Who's Who in Communist China*, Hong Kong, 1966.

[77] See the section on "The Judicial Reform," in Chapter 2.

[78] See "Defective Administration of Justice" in Chapter 3.

[79] *Jen-min jih-pao*, August 22, 1957.

of peasant and worker background.[80] Of the judicial personnel in the province of Szechwan, only 36.2% had received legal training before. The meagre knowledge and limited experience of the judges were reflected in their trial work. Only 26.5% of appealed judgments in criminal cases and 44% of appealed judgments in civil suits were upheld by the Provincial Higher People's Court of Szechwan.[81] Speaking before the National People's Congress, even Tung Pi-wu admitted that the lack of adequate training and education of certain judicial cadres had contributed to some errors and defects in the administration of justice in the Chinese People's Republic.[82]

To train judicial personnel, two types of schools are available in Communist China. One is university law schools; the other special training schools and classes. A number of comprehensive universities, such as China People's University, Peking University, Northwest University, Kirin University, and Hupei University, have faculties of law within their structure. There are also several institutes of political science and law operating in the country. Peking, Shanghai, Kirin, Wuhan, Sian, and Chungking are the centers where major law schools and institutes are located.[83] Usually, it takes a student from four to five years after high school to complete his legal study. The enrollment figure in the law schools was estimated in 1961 to be three thousand.[84]

The other type of schools consists of the Central Political-Judicial Cadres' School, its branch schools, and various legal training classes in the provinces. The Central Political-Judicial Cadres' School in Peking, for example, has both regular and advanced classes. Each regular class runs for a year and takes as trainees leading administrative, judiciary, and procuratorial officials at the county level who are between twenty-

---

[80] *Ch'ang-chiang jih-pao* (Yantze Daily), Hankow, October 5, 1957.

[81] Stated before the National People's Congress by Liu Wen-hui, a former worlord of Szechwan, in *Hsin-hua pan-yueh-k'an,* No. 15, 1957, p. 78.

[82] *New China News Agency*, March 2, 1957.

[83] According to the Minister of Higher Education's "Guide to Institutions of Higher Education" in 1957, there were six law faculties in the comprehensive universities and four institutes of political science and law. American Consulate General, Hong Kong, *Current Background*, No. 462, July 1, 1957. Since then some reorganization and consolidation have taken place. Consult The Japanese Association of International Jurists (ed.), *Chugoku no ho to shakai* (Law and Society in China), Tokyo, 1960, p. 87; also Luke T. Lee, "Chinese Communist Law: Its Background and Development," *Michigan Law Review*, Vol. 60, 1962, p. 464.

[84] Woodsworth, p. 307.

five and thirty years of age. Each advanced class operates for a term of two years and has as trainees top administrative, judiciary, and procuratorial officials at the provincial level who are between thirty-five and forty-five years of age. The objective of the Central Political-Judicial Cadres' School is to retrain current leading cadres from the counties up and make use of their practical experiences for future improvement.[85] Beside the various judicial cadres' schools and training classes in the country, there are also special institutes set up to train judges and court officials among the national minorities.[86]

So far as legal curricula are concerned, individual variations, of course, exist from one school to another. However, the following seem to constitute the nucleus of subjects generally taught in all the legal institutions in Communist China: Marxism-Leninism, thought of Mao Tse-tung, theory of state and law, Russian legal system, history of the Chinese revolution, the constitution, judicial organization, the procuracy, land law, labor law, marriage law, civil law, and criminal law.[87]

Given the fact that certain important codes are still lacking in China and that political education and activities often encroach upon the time for academic learning, technical legal training received by judicial personnel would appear to be of rather limited scope. This, on the other hand, may not matter too much at the present stage of development in China when Party policy is considered the soul of the legal system and Party leadership is exercised even over trial work. Under the current slogan of "politics in command," ideological considerations obviously outweigh professional expertise in the application of the "red and expert" line in the judicial field.

Independence of the Courts?

In the Soviet Union there is a constitutional guarantee for the independence of *judges*.[88] In Communist China the independence guaranteed is that of the *courts*. Article 78 of the Constitution, as well

---

[85] Masao Fukushima, Naokichi Ubukata, and Ryoichi Hasegawa, *Chugoku no saiban* (Justice of China), Tokyo, 1957, p. 44.

[86] Shih Liang, *People's China*, No. 12, 1957, p. 19.

[87] See *Chugoku no saiban*, p. 45; L. T. Lee, pp. 465-466; *Kung-fei szu-fa chih yen-chiu* (A Study of the Judicial System of the Communist Bandits), Taipei, 1957, p. 60; Tieh Kuang, "Our Fighting Duties on the Battle-Front of Legal Theory," *Cheng-fa yen-chiu*, No. 2, 1964, p. 4.

[88] Article 112 of the 1936 Soviet Constitution reads: "Judges are independent and subject only to the law." Denisov & Kirichenko, p. 402.

as Article 4 of the Organic Law of the People's Courts, provides that "in administering justice the people's courts are independent, subject only to the law." This provision is interpreted to have two meanings: on the one hand, the courts reject any "illegal interference" in their work by government authorities, public organizations, or individuals, and, on the other hand, they must submit to the will and control of the people.[89] In other words, the "independence" of the courts is a rather restricted one and does not mean independence from the state and the Party. Spokesmen for the Peking regime have attacked the Western concepts of "judicial independence" and "separation of judges from politics" as reactionary and incompatible with the Dictatorship of People's Democracy. Being an instrument of the state, argues the official line, the "people's courts" must accept as do all other state organs the leadership and direction of the Chinese Communist Party.[90]

To be sure, the members of the courts have, in theory, the right to try cases without having judgments dictated to them. They are, however, obviously subject to various types of influence and control stemming from the channels of appointment, accountability, and supervision. Under the law the presidents of the "people's courts" are elected and removed by the corresponding "people's congresses"; judges and the powerful judicial committees are appointed and removed by the corresponding "people's councils."[91] Also legally, the courts are responsible to the "people's congresses" at the same level and have to report to the latter on their work.[92] Moreover, judicial supervision is exercised by the higher courts and the procuratorates to see that the lower courts function according to the law and perform their tasks properly.[93]

Additional checks on the judiciary are provided by the often-mentioned "mass line" devices and the press. To the extent that it handles legal questions and comments on cases and court decisions, the

---

[89] Shih Liang, *People's China*, No. 12, 1957, pp. 17-18, Wang Hui-an "Superiority of Our Judicial System," *Jen-min jih-pao*, October 16, 1954.

[90] Huang Yuan, pp. 19-20; Ch'i Wen, "We Must Thoroughly Liquidate the Influence of the 'Judicial Independence' Concept of the Bourgeois Class," *Cheng-fa yen-chiu*, No. 2, 1960, pp. 52-58. For additional discussion of the question of judicial independence, see the section on "the reversal in 1957" in Chapter 3.

[91] Articles 10, 32, 34 of the Organic Law of the People's Courts.

[92] Article 14 of the Organic Law.

[93] Articles 11, 12, 14 of the Organic Law. For a full account of the role of the procuratorates, see the following chapter.

Chinese press plays an influential role in the system of "people's justice." Suffice it here to cite a few examples. In reply to individual inquiries, the editor of the *Daily Worker* discussed questions concerning slander, inheritance, and the adoption of children.[94] In answering a letter to the editor, the *Chinese Youth Journal* expressed the view that sterility should not constitute a jusifiable ground for divorce.[95] There was a rape case in Shanghai in which the plaintiff, Chung Chin-mei, was dissatisfied with the municipal court's decision and wrote a letter of appeal directly to the *Liberation Daily*. Under the pressure of criticism published in the paper, the court sentenced the accused to jail and conducted a self-examination of its own "bureaucratic attitude."[96] Another case involved an army veteran, Kuo Chin-sheng, whose father was forced to commit suicide by local cadres in a village of Hopei province. After one year and a half, during which Kuo's persistent efforts to file the complaint before the courts bore no fruit, the case was finally "exposed" by the *Hopei Daily* and properly dealt with by the provincial Party committee.[97] Still another case was concerned with a peasant woman, Chung Kuei-lan, who had been wrongfully imprisoned three times by the "people's court" of Pihsien in Szechwan. Seeing its educational value, the *People's Daily* publicized this case to warn against bureaucratism and the miscarriage of justice.[98]

In the last two cases mentioned above, direct Party intervention was also reported. We may recall the Article 78 of the constitution only requires the courts to administer justice *according to the law*. Ironically, the lack of complete codes in Communist China has been used to justify the Party's interference in judicial functions. As stated by a writer in the leading legal journal, *Cheng-fa yen-chiu*, law is no more than a "concretization of Party policy." Since the existing laws cannot be "comprehensive enough to regulate everything in a detail," and since some of the laws are not "keeping pace with the ever-changing conditions of the class struggle," only through the accept-

[94] *Kung-jen jih-pao*, December 15, 1956; March 9, 1957; April 11, 1957.
[95] *Chung-kuo ch'ing-nien* pao (Chinese Youth Journal), Peking, November 3, 1962.
[96] *Chieh-fang jih-pao*, Shanghai, May 23, 26, 30, 1950, in W. Allyn Rickett (ed.), *Legal Thought and Institutions of the People's Republic of China: Selected Documents* (mimeograph for limited circulation), Philadelphia, 1964, pp. 188-197.
[97] *Jen-min jih-pao*, November 22, 1952.
[98] *Ibid.*, January 10, 1957.

ance of Party guidance in trial work are the courts able to "implement Party policy and observe the law of the state correctly."[99]

Indeed, as a result of the 1957 reversal of the trend toward legal stability, frequent and direct Party interference with individual judicial decisions in recent years has rendered the constitutional provision for the courts' independence rather academic. Judges in Communist China now find it prudent to consult local Party leaders on issues of any importance. The story of Liu Tse-chün, a county judge in Hopei province, is a case in point.[100] Liu began his judicial work in 1953 without any previous legal training or experience. However, in the years he served as a judge in a number of places, Liu always asked for instructions from Party committees on matters ranging from the conduct of trials to the writings of verdicts. Punctiliously he carried out all instructions of his Party superiors, and the result was astonishing. In the 1,592 cases he handled through his legal career, not a single mistaken judgment was found!

Besides the aforesaid story, there are some other instances where the domination of the Party over the courts is even more complete. In an editorial article highly critical of Peking, Russia's *Izvestia* on May 17, 1964 charged that "the violation of socialist legality has become a practice in the state life of China." Among other things, it pointed out that the Chinese policy has resulted in such a strange situation "when the secretary of a district Party committee ousts the judge, sits at the bench himself and starts to decide cases."[101] According to an account of the *People's Daily* on November 14, 1964, a dispute between two production brigades over the ownership of a mountainous tract of forest land was reported by a peasant to the Party committee (not to the court) of T'aihu county in Anhwei province. After dispatching an investigator to examine the situation, the assistant secretary of the Party committee promptly settled the dispute in accord with the established policy relating to this matter.[102]

---

[99] Ch'i Wen, "We Must Thoroughly Liquidate the Influence of the 'Judicial Independence' Concept of the Bourgeois Class," *Cheng-fa yen-chiu*, No. 2, 1960, p. 54.

[100] Liu Tse-chun, "My Experience in Judicial Work," *Cheng-fa yen-chiu*, No. 1, 1959, pp. 48-51.

[101] *The Current Digest of the Soviet Press*, Vol. 14, No. 21, 1964, p. 5.

[102] "Handle on a Priority Basis Letters and Calls from Poor and Lower-Middle Peasants," *Jen-min jih-pao*, November 14, 1964.

Chapter 5

The People's Procuracy

The Procuracy is one of the major institutions of the judicial system in the People's Republic of China. It has an all-embracing supervisory authority over the observance of law throughout the country. Although closely patterned upon the Soviet model, this institution does not seem to be entirely divorced from the political heritage of old China. Just as the Soviets have adapted the old Russian Procuracy to their own needs,[1] so could the Chinese Communists draw upon the experience of the traditional Censorate, known as the "eyes and ears of the Emperor."[2]

Before 1949 the Chinese Communists did not have a separate procuratorial system in the areas under their control. There were, however, individual procurators attached to the "people's courts" even during the Kiangsi period of the early 1930's. Their primary function was to investigate and prosecute criminal cases, while the State Political Security Bureau was given the main responsibility of detecting and suppressing the counterrevolutionaries.[3] During the Yenan period the "people's courts" of the Border Regions had procurators at all levels, whose duty was to conduct investigations, institute criminal proceedings, and supervise the execution of court decisions. In addition, the procuratorates as well as public security organs had the authority to make and approve arrest.[4] It was after the People's Republic of China came into being in late 1949 that

[1] See Harold J. Berman, *Justice in the U.S.S.R.*, New York, 1963, pp. 238-247.

[2] An interesting comparison between the People's Procuracy and the Censorate is attempted in Charles O. Hucker, "The Traditional Chinese Censorate and the New Peking Regime," *American Political Science Review*, Vol. 45, No. 4, 1951, pp. 1041-1057. As expected, the Chinese Communists dogmatically deny any link between the old system and the new Procuracy. See Ch'en Ch'i-yü, *Hsin-chung-kuo chien-ch'a chih-tu kai-lun* (A Sketch of New China's Procuracy), Peking, 1950, p. 33.

[3] Consult the section on "The Soviet Period" in Chapter 1 of this book.

[4] See the section on "The Yenan Period" in Chapter 1; also V. Ye. Chugunov, *Criminal Court Procedures in the Chinese People's Republic* (Trans. from Russian) JPRS (Joint Publication Research Service), No. 4595, 1961, pp. 4-5.

steps were taken to develop the People's Procuracy as an entity independent of the courts.

Pre-Constitutional Development, 1949-1954

The Organic Law of the Central People's Government, adopted on September 29, 1949, established the People's Procurator-General's Office with the "supreme supervisory power to ensure the strict observance of the law by all government institutions and public functionaries as well as by nationals of the country."[5] Following this, the Communist authorities proceeded to organize a new system of procuracy throughout China. In September 1951, the Central People's Government Council promulgated the Provisional Regulations Governing the Organization of the Office of the People's Procurator-General and the General Regulations Governing Organization of Offices of People's Procurators of Various Levels.[6]

According to these regulations, the People's Procurator-General's Office was the highest prosecuting organ, directly under the jurisdiction of the Central People's Government Council. Beneath this Office stood local offices of "people's procurators" at various levels. The local procuratorate was subject to the dual control of the next highest procuratorate and the "people's government" of the corresponding level. Among the chief functions of the procuratorate were to examine the legality of the actions of individuals and government organs, to investigate and institute legal proceedings against counterrevolutionary and other criminal elements, to oppose unwarranted or improper judgments and appeal them to a higher court, to supervise the management of prisons and labor reform institutions, and to participate in any important civil cases in which the interests of the state were involved. In areas where procuratorates had not yet been formed, the responsibilities of prosecuting crimes and opposing wrong judgments were "pro-

[5] Article 28 of the Organic Law. The English text of this document is in *The Important Documents of the First Plenary Session of the Chinese People's Political Consultative Conference,* Peking, 1949, pp. 29-44.

[6] For English translation of these two regulations, see American Consulate General, Hong Kong, *Current Background,* No. 183, May 26, 1952. A detailed discussion of the People's Procuracy before 1952 is in George Ginsburg and Arthur Stahuke's "The Genesis of the People's Procuratorate in Communist China 1949-1951," *The China Quarterly,* No. 20, October-December 1964, pp. 1-36.

visionally entrusted" to public security organs under the leadership of the procuratorates of higher levels.

Besides organizing the procuratorates, the Communists also set up the "people's procuratorial correspondents," "denunciation boxes," and reception offices to mobilize the masses to aid the work of detecting and prosecuting unlawful acts.[7] Active in the Three-Anti, Five-Anti, Judicial Reform and Suppression of Counterrevolutionaries Campaigns, the People's Procuracy served as a useful weapon for the Peking regime to deal with its enemies. The procuratorates in East China alone were reported to have prosecuted by 1953 over 14,000 counterrevolutionary cases.[8] Through the "procuratorial correspondents" and "denunciation boxes," the authorities in East China and the Northwest received in 1952 altogether 56,448 letters exposing bureaucratism and illegal activities.[9]

On the other hand, the whole system of procuracy was still in its infancy and left much to be desired in terms of organization and experience. First of all, many localities were still without any procuratorial organs. Up to early 1954 only one third of the administrative units on or above the county level had established the People's Procuratorates.[10] Furthermore, as pointed out by the Communists, there was a lack of understanding among many procuratorial cadres about the natures of their work.[11] Some still clung to the "old legal concept of separation of powers" and failed to appreciate the importance of cooperating closely with the courts and police. Others regarded their work as insignificant and their office as subservient to the court. Still others considered themselves occupying a privileged position as the "supreme supervisor." In the words of Vice Procurator-General Lan Kung-wu, "What to do and how to do it?" remained an unsolved problem in the procuratorial work of many places.[12]

---

[7] For reports on these devices, see *Hsin-hua jih-pao* (New China Daily), Chungking, September 4, 1952 and *Kuang-ming jih-pao* (Kuang-ming Daily), Peking, October 25, 1952.

[8] *Jen-min jih-pao* (People's Daily), Peking, April 25, 1953.

[9] *Ibid.*

[10] "Resolution of the Second National Procuratorial Conference," *Jen-min jih-pao*, May 21, 1954.

[11] "Strengthen Procuratorial Work and Protect National Construction," *Ibid.*, May 21, 1954; Lan Kung-wu, "People's Procuratorates of All Levels Should Actively Participate in the Judicial Reform Movement," *Ibid.*, September 7, 1952.

[12] *Ibid.*

Development under the 1954 Constitution

The Constitution of the People's Republic of China, adopted on September 20, 1954, strengthened the People's Procuracy greatly by making it independent of the rest of the government machinery in a highly centralized hierarchy without lateral lines of responsibility and control. Article 84 of the Constitution provides that the Supreme People's Procuratorate is accountable only to the National People's Congress or its Standing Committee. Articles 81 and 83 replace the principle of dual leadership with that of "vertical leadership" at local levels. According to them, the local procuratorates work solely under the guidance of the higher procuratorates and the overall leadership of the Supreme People's Procuratorate; they are independent in the exercise of their authority, free from any local state organs' interference.[13]

On the basis of the constitutional principles, the National People's Congress passed on September 21, 1954 a new Organic Law for the People's Procuratorates to define clearly their structure, power, and activities.[14] In an editorial on the implementation of this Law, the *Kuang-ming Daily* on May 27, 1955 called for the summing up of experience in procuratorial work and the establishment of all local "people's procuratorates" at the earliest possible time.

Evidence available indicates that considerable progress has been made in the systematic development of the People's Procuracy since 1954. Chief Procurator Chang Ting-ch'eng of the Supreme People's Procuratorate reported on July 22, 1955 the increase from 1,199 to 1,963 in the number of "people's procuratorates" and from 6,963 to 12,155 in the number of procuratorial cadres since the promulgation of the Constitution.[15] The *People's Daily* on September 5, 1956 also reported the increase of the number of "people's procuratorial correspondents" to 94,000. In another speech before the National People's Congress, Chang Ting-ch'eng pointed out that out of 1,400 court decisions protested by the pro-

---

[13] The text of the Constitution is contained in *Chung-hua jen-min kung-ho-kuo a-kuei hui-pien* (Compendium of the Laws and Regulations of the Chinese People's Republic), Peking, Vol. 1 (1956), pp. 4-31.

[14] The text of the Organic Law is in *ibid.*, pp. 133-138. For English texts of the Constitution and the Organic Law, see *Documents of the First Session of the First National People's Congress of the People's Republic of China,* Peking, 1955, pp. 131-163 and 201-211 respectively.

[15] *Ch'ang-chiang jih-pao* (Yantze Daily), Hankow, July 25, 1955.

curatorates in 1956, 1,159 were either over-ruled or sent back for new trials.[16] Although some prominent procurators were denounced as "rightist" during the latter part of 1957, and although relatively little statistical information has come out of the mainland in recent years, Communist spokesmen have continued to stress the expansion and success of procuratorial work throughout the country.[17] The People's Procuracy has been specially praised for its active role in the struggle for the suppression of counterrevolutionaries.[18] Because China is in a different stage of development from the Soviet Union, explains one writer, the People's Procuratorates have to be primarily concerned with prosecution against criminals in general and against counterrevolutionaries in particular.[19] According to Chang Ting-Ch'eng's latest report to the NPC, the procuratorial organs have so thoroughly carried out the task of consolidating the Dictatorship of People's Democracy that there have been a general and constant decline of criminal cases in China.[20]

Structure of the People's Procuracy

The hierarchy of the Procuracy established by the Organic Law of 1954 consists of the Supreme People's Procuratorate, local "people's procuratorates," and special "people's procuratorates." As the highest organ of the hierarchy the Supreme People's Procuratorate directs and supervises the work of all the local and special procuratorates in Communist China. Its Chief Procurator is elected by the National People's Congress for a term of four years. Its Deputy Chief Procurators and, upon the recommendation of the Chief Procurator, other procurators are appointed and removed by the Standing Committee of the National People's Congress (Article 20).

[16] *Ta-kung pao* (L'Impartial), Peking, July 2, 1957.

[17] In a report to the National People's Congress in June, 1956, Huang Shao-hung, however, made the following statement: "Since the system of procuracy is newly erected, its organization on every level is as yet unsound and the staffs are insufficient. In some of the counties in Chekiang there are only three procurators in the whole county and their knowledge of their work is defective." *China News Analysis,* Hong Kong, No. 140, July 20, 1956, p. 6.

[18] For instance, see Chuang Ting-ch'eng, "Firmly Maintain the Correct Line of the People's Democratic Dictatorship," *Hung-ch'i* (Red Flag), Peking, No. 20, October 16, 1959, pp. 32-33.

[19] Ch'en Ch'i-yü, p. 38.

[20] *Jen-min jih-pao,* January 1, 1965.

Local "people's procuratorates" are organized in provinces, autonomous regions, municipalities directly under the central authority, autonomous *chou* (prefectures), counties, municipalities, and autonomous counties. Some of the procuratorates may also set up branches if needed (Article 1). At each level, there are a chief procurator and a number of deputy chief procurators and other procurators. The chief procurator is in charge of the work and directs a procuratorial committee specifically formed to deal with important questions (Article 2). In the words of official spokesmen, the establishment of the latter committee ensures collective discussion of problems and enables the procuratorate to proceed with its work more efficiently. At the same time, the committee is subject to the guidance of the chief procurator, who has a decisive voice in case of disagreements among committee members. The whole arrangement, in short, stands as a combination of the system of collective leadership and that of individual responsibility —"a concrete utilization of the principle of democratic centralism."[21]

The personnel of the procuratorates of provinces, autonomous regions, and municipalities directly under the central authority are appointed and removed by the Supreme People's Procuratorate with the approval of the Standing Committee of the National People's Congress. Those at lower levels are appointed and removed by the Provincial-level procuratorates with the approval of the Supreme People's Procuratorate (Article 21). This procedure of appointment as well as the lineal accountability provided by the Constitution makes the People's Procuracy a single centralized system, under which the lower procuratorates are subordinate solely to the higher ones and are free from interference by the State Council or the local people's councils or congresses.

The Organic Law empowers the Standing Committee of the National People's Congress to prescribe the organization of special "people's procuratorates" (Article 1). Directly under the

---

[21] Chang Chien and others, "Some Understanding of the Principle under Which the People's Procuracy Implements the System of Responsible Chief Procurator," *Cheng-fa yen-chiu* (Studies of Political Science and Law), Peking, No. 1, 1956, p. 17. See also Li Chi-hsü, "People's Procuracy in Our Country," *Chung-kui ch'ing-nien pao* (Chinese Youth Journal), Peking, November 11, 1954; Lui Shao-chi, "Report on the Draft Constitution of the People's Republic of China," *Documents of the First National People's Congress,* p. 64.

Supreme People's Procuratorate, special Military Procuratorates and Railway and Water Transportation Procuratorates have been established with a structure similar to that of regular procurator- ates. In an article in the *Kuang-ming Daily* on August 1, 1956, a high procuratorial official gave three reasons for the establish- ment of the Transportation Procuratorates: (1) the need for better supervision; (2) the complicated and technical nature of cases involving the transportation system; (3) the importance of railway and water transportation in national construction.[22] Without any official explanation, however, the Chinese Commun- ists abolished the Transportation Procuratorates in 1957, leaving the Military Procuratorates the only special procuratorial organs still in operation at present.[23]

Buttressing the hierarchy of the highly centralized system of procuracy are the "people's procuratorial correspondents," "de- nunciation boxes," and other devices for building up a nation- wide and closely-knit network of supervision and control. At- tempts have been made to establish "people's procuratorial corres- pondents" at every point and in every section of society. Accord- ing to a 1956 report, for example, Hopei province planned to ex- pand the number of its "procuratorial correspondents" from 944 to 20,000 within the year so that they might be present in all collective farms, mines, factories, enterprises, etc.[24] Encourage- ment has also been given to the masses to write letters and visit the reception centers to report any guilty individual or any activity contrary to the law or interests of the regime. In Canton alone, the number of letters answered and calls attended to by the pro- curatorial authorities totalled 7,637 for the two years between 1956 and 1958.[25]

----

[22] Liu Hui-chi, "Task of the Railway Transportation Procuratorates," *Kuang-ming jih-pao*, August 1, 1956.

[23] The abolition of the Transportation Procuratorates was rather casually announced. In a newspaper notice, for example, the Chungking Branch Office of the Yantze Water Transportation Procuratorate announced in September 1957 that it had been ordered to cease operation and that from now on any case involving water transportation along the upper Yantze should be referred to the procuratorate of a given locality where the case had occurred. *Ch'ung-ch'ing jih-pao* (Chungking Daily), September 27, 1957.

[24] *Kuang-ming jih-pao*, May 18, 1956.

[25] Tseng Ch'any-ming, "Report on the Work of the People's Procura- torate of Canton since 1956," *Kuang-chou jih- pao* (Canton Daily), May 29, 1958.

Functions of the Procuracy

While a little more extensive than before, the functions of the People's Procuracy after the adoption of the Constitution remain essentially the same: to protect the interest of the state, to ensure the observance of the law, and to prosecute counterrevolutionary and other criminal elements. In the following pages we shall examine in some detail the Procuracy's functions as well as its relations with other state organs under the headings of general supervision, supervision over investigation, judicial supervision, and supervision over the execution of judgments.

A. General Supervision

Pursuant to the Organic Law of 1954, the People's Procuratorates exercise procuratorial authority over all departments of the State Council, all local organs of state, persons working in the government, and citizens at large, to ensure the observance of the law (Articles 3 and 4). If they find any decisions, orders, or measures of the organs of state to be illegal, the People's Procuratorates have the right to protest or demand the rectification of the situation. Although having no direct authority to annul, modify, or suspend the decisions protested, they can expect the governmental agencies concerned to answer their protests or demands (Article 8). Furthermore, the procurators have the right to attend the meetings, participate in the proceedings, and examine the orders, files, or other documents of any agencies or organizations (Article 19). They are also obliged to ascertain the criminal responsibility for illegal acts committed by any officials or citizens (Articles 9 and 10).

Before the abolition of the Ministry of Supervision in 1959, the Chinese Communists had tried to define the "division of labor" between that Ministry and the Procuracy as follows:

> The supervision offices are administrative supervisory organs with duties to oversee how state organs and personnel carry out government decisions and whether they break laws, neglect duties, or violate administrative discipline in their work. These organs have no responsibility for supervising non-government workers, and the only sanctions at their disposal are administrative penalties. The procuratorates, on the other hand, are legal supervisory organs with duties to prosecute both government and non-government personnel for any law-breaching and criminal acts; their activities are character-

ized by emphasis on legal sanctions. In the process of dealing with concrete cases, the supervision organ will refer the case to the procuratorate for prosecution if there is a crime to warrant criminal action; similarly, the procuratorate will refer the case to the supervision organ if there is delinquency of duties to warrant disciplinary action.[26]

In April 1959, the National People's Congress abolished the Ministry of Supervision and ordered that its work be carried on thereafter by the executive organs of state.[27]

B. Supervision over Investigation

Before the development of the Procuracy, many of its functions were performed by the public security organs. Even now the public security organs still investigate far more cases than the procuratorates. Although there is no legislative delimitation, in practice the public security organs conduct investigations over a wide variety of criminal cases ranging from theft to treason whereas the procuratorates only investigate certain specific categories of crimes.[28]

The Organic Law of the People's Procuracy, nevertheless, gives the procuratorates the supervisory power over investigative activities in a number of ways.[29] 1. If a procuratorate finds that a crime has been committed, it can investigate the case itself or transfer it to a public security organ for investigation (Article 10). 2. If a procuratorate discovers an infraction of the law in the investigative activities of a public security organ of the corresponding level, it should notify that public security organ to rectify its illegal practices (Article 11). 3. The procuratorate has the right to decide as to whether criminal proceedings should be instituted in a given case, and the public security organ is required to turn over the case to the procuratorate for decision on prosecution (Articles 11 and 12). 4. Arrest of any citizen must be first approved by the procuratorate unless it has been authorized by a "people's court" (Article 12). The public security organs may, according to the Regulations on Arrest and Detention, take emergency meas-

[26] Li Chi-hsü, *Chung-kuo ch'ing-nien pao,* November 11, 1954.

[27] The decision is in *Chung-hua jen-min kung-ho-kuo fa-kuei hui-pien,* Vol. 9 (1959), pp. 108-109.

[28] The procuratorates usually investigate cases of crimes committed in office, violation of industrial safety regulations, serious infractions of labor discipline, crimes against marriage or the family, certain cases of crimes against the person, rights, and lawful interests of citizens. Chugunov, p. 61.

[29] Consult Li Ya-hsi, "My Concept of the Work of the People's Procuracy in Regard to Supervision over Investigation," *Cheng-fa yen-chiu,* No. 2, 1957, pp. 49-52.

ures to make arrest without prior authorization when a person is discovered making preparations for a crime, in the act of perpetrating a crime, or apprehended immediately after commission of a crime.[30]

No sooner had the Organic Law of the People's Procuracy been promulgated than the procuratorates began to exercise supervision over the activities of the public security organs. During 1955 the procuratorates in Shanghai granted eighty-one percent of the police demands for warrants and refused thirteen percent; for the remaining six percent, further investigation was asked. In Chekaing province, sixty-four percent of the requests were granted, twenty-two percent were refused, and fourteen were held up for further investigation.[31] In order to maintain the system of "division of labor" and mutual restraint, the Organic Law of the People's Procuracy also confers upon the public security organ the right to object to a procuratorate's decision and appeal it to a higher office in the Procuracy (Article 13). Between January and April of 1957, the Provincial People's Procuratorate in Hunan reversed the decisions of the lower levels in twenty-one cases out of sixty-three appealed by public security organs.[32]

C. Judicial Supervision

Through their participation in the judicial process, the procuratorates supervise the legality of the activities of the courts in handling criminal and civil actions. As provided by Article 4 of the Organic Law, the People's Procuracy has the power not only to prosecute criminal cases but also to institute or intervene in legal actions with regard to important civil cases. Such intervention in civil suits is called for only when the state or public interest or the rights and legitimate interests of the people are involved.[33]

The Chinese Communists have often referred to the relationship between the "peole's procuratorates" and the "people's courts" as one of cordination and mutual restraint. It would be useful here to outline the formal procedure through which judicial supervision may be exercised by the procuratorates.

[30] Article 5. The text of the Regulations is in *Chung-hua jen-min kung-ho-kuo fa-kuei hui-pien*, Vol. 1 (1956), pp. 239-242.

[31] *China News Analysis*, No. 140, p. 6.

[32] Chang Ting-ch'eng's report to the National People's Congress, *Ta-kung pao*, July 2, 1957.

[33] For discussion of the Procuracy's supervision of civil suits, see Kao Hsin-tien, "The Chief Procurator's Participation in Civil Actions," *Fa-hsüeh* (Jurisprudence), Shanghai, No. 4, 1957, pp. 55-59.

1. Participation in the preparatory session. The main task of the procurator at the preparatory session of the court consists in presenting all the facts and evidence of the case, explaining the indictment, and answering the questions raised by the court. In addition, he has the task of supervising the legality of the hearing. Upon discovery of any violation of the legal proceedings by the judges, the procurator has the right to demand rectification or to ascertain the responsibility. If he disagrees with the court in its decision, the procurator has the right to submit a protest to the judicial committee of this court or to a court at the next higher level.

On the other hand, the "people's court" can decide during the hearing to return the case to the procuratorate for further investigation on the ground of defective information. It can decide to drop the case upon discovery of insufficient evidence or unjustifiable nature of prosecution. It can also order the revision of the indictment by the procuratorate if this document has been improperly formulated.[34]

2. Presence at the trial. Article 14 of the Organic Law gives the procurator the power as well as the responsibility to act as state prosecutor to prosecute cases at the court of trial. As explained by Communist writers, it is the task of the procurator to aid the court in verifying the entire circumstances of the case and to establish the guilt of the accused. He is allowed or even obliged to question the accused, the witnesses, and the experts when the accused tries to use deceptive arguments to evade the criminal responsibility. During the debates in court, the procurator should show not only that the accused committed the crime but that the crime he is accused of is dangerous to the state and society.[35]

Besides the function of prosecution, the procurator also performs supervisory functions at the trial. In the capacity of upholder of the law, the procurator supervises the activities of the court and the parties to a lawsuit to ensure their legality and to protect the legal rights of the defendant. He has the right, for instance, to demand the court to correct any of its activities contrary to the legal procedure or to change its improper ruling on the request made by the accused.[36]

---

[34] See Chang Fu-hai, "Supervision of the People's Procuracy over the Judiciary," *Cheng-fa yen-chiu,* No. 2, 1955, p. 16.

[35] *Ibid.;* Li Ting, "The Tasks of the Chief Procurator and other Procurators in the Court," *Kuang-ming jih-pao,* March 27, 1955.

[36] *Ibid.*

3. Protest against judgments. This is another important aspect of the procuratorate's supervision over the judiciary. Under the Organic Law, a local procuratorate has the right to protest a judgment of first instance and demand its review by a higher court (Article 15).[37] An upper procuratorate can lodge a protest even against a legally effective judgment of a lower court; the Supreme People's Procuratorate can do this against a similar judgment of any court (Article 16).

It should be added in this connection that the Chief Procurator of the Supreme People's Procuratorate is empowered by the Organic Law to participate in the meetings of the Judicial Committee of the Supreme People's Court. If he disagrees with a decision of the Judicial Committee, he has the right to refer it to the Standing Committee of the National People's Congress for examination and decision. Chief procurators at local levels have the same right in relation to the corresponding local judicial committees (Article 17).

D. Supervision over the Execution of Judgments

According to Articles 4 and 18 of the Organic Law, the People's Procuracy has the supervisory authority to see that the execution of judgments and the activities of corrective labor institutions conform to the law. To exercise such supervision, the procurator is expected to examine carefully appeals and petitions from the masses or convicts, to check regularly how court decisions are carried out, and to inspect personally the places of confinement and institutions of labor reform.

Upon discovery of any violation of the law in the execution of judgments or in the activities of corrective labor institutions, the procurator should notify the responsible organs to correct such violation. If real difficulties are detected in the execution of judgments, he should refer these problems to the courts for disposal. In case that defects are found in the administrative or "re-educational" measures of corrective labor institutions, he should also make suggestions for their improvement.[38]

---

[37] See also Article 11 of the Organic Law of the People's Courts in *Chunghua jen-min kung-ho-kuo fa-kuei hui-pien*, Vol. 1, pp. 125-126. For a detailed discussion of the procedure used by the procuratorates to protest judgments, consult Chang Fu-hai, pp. 16-17.

[38] Chang Fu-hai, p. 17; Ch'en Chi'i-yü, p. 44.

Recent Trends

By virtue of its centralized structure and broad authority of supervision, the People's Procuracy is undoubtedly one of the most powerful organs of the state machine. Like the whole legal system of Communist China, however, it is still in the process of development and has its share of problems and mistakes. There have been reports about the procurators' erroneous approval of arrests or prosecution of innocent men. Red tape, bureaucraticism and failure to follow the proper procedure have also been reported in other instances.[39] More important has been the question whether or not the procurators, always subject to the leadership of the highest Communist Party circles, should be interfered with in their work by local Party bosses.

The procurators who interpreted their functions too literally according to the legal provisions and dared to voice their objection to interference by local Party Committees were branded as "rightist" during the Anti-Rightist Campaign of 1957-1958. Among those attacked were Liu Hui-chih, Deputy Chief Procurator of the Procuratorate of Transportation, and Wang Li-chung, Director of the First Office of the Supreme People's Procuratorate[40] As a result of this Campaign, six "rightist" procurators of the Supreme Procuratorate along with fifty-seven other procurators at the central and local levels were dismissed in 1958.[41]

The mood of the Peking regime probably can be best detected through an examination of the arguments used by its spokesmen to refute the "rightist" ideas. First of all, the regime has strongly attacked the objection to Party cadres' interference wih procuraorial work. During the "Hundred Flowers" period, one high procuratorial official expressed the opinion that "local Party committees should exercise their leadership over policies and programs only, and should not interfere in matters of a purely technical nature. Otherwise, the absence of any distinction between the Party and the government would have a demoralizing effect on the procuratorial workers." Another procurator opposed the sending of

---

[39] Tseng Ch'ang-ming's report in *Kuang-chou jih-pao*, May 29, 1958; Chang Ting-ch'eng's report in *Ta-kung pao*, July 2, 1957; Li Shih-wen, "The Dictatorship Nature and Supervisory Function of the Procuratorates Are United," *Cheng-fa yen-chiu*, No. 5, 1958, pp. 56-57.

[40] See the editorial of *Jen-min jih-pao*, December 20, 1957.

[41] American Consulate General, Hong Kong, *Survey of China Mainland Press*, No. 1829, August 11, 1958.

large numbers of Party members to serve on the staff of the procuratorates on the ground that they were not legal experts and
could not possibly handle the problems of their work. Both views
have been denounced by the Communists as attempts to restrict
the scope of Party leadership and to undermine the foundation
of the Dictatorship of People's Democracy.[42]

Also under attack has been the theory of "supreme supervision,"
advocated by Liu Hui-chih and other "rightists." According to this
theory,

> violations of the law by state organs and functionaries have reached
> serious proportions in China. Not only have the administrative
> authorities and supervisory departments failed to exercise any effec-
> tive supervision, but they have violated laws themselves. . . . There-
> fore, there is a need to establish a new, all-embracing system of
> supervision, with the procuratorates given the power of "supreme
> supervision" over all governmental agencies and activities throughout
> the country.[43]

By way of refutation, Communist writers and jurists have warned
that the adoption of this theory would inevitably lead to two serious consequences: (1) the weakening and negation of the dictatorship over class enemies by tying the hands of such organs as
the courts and police; (2) the usurpation of the Party's overall
supervisory power by the Procuracy through the latter's being free
from any control. As pointed out by the Communists, the procuratorates, courts, and public security organs are all important
weapons for the People's Democratic Dictatorship. They should
work together, coordinate their activities, and follow Party leadership in the struggle against counterrevolutionary and other criminal elements engaged in the sabotage of socialist construction.[44]

Attention has been further called to the basic difference between

---

[42] *Jen-min jih-pao,* December 12, 1957; *Kuang-hsi jih-pao* (Kwangsi
Daily), Nanning, August 31, 1957.

[43] Wang Kuei-wu, "Refute Liu Hui-chih's 'Theory of Supreme Supervision'," *Jen-min jih-pao,* January 1, 1958.

[44] *Ibid.;* Ch'eng Ch'ao-ming, "The Struggle Between the Two Lines on
the Battlefront of Procuratorial Work," *Cheng-fa yen-chiu,* No. 1, 1958,
pp. 33-36, 39; T'an Cheng-wen, "Absorb Lessons from Experience and Push
Forward the Big Leap of Procuratorial Work," *Ibid.,* No. 3, 1958, pp. 40-42;
Ts'ui Tz'u-feng, "Eliminate Superstition, Liberate Thought, and Liquidate
Thoroughly the Influence of Doctrinarism in Procuratorial Work," *Ibid.,*
No. 1, 1955, pp. 44-47; Ch'i Wen, "We Must Thoroughly Liquidate the
Influence of the 'Judicial Independence' Concept of the Bourgeois Class,"
Ibid., No. 2, 1960, pp. 56-57.

"contradictions among the people" and "contradictions between the enemy and ourselves." Thus, infractions of the law by state organs and functionaries are generally "individual incidents, different in nature from the acts of sabotage perpetrated by the reactionaries and counterrevolutionaries." The former, "contradictions among the people," should be handled with the "method of democracy and persuasion," while the latter, "contradictions between the enemy and ourselves," should be handled with the "method of dictatorship and force." These two must not be confused.[45]

Another "rightist" idea that has been refuted by the Chinese Communists is the principle of presumption of innocence. Their reasoning is that if the procuratorate or the court approves the arrest of a person by the police, there must be sufficient evidence about his guilt. Therefore, it would be meaningless to talk about the presumption of innocence, a "bourgeois principle" which can serve only the enemy but not the people nor the revolution.[46] One "rightist" procurator was thus accused of siding with the landlords for his frequent protests of their innocence and his demands for a thorough examination of their cases.[47]

The stand taken by the Peking regime against the "rightists" reflects clearly its current rigidity and a reversal of the trend toward legality and moderation during the years between 1954 and 1957. This is also evident in the following features of procuratorial work that have been specifically emphasized since 1958 when the ill-fated Big Leap Forward Movement was launched.

Suppression of Counterrevolutionaries. At the Fourth National Procuratorial Work Conference held in 1958, the primary task of the People's Procuracy during the Big Leap was declared to be the suppression of counterrevolutionaries and the protection of the implementation of the Party line for socialist construction.[48] Subsequently, high procuratorial officials reported on different occasions the active role played by the procuratorates in the struggle against the counterrevolutionaries and the great victory scored

[45] Li Shih-wen, pp. 55-56; Ch'eng Ch'ao-ming, pp. 35-36.

[46] T'an Cheng-wen, p. 37; "Refute the Principle of Presumption of Innocence," *Kuang-ming jih-pao,* December 13, 1957.

[47] "The Way That Chang P'ing Has Degenerated Into a Rightist," *Nan-fang jih-pao* (Southern Daily), Canton, November 13, 1957.

[48] *New China News Agency,* Peking, August 24, 1958.

by the policy of "combining punishment with leniency" toward the enemy. While pointing out the fact that "the counterrevolutionaries have become fewer, weaker and more isolated," these officials at the same time stressed the need for continuing vigilance against "disruptive enemy activities."[49] One of the widely publicized "espionage and counterrevolutionary" cases in recent years was the prosecution and trial of Catholic Bishops James Walsh and Kung P'in-mei in 1960.[50] Writing in *Cheng-fa yen-chiu* in 1963, one Communist author warned all political and legal workers that the struggle against the counterrevolutionaries was complex, violent and of a long duration:

> Although with their backs against the wall or on the verge of total destruction, our class enemies will intensify their hatred against us and fight fiercely in the hope of regaining the "lost paradise" whenever certain difficulties occur during the transitional period of socialist construction or whenever there is an anti-Communist, anti-Chinese movement on the international scene. . . . It is, therefore, necessary for us to move a step further to strengthen the People's Democratic Dictatorship and carry out the class struggle.[51]

The Mass Line. The pursuit of the mass line has been another prominent feature in procuratorial work during the past few years. As applied in all kinds of work, the mass line is a convenient device to keep the people on a close watch and to mobilize them to support Party policy and wage the class struggle. According to the official line in this instance, it is designed to improve the quality of procuratorial work, ensure the correct handling of cases, and raise the revolutionary consciousness of the masses. To implement the mass line, the procuratorates have been brought to the people, and investigation and prosecution have been conducted on the spot. With such slogans as "Link with the masses" and "Safeguard production," procuratorial personnel have gone to the countryside or factories to mingle with the masses, eat and live with them, and participate in production and handle cases at the

---

[49] Chang Ting-ch'eng, "The Work of the People's Procuratorates," *New China News Agency*, April 24, 1959; Chao P'o, "The Work of the People's Procuratorates of Szechwan Province," *Szu-ch'uan jih-pao* (Szechwan Daily), Chengtu, June 24, 1959.

[50] For materials on this case, see *Trials of Catholic Bishops James Welsh and Kung P'in-mei*, JPRS, No. 5469, 1960.

[51] Pien Hsi-wen, "Grasp the Rules for the Class Struggle in the Transitional Period," *Cheng-fa yen-chiu*, No. 1, 1963, pp. 4-5.

same time.[52] As reported by twenty-four procuratorates of provinces, municipalities, and autonomous regions, eighty three "work teams" were sent to the basic levels during the first half of 1964 to conduct investigation, sum up experience, and guide procuratorial activity.[53]

The people, on the other hand, have been urged to formulate and observe "socialist patriotic pacts," to write or visit the procuratorates, to detect and report criminals, and to exercise supervision over undersirable elements. In the year 1962 alone, Party and government organizations in Kiangsu province reportedly contacted some 500,000 people through receiving letters and visitors.[54] Also, as a part of the mass line to eliminate "bureaucratism, doctrinarism, and subjectivism," procedures have been simplified and outmoded systems have been discarded by individual procuratorates to achieve greater efficiency. The Chief Procurator of Canton, for instance, reported in 1958 that his office was able to do away with thirty-two kinds of unnecessary procedures as a result of certain experiments. "Now, on the average," he declared, "only three hours are needed to dispose of a case, involving all procedures for effecting arrest, examination of findings, and prosecution at the court."[55]

Absolute Party Leadership. Most illustrative of the regime's rigid response to liberal criticism and internal difficulties in recent years is the strong emphasis placed on absolute Party leadership over procuratorial work at all levels. Official pronouncements and individual writings have been repeating the same theme ever since 1957. Typical are the following statements made respectively by T'an Cheng-wen and Chang Ting-ch'eng of the Supreme People's Procuratorate:

> The Communist Party is the highest organizational form as well as the vanguard of the proletarian class. It is also the central and guiding force of the proletarian dictatorship. As one of the instru-

[52] See the reports of Chang Ting-ch'eng and Chao P'o, cited in note 49. In his report to the Third Session of the Second National People's Congress in 1962, Premier Chou En-lai also stated: "Government functionaries should constantly make on-the-spot investigations, develop a working style characterized by seeking truth from facts and adhering to the mass line . . ." *Peking Review,* April 20, 1962, pp. 6-7.

[53] Chang Ting-ch'eng, "Report on the Work of the Supreme People's Procuratorate," *Jen-min jih-pao,* January 1, 1965.

[54] *New China News Agency,* Nanking, February 20, 1963.

[55] Tseng Ch'ang-ming, *Kuang-chou jih-pao,* May 29, 1958.

ments of the proletarian dictatorship, the Procuracy therefore must obey absolutely the leadership of the Party and become the Party's tractable and convenient tool. Only when put under the Party's absolute leadership, can the Procuracy fully develop its work and power in the struggle against the enemy, and eliminate or reduce significantly the chances of confusion and mistakes. Consequently, to obey Party leadership is the most basic condition and the highest principle for good procuratorial work.[56]

The procuratorates must place their work entirely under the leadership of the Party Central Committee and the Party Committees at different levels in the service of the central task of the Party, and use continuously the ideology of the Party, the ideology of Marxism-Leninism, to arm the cadres mentally and to develop their Party character more intensively before they can successfully fulfill their tasks.[57]

The above quotations have clearly defined the current role of the People's Procuracy and its subordinate position to Party leadership.[58] There is no question that the Procuracy is equipped, by the Constitution and its Organic Law, with a broad supervisory authority over the observance of law throughout the country. But its functions to check upon the legality of activities of other governmental organs have to be secondary to its duties to prosecute and suppress the counterrevolutionaries. Its power to protect the people's "democratic rights" is necessarily conditioned by the requirements of national security. As the "eyes and ears" of the Communist regime, the procurators are expected to carry out its will and to enforce the People's Democratic Dictatorship over the enemy.

---

[56] T'an Cheng-wen (the late Deputy Chief Procurator), "Consolidate the Victory of Procuratorial Work in the Struggle Between the Two Lines; Strive to Liquidate Thoroughly the Remnant Legal Concept of the Bourgeois Class," *Cheng-fa yen-chiu*, No. 6, 1958, p. 29.

[57] Chang Ting-ch'eng, *Hung-ch'i*, No. 20, 1959, p. 36.

[58] David C. Buxbaum, "Preliminary Trends in the Development of the Legal Institutions of Communist China and the Nature of the Criminal Law," *The International and Comparative Law Quarterly*, Vol. 11, January 1962, pp. 25-26, points out that there is a close tie between the Control Committee of the Party and the Procuracy of the government.

Chapter 6

The Police

Justice in Communist China is not only administered by the judicial organs but also by a host of administrative agencies and social organizations. Exceedingly important among the nonjudicial organs are the police. According to Mao Tse-tung, the police along with the courts and the army are the oppressive instruments of the state which the ruling class uses against its class enemies.[1]

In terms of organization, power, and activity, the Chinese Communist police (public security organs) bear a strong influence of the Soviet model. To be sure, they have not attained the same degree of notoriety as the NKVD-MVD and their predecessors in Russia.[2] On the other hand, the Chinese police are just as effective and powerful as their Soviet counterpart in enforcing social control and suppressing the enemies of the state. During the mid-1950's when China was moving in the direction of legal stability, some efforts were made to curb the power of the police. Since the Anti-Rightist Campaign of 1957-1958, however, such efforts have been discontinued and police control has been omnipresent in the Chinese mainland. Little change can be expected under current conditions as Peking is busy combatting revisionism abroad and anti-Party elements at home.

The Public Security Structure

As in the case of the U.S.S.R., the police system in Communist China consists of both public and secret units. During the period of the Kiangsi Soviet Republic, the Chinese Communist police were under the administration of the State Political Security Bureau.[3]

---

[1] Mao Tse-tung, *On People's Dictatorship*, Peking, 1951, p. 17.

[2] The Soviet police system has been transformed several times: Cheka, 1917-1922; GPU and OGPU, 1922-1934; NKVD (the People's Commissariat for the Interior), 1934-1946; MVD (Ministry of Interior) and MGB (Ministry of State Security); and KGB (Committee of State Security), 1954-. For details, consult V. Gsovski and K. Grzybowski, *Government, Law and Courts in the Soviet Union and Eastern Europe*, New York, 1959, Vol. 1, pp. 564-585; also Harold J. Berman, *Justice in the U.S.S.R.*, New York, 1963, pp. 391-392, note 22; p. 403, note 40.

[3] See *supra* Chapter 1, Section on "The Soviet Period."

Since the formation of the People's Republic of China, they have been organized into a hierarchical structure of public security organs.

At the top of the hierarchy is the Ministry of Public Security in the State Council. Under this Ministry are four levels of public security organs in the following descending order: the public security department at the provincial and special municipal level; the public security bureau at the county and municipal level; the public security sub-bureau at the rural or urban district level; and the public security station at the village and city street office level.[4] In addition there are within the public security system the secret police and units of the public security armed forces, known since 1955 as the "people's armed police," to provide the regime with further protection against hostile elements.[5]

Below the official structure and supplementing the work of the police are mass security organizations which penetrate into every aspect of life. On the basis of the regulations issued by the Ministry of Public Security on August 10, 1952, security committees have been set up within factories, enterprises, schools, offices, streets, villages, communes, and production brigades.[6] Composed of three to eleven members each, these committees are subject to the direction of the basic-level governmental and public security organs and may establish

---

[4] For the public security structure, see "Organic Law of the Local People's Congresses and Local People's Councils of the Chinese People's Republic," *Chung-hua jen-min kung-ho-kuo fa-fuei hui-pien* (Compendium of Laws and Regulations of the Chinese People's Republic), Peking, Vol. 1 (1956), pp. 139-150; "Regulations for the Organization of Public Security Stations," *ibid.*, pp. 243-244; Chu Pu-fu, *Chung-kung jen-min ching-ch'a t'ou-shih* (Perspective on the "People's Police" in Communist China), Hong Kong, 1955, pp. 23-40.

[5] Little information is available about the secret police system. Some discussion of it and the public security armed forces is found in Peter S. H. Tang, *Communist China Today*, New York, 1957, pp. 235-236. A more detailed description of the public security armed forces is in Chu Pu-fu, pp. 116-132. It should be noted that by a decree of the State Council in July 1957 the public security troops have been transformed into the "people's armed police" to be controlled directly by the Ministry of Public Security and disconnected with the Ministry of National Defense. *Chung-hua jen-min kung-ho-kuo fa-kuei hui-pien*, Vol. 2 (1956), p. 449.

[6] "Provisional Regulations Governing Organization of Security Committees," *Chung-yang jen-min cheng-fu fa-ling hui-pien* (Compendium of the Laws and Regulations of the Central People's Government), 1952 (Peking, 1954), pp. 56-58. Since 1958 security committees have been organized in communes and production brigades. Consult Edgar Snow, *The Other Side of the River*, New York, 1962, p. 351.

small security teams of "three to five activists" with the approval of appropriate public security authorities. The major duty of these committees is to assist the organs of public security in combating treasonable, espionage, counterrevolutionary, and other criminal activities. Obviously, the security committees are another striking example of the Chinese Communists' "mass line" strategy designed to maximize the effectiveness of official policies by bringing the general masses into direct participation and by using them as an instrument of supervision and control. Reports from mainland China indicate that such grassroots security committees have been used with considerable success. In March 1965, for example, the Canton Municipal Bureau of Public Security commended 35 committees and 219 activists for maintaining law and order. They were particularly cited for their role in dealing severe blows to enemy agents and criminal offenders and in safeguarding the socialist cause and the lives and property of the people.[7]

Powers and Functions of the Police

As an important instrument of the People's Democratic Dictatorship, the "people's police" perform a wide variety of tasks in Communist China. They are competent to arrest, detain, and investigate suspected counterrevolutionaries and other criminals in accordance with the law. They have the authority to impose as well as administer punishment. They direct the system of "reform through labor" institutions and may use their discretion in deciding whether to release a prisoner at the end of the term.[8] They are also in charge of traffic control, fire prevention, public health, census registration, and protection of important military and economic establishments.[9]

[7] *Nan-fang jih-pao* (Southern Daily), Canton, March 13, 1965. In October 1962 490 security activists received similar commendations from the Canton Municipal Public Security Bureau. *Yang-ch'eng wan-pao* (Canton Evening News), October 13, 1962.

[8] Articles 6, 62, and 72 of the Regulations on Reform through Labor (September 1954). The text of the Regulations is in *Cheng-yang jen-min cheng-fu fa-ling hui-pien*, 1954, pp. 33-43. See also Provisional Measures Concerning the Release of Prisoners and Their Employment (September 1954), *ibid.*, pp. 44-45.

[9] See "The People's Police Act" (June 25, 1957) in *Chung-hua jen-min kung-ho-kuo fa-kuei hui-pien*, Vol. 5 (1957), pp. 113-116. Other activities of the police are described in Gene T. Hsiao, "Communist China: Legal Institutions," *Problems of Communism*, Vol. 14, No. 2, March-April 1965, pp. 118-119.

Under the Penal Regulations on Security Control (October 1957), the police are empowered to impose administrative sanctions against individuals violating public security but committing no criminal offenses. Among the punishable acts listed are disturbance of public order (scuffle, gambling, or prostitution), breach of safety and health regulations, violation of the rights of a citizen's person (assault or abuse), and infliction of property damage (fraud or petty theft). The punishments that the public security organs may impose on the offenders consist of (1) warning, (2) modest fine, and (3) short detention.[10]

A 1952 regulation gave the police the authority to impose, without court trial, "control" over counterrevolutionaries, landlords, and other reactionary elements "who have not shown adequate repentance for their past offenses but who have not commited any new criminal activity to warrant their arrest."[11] In November 1956 the National People's Congress, by a decision, transferred this authority to the courts while leaving the public security organs with the responsibility of executing the punishment.[12] Persons subject to "control" measures may be deprived of political rights for periods up to three years or more, during which time they are required to engage in compulsory labor and ideological reform under police supervision and mass surveillance.

The State Council adopted a decision on "Re-education and Rehabilitation through Labor" on August 3, 1957, granting the police, civil administrative organs, as well as social groups a far-reaching power, subject only to the approval of the local "people's committees," to confine without court trial a wide range of undesirable elements to special labor camps for an indefinite period of time.[13] Comparable to the Soviet anti-social parasitic laws adopted in recent years,[14]

---

[10] The text of the Penal Regulations is in *ibid.*, Vol. 6 (1957), pp. 245-254.

[11] Articles 3 of the Provisional Measures for the Control of Counterrevolutionaries (June 1952), *Chung-yang jen-min cheng-fu fa-ling hui-pien*, 1952, p. 53.

[12] *Jen-min shou-ts'e, 1957* (People's Hankbook, 1957), Peking, 1952, p. 356.

[13] The text of this decision is in *Chung-hua jen-min kung-ho-kuo fa-kuei hui-pien*, Vol. 6, pp. 243-244. According to some former police officials of Communist China, the period of confinement may have been limited after 1962 to three years. Jerome A. Cohen, "The Criminal Process in the People's Republic of China: An Introduction," *Harvard Law Review*, Vol. 79, No. 3, January 1966, pp. 491-492.

[14] For the Soviet anti-social parasitic laws, see Berman, pp. 291-298.

this decision is directed against the following four categories of individuals: (1) Vagrants, rascals, petty thieves and swindlers who incur no criminal liability, or persons who violate rules of public order and fail to mend their ways despite repeated warnings; (2) counterrevolutionary and anti-socialist reactionary elements whose offenses are of a minor nature, not subject to criminal punishment, and who have been dismissed from their jobs and cannot earn a living; (3) persons who are able to work but refuse to do so in government organs, groups, enterprises, and schools, or who violate discipline, disturb the peace, and, having been expelled, have no means of existence; (4) persons who refuse to accept specific work assignments, or who refuse to be directed in production labor, engage in disorderly conduct, interfere with public tasks, and fail to mend their ways despite repeated warnings.

By virtue of this decision, administrative agencies, particularly the police, can send practically anyone to labor camps without regard to legal procedures and constitutional guarantees. According to *Izvestia's* editorial on May 17, 1964, many hundreds of thousands of people in China suffered from this "crude violation of the elementary democratic rights and liberties of the citizen." In pursuit of the "mass line" strategy, the Ministry of Public Security and its agencies at all levels have made periodic efforts to better relations with the people and to improve the system of intelligence and control. During the traditional Spring Festival, for instance, the "love the people month" campaign is regularly launched each year. All public security personnel are expected to solicit the views of the masses, listen to their complaints, study the Party's guidelines and policies, and review the "eight rules of discipline" and "ten points of attention" for the police. Furthermore, they are required to perform good deeds, understand the hardships of the masses, and do their best to help solve these problems.[15] All in all, the "love the people month" movement illustrates what one observer describes as "both the intimacy of security links with the household and the Party's basic assumptions as father and protector."[16]

---

[15] See, for example, the Ministry of Public Security's circular on launching the "love of the people month" movement during the 1965 Spring Festival in *Jen-min jih-pao* (People's Daily), Peking, December 29, 1964.

[16] Snow, p. 351.

Other Extrajudicial Apparatus

Besides the police, there are many other extrajudicial agencies which also participate in the process of resolving conflicts and applying administrative sanctions. These institutions indeed form important parts of Communist China's highly effective system of control over the lives of the people. At the basic levels of the Chinese control structure are street offices, residents' committees (100-600 families) and residents' groups (15 to 40 families) in the cities and "people's communes," production brigades, and production teams in the countryside.[17] Individuals are further subject to administrative and social pressures from state organs, schools, enterprises, factories, political parties, and mass organizations. Each of these institutions handles minor disputes and settles internal contradictions through the methods of persuasion and conciliation. It also has the power to impose such administrative and disciplinary sanctions as warnings, criticism, self-criticism, struggle, demotion, and dismissal.[18] According to Article 3 of the afore-mentioned decision of the State Council on August 3, 1957, parents, guardians, or any organization to which the offender belongs can place him in a labor camp for "re-education and rehabilitation."

The handling of large numbers of minor contradictions and offenses by administrative authorities and social groups undoubtedly does much to relieve the burden of the judiciary proper. At the same

[17] For the regulations on street offices and the regulations on residents' committees, see *Chung-ha jen-min kung-ho-kuo fa-kuei hui-pien*, Vol. 1, pp. 171-172 and 173-175 respectively. For an analysis of the "people's commune" and its subordinate production units, see Cheng Chu-yuan, "The Changing Pattern of Rural Communes in Communist China," *Asian Survey*, Vol. 1, November 1961, pp. 3-9; Henry J. Lethbridge, *The Peasant and the Communes*, Hong Kong, 1963. Wang Shu-wen, "A Study of the Three-Level Ownership System with the Production Brigade as Its Foundation in the Rural People's Communes," *Cheng-fa yen-chiu* (Studies of Political Science and Law), Peking, No. 1, 1961, pp. 29-32. For a comprehensive discussion of the Chinese Communist Methods of Organization and Control, see Franz Schurmann, *Ideology and Organization in Communist China*, Berkeley, 1966.

[18] Consult Articles 5-8 of the "Provisional Regulations of the State Council Concerning Rewards and Punishments for Administrative Personnel" in *Chung Hua jen-min kung-ho-kuo fa-kuei hui-pien*, Vol. 6, pp. 198-200; Article 10 of the "People's Police Act," *ibid.*, Vol. 5, p. 116; Article 13 of the "Constitution of the Communist Party of China," *Eighth National Congress of the Communist Party of China*, Peking, 1956, Vol. 1, p. 149; Article 5 of the "Constitution of the Trade Unions," *Labor Laws and Regulations of the People's Republic of China*, Peking, 1956, p. 20; Cohen, pp. 490-491.

time, abuses of power and violations of human rights have occurred not only among the police but also the other extrajudicial organs. Illuminating are cases revealed in the recently published secret documents of the Chinese Red Army, which cover the events of 1960-1961. In one case, the production group of an army unit seized a local woman commune member and her husband for stealing cabbage. First, the couple were cruelly beaten and hung by the wrists from the basketball goal. Later, they suffered the indignities of having their clothes taken off at the struggle meeting.[19] In another army unit, offending soldiers were often treated rudely and put through a series of humiliating experiences. As a result, there happened successively in three months three incidents that led quickly to suicides. The first two involved just petty theft and the third a soldier's complaint about the grain situation.[20]

In the last analysis, the Communist Party is the decision-making center in China and the final arbiter of right and wrong. Its members staff key positions in government and society, and its network penetrates the courts, administrative agencies, and mass organizations at all levels. Its will is enforced and its enemies are punished by the vast system of judicial and extrajudicial apparatus or by Party committees themselves. In 1957-58 the "rightist" elements were subject to various forms of attacks and sanctions from both official and semi-official organs.[21] Currently, the same is happening to the "anti-Party" and "anti-socialist" elements in the nation-wide purge of dissenters.[22] One certainly cannot understand the true nature of "people's justice" without examining its formal as well as informal institutions and processes.

[19] J. Chester Cheng (ed.), *The Politics of the Chinese Red Army*, Stanford, 1966, pp. 146-147.

[20] *Ibid.*, pp. 356-358.

[21] See Francis Harper (ed.), *Out of China: A Collection of Interviews with Refugees from China*, Hong Kong, 1964, Chapter 7; "Interview with Chinese Medical Doctor," *Current Scene*, Hong Kong, Vol. 1, June 12, 1961, pp. 9-10; Mu Fu-sheng, *The Wilting of the Hundred Flowers*, New York, 1963, pp. 168-175; Theodore H. E. Chen, *Thought Reform of the Chinese Intellectuals*, Hong Kong, 1960, Chapters 18-19.

[22] It is still too early to tell with certainty the nature and scope of the current purge, but some clues can be found in *Jen-min jih-pao*, April 15, 1966 (editorial); *Chieh-fang-chün pao* (Liberation Army News), Peking, May 4, 1966 (editorial); "Peking Party Rift Appears to Deepen," *New York Times*, May 10, 1966; "Titanic Struggle Seen in Red China," *ibid.*, June 26, 1966.

Chapter 7

The People's Lawyer

The institution of legal defense is of a very fluid nature in the Chinese People's Republic. Officially, there are "people's lawyers" who can participate in the administration of justice. In reality, however, their number is quite small and their role in the judicial process is but a nominal one.

In the pages that follow, an attempt will be made to examine the Chinese system of legal counsel along two major lines. One is the development of the Communist attitude toward the bar in terms of proclaimed policy as well as practice. The other is the organization and activity of the Chinese lawyers and the problems that they are confronted with in performing their duties.

Absence of Lawyers in the Early Years of the Communist Rule

Even prior to the advent of the Communist regime, the Chinese never held the bar in the same esteem as the people in the West. The underlying reason would seem to be a combination of their time-honored tradition of subordinating law to morality with the underdeveloped status of the legal profession in Chinese society.[1] It should be noted that the role of advocates was practically unknown in old China. Persons offering their service to the public in litigations were usually disreputable individuals, who used all kinds of unethical methods to achieve their objectives. The fact that they were often referred to as *"sung-kun"* (brigands of lawsuits) testified to the unpopularity of these men.[2] During the modern era a regular profession of advocates was established by the Nationalist government. Unfortunately, few properly qualified persons were admitted to the bar, and some lawyers also disgraced

---
[1] For discussions of the Chinese concept of law, see Jean Escarra, *Le Droit Chinois,* Peking, 1936, pp. 3-84; Derk Bodde, "Basic Concepts of Chinese Law: The Genisis and Evolution of Legal Thought in Traditional China," *Proceedings of the American Philosophical Society,* Vol. 107, No. 5, 1963, pp. 375-398.

[2] Escarra, p. 326.

their profession through devious and reprehensible practices.[3]

While paying lip service to the right of defense for the accused, the Chinese Communists in the past frequently maintained such a hostile and suspicious attitude toward the legal profession that there was no place for the lawyer in the new order they were building. This can be traced back to the early days of the Communist revolutionary movements.

Dominated by the Communists, the First Peasant Congress of Hunan Province adopted a number of resolutions in late 1926. In a resolution on the judicial problem, the Congress attacked the complexity of the legal procedure and the treachery of the *"sung-kun"* in the old system. Among other things, it resolved to place the *"sung-kun"* under a strict ban and to grant the Peasant Associations the right to represent their members in litigation.[4]

In the Provisional Regulations on the Organization of Courts and Judicial Procedures, promulgated in 1932 by the Central Executive Committee of the Chinese Soviet Republic in Kiangsi, the right of the accused to have his interest defended was officially recognized.[5] As may be recalled, one of the important judicial practices developed in the Chinese Soviet area was mass trials (*kung-shen*). At such a trial anyone present could come forward with charges against the accused. The latter or someone else was also theoretically "free" to speak and argue against the accusations.[6] There is, nevertheless, little evidence that any meaningful defense actually took place. Still less can we find any instance in which lawyers had a role to play.

During the period of the National United Front against Japan, the Communist regime in Yenan seemed to be more tolerant of the idea of defense counsel. According to a leading Communist Chinese jurist, the "people's courts" in the Shensi-Kansu-Ninghsia

---

[3] For comments on Chinese lawyers under the Nationalist regime, see *ibid.,* pp. 333-334; Ch'ien Tuan-sheng, *The Government and Politics of China,* Cambridge, 1950, pp. 260-261.

[4] *Ti-i-tz'u kuo-nei ko-ming chan-cheng shih-ch'i ti nung-min yün-tung* (The Peasant Movement in the Period of the First Revolutionary Civil War), Peking, 1953, pp. 355-356.

[5] Ch'u Huai-chih & Chang Min-fu, "Toward an Understanding of the System of Defense in Criminal Proceedings in Our Country," *Hsin chien-she* (New Construction), Peking, No. 5, 1956, p. 14.

[6] See the discussion of *kung-shen* in the section on "The Soviet Period" in Chapter 1. Also consult L. M. Gudoshnikov, *Legal Organs of the People's Republic of China,* (Trans. from Russian) JPRS (Joint Publication Research Service), No. 1698-N, 1959, p. 9.

Border Region permitted parties in litigation to ask relatives or persons with legal knowledge to serve as defense counsel or legal representatives. Furthermore, people's organizations were allowed to designate certain people as legal counsel or representatives in suits involving their members.[7] Despite all this, it is said the situation then did not warrant the instituting of a system of lawyers in the Border Region.[8]

In February 1949, shortly before its complete victory over the Kuomintang, the Central Committee of the Chinese Communist Party issued a directive abolishing the six codes of law of the Nationalists and prescribing the principle of the judicial system for the "liberated" areas.[9] On the eve of the establishment of the new People's Republic of China in the fall of the same year, the Common Program of the Chinese People's Political Consultative Conference again declared the abolition of all Nationalist laws and courts: "All laws, decrees and judicial systems of the Kuomintang reactionary government oppressing the people are abolished and laws and decrees protecting the people shall be enacted and the people's judicial system shall be set up." (Article 17)[10]

Along with other institutions of the Kuomintang regime, the bar was swept away by this drastic change of the country's legal structure. Law offices were closed and private lawyers were prohibited from practicing. Reports ranging from Harbin to Shanghai all stressed the accessibility of the "people's courts" to the common man, the simplicity of the new judicial procedure, and the disappearance of old-style lawyers in litigation.[11] In Communist minds, these lawyers only served the interest of the privileged few

---

[7] Ma Hsi-wu, "The Work of the People's Judiciary in the Shensi-Kansu-Ninghsia Border Region in the Stage of the New Democratic Revolution," *Cheng-fa yen-chiu* (Studies of Political Science and Law), Peking, No. 1, 1955, p. 10.

[8] Masao Fukushima and others, *Chugoku no saiban* (Justice of China), Tokyo, 1957, p. 167.

[9] Tung Pi-wu, "The Legal System of China," *New China News Agency*, Peking, September 20, 1956.

[10] For the English translation of the Common Program by NCNA, see *China Digest*, Hong Kong, October 5, 1949, pp. 3-4.

[11] *China Weekly Review*, Shanghai, August 20, 1949, p. 218; January 14, 1950, p. 113; *China Monthly Review*, Shanghai, November 1950, pp. 78-79. The Ministry of Justice further ordered in 1950 the suppression of the activity of private lawyers. Lin Ch'eng, "Strictly Prohibit the Illegal Activities of the Underground Lawyers," *Jen-min jih-pao* (People's Daily), Peking, September 14, 1952.

and were too wedded to the old forms of law and procedures to be fitted to act as people's attorneys.[12]

On the other hand, the Communist regime continued to recognize officially the defendant's right to defense in a lawsuit. Reference also was made to the preparation of the introduction of a system of "people's lawyers." All seemed to be a part of the regime's efforts to stabilize its rule and to institute a new legal order in place of the one abolished. For instance, Article 12 of the "Provisional Regulations of the Shanghai People's Court Governing the Disposal of Civil and Criminal Cases" (promulgated on August 11, 1949) provided that the accused in a criminal case might ask either the presiding judge to assign a public defender or the people's organization concerned to send a representative as defense counsel. In a civil action, the litigants might, with the permission of the presiding judge, designate their closest relatives as agents to appear in court.[13] A similar provision on the right of defense was contained in the "Organic Regulations of People's Tribunals" promulgated on July 20, 1950. An *ad hoc* institution, the "people's tribunals" (*jen-min fa-t'ing*) were instruments used to enforce agrarian reform and later the "3-anti" and "5-anti" campaigns; but Article 6 of their Organic Regulations read: "When a *hsien* (or municipal) people's tribunal and its branches conduct a trial, they shall guarantee the right of the accused to defend himself and to have defense counsel. The counsel must be approved by the Tribunal before he can argue the case."[14]

Although no stipulation concerning the right of defense was included in the "Provisional Organic Regulations of the People's Courts of the Chinese People's Republic" (promulgated on September 3, 1951), the Acting Chairman of the Law Codification Committee made the following statement in his explanatory report on the "people's courts" (*jen-min-fa-yüan*): "In an open trial, the litigants and their approved counsel should be given full rights of voice and defense."[15] Reviewing the judicial work between 1949 and 1951, one Communist writer also stated that

[12] Shih Liang, "The Judicial System in New China," *People's China,* Peking, No. 12, 1957, p. 16.

[13] For the text of these Regulations, see *Shang-hai chieh-fang i-nien* (One Year after Shanghai's Liberation), Shanghai, 1950, Part III, pp. 13-16.

[14] The text of these Regulations is in *Jen-min shou-ts'e. 1951* (People's Handbook, 1951), Shanghai, Section 6, pp. 46-48.

[15] Hsu Te-heng, "Explanatory Report on 'Provisional Organic Regulations of the People's Courts of the Chinese People's Republic'," *Jen-min jih-pao,* September 5, 1951.

progress had been made in the direction of introducing "people's attorneys" to China. "To manifest the democratic spirit of our judicial work and to protect the right of defense of the accused as well as the legitimate interest of the civil litigants," said Ch'en Chi-yü, "we have instituted public defenders to perform for the accused or one of the litigant parties such tasks as gathering evidence, examining the circumstances of the case, studying problems, and taking part in the trial in order that experience can be accumulated to establish a new system of people's lawyers."[16]

The above regulations and pronouncements notwithstanding, there was no evidence that the defendant ever exercised the right of defense in the first few years of the People's Republic. This conspicuous discrepancy between the regime's proclaimed policy and its actual practice reflected the fact that the pull toward arbitrary and repressive methods of control was much stronger than the attempt to establish a more orderly rule at a time of intensive struggles against landlords, counterrevolutionaries, foreign imperialists, and the others. Contrary to what was legally guaranteed, the common practice was for the accused to yield and to confess his guilt. Neither in the trials reported by Communist publications, nor in the testimonies given by Chinese as well as foreign witnesses, was there a single case in the pre-constitutional period where the accused was defended by himself or by a defense attorney.[17] Speaking from personal experience, a former Dean of the Faculty of Law at the University "l'Aurore" of Shanghai pointed out that in the Communist court procedure

> not only is the accused presumed guilty, but he is forbidden to prove the contrary: to try, is to revolt . . . In the presence of such a conception of procedure, can we be astonished at the complete suppression of lawyers? The conception is rooted in the logic of the system, and the services of a lawyer before such tribunals becomes not only superfluous but absolutely unthinkable. *Defense amounts to revolt.* Who would dare, even as a lawyer appointed by law, to oppose the "government" in the defense of an accused. The words of the lawyer would die in his throat and he would feel equally as guilty as his client. The absence of defense counsel in the criminal

16 Ch'en Chi-yü, "People's Judicial Reconstruction in the Past Two Years," *Hsin chung-hua pan-yüeh-k'an* (New China Semimonthly), Shanghai, Vol. 14, No. 19, 1951, p. 10.

17 Consult Henry Wei, *Courts and Police in Communist China to 1952,* Lackland Air Force Base, 1955, Chaps. III-V, and Commission Internationale Contre Le Régime Concentrationnaire, *White Book on Forced Labour and Concentration Camps in the People's Republic of China,* Paris, 1957, Vol. II, pp. 44-48.

process is not, therefore, accidental, but, on the contrary, impera-
tively solicited by the fundamental conceptions of communist penal
law.[18]

Purge of "Underground Lawyers" during the Judicial Reform

Former private lawyers in China, already banned from practice
of law, received a further blow when the Communist regime
launched a drive against their "illegal, underground activities"
during the Judicial Reform Movement of 1952-1953. Although
the regime abolished the whole legal system of the Kuomintang
from the outset, it was forced to retain until 1952 many of the
old judicial personnel because of the shortage of cadres trained in
law. Having had only a brief experience of Communist indoctrination, these former Kuomintang personnel understandably still kept
much of their traditional judicial concepts and practices. The existence of such "serious political and organizational defects" in
the "people's courts" was revealed during the Three-Anti and
Five-Anti Movements. In a report to the Government Administrative Council on August 13, 1952, Miss Shih Liang, Minister of
Justice, pointed out: "There are twenty-eight thousand judicial
cadres in the country, of whom six thousand, or approximately 22
per cent, had worked under the old regime. In large and medium-
sized cities particularly, these people make up the majority of
judges in the people's courts."[19] Of these old judicial personnel,
it was estimated, sixty to eighty per cent were anti-Party and "depraved" elements, many having been members of the Kuomintang and its secret police. Their "corrupting influence" was found
to be considerable even on the old Party cadres.[20]

It was under such conditions that the Chinese Communist government decided to launch a nation-wide Judicial Reform Movement, which lasted from August 1952 to April 1953.[21] The Objective of this Movement was to combat the old legal concepts,

[18] André Bonnichon, *Law in Communist China*, The Hague, 1956, pp.
8-11.

[19] Shih Liang, "Report Concerning the Thorough Reform and Reorganization of the People's Courts at All Levels," *Ch'ang-chiang jih-pao* (Yantze
Daily), Hankow, August 24, 1952.

[20] *Ibid.* See also T'ao Hsi-chin, "On the Judicial Reform," *Cheng-fa yen-
chiu*, No. 5, 1957, p. 12.

[21] The public had been prepared for the Movement since June 1952.
Two opposing interpretations of the Judicial Reform are represented by
T'ao His-chin, pp. 12-16, and Ch'en Shu-fang, *Chung-kung ti szu-fa kai-ko*
(The Judicial Reform of the Chinese Communists), Hong Kong, 1953.

to purge the old judicial personnel, and to liquidate the "under-ground lawyers." The Reform was carried out with great vigor, and as a result only twenty per cent of the judicial personnel who had worked under the Nationalist regime were retained in their posts.[22]

One of the primary targets of the Judicial Reform was "hei lü-shih" (underground lawyers). Since the "liberation" members of the bar had been compelled to give up their law practice. Many of them had set up offices to handle accounting, to do translation, or to draw up documents for people in urban areas. Others had become trustees, managers, secretaries, or clerks in privately-owned enterprises. However, during the Judicial Reform the Communists charged that former lawyers had been using their new positions as a screen to carry on "underground" activities to the injury of the people and the state. Through ties with relatives, friends, old schoolmates, and former colleagues, the *"hei lü-shih"* and the *"sung-kun"* (pettifoggers) were said to have organized them-selves in groups and to have worked closely with the old judicial officials in a conspiracy against New China's legal system. Their illegal acts, according to official reports, included bribery and cor-ruption, fraud and blackmail, perversion of justice, monopoly of lawsuits, incitement to strifes and disputes, and confounding of right with wrong.[23]

As a part of the Reform campaign, the Communist press played up the stories of the "anti-people" activities of the "underground lawyers". For instance, in a case reported in Wuhsi, Kiangsu, a lawyer (father) and a judge (son) were accused of having teamed together to commit between 1949 and 1951 over one hundred criminal acts, ranging from selling confidential information to harbouring counterrevolutionaries.[24] In another case, an "under-ground lawyer" in Canton was found to have extorted from a litigant in one lawsuit alone some 120 million yuan.[25] "The under-ground lawyers," commented a writer in the *People's Daily*, "are loyal 'body-guards' of the criminal elements and, at the same time, the accomplices of the corrupt personnel in the people's courts.

---

[22] *Kuang-ming jih-pao* (Kuang-ming Daily), Peking, August 31, 1957. For details, consult the section on "The Judicial Reform" in Chapter 2.

[23] Lin Ch'eng, *Jen-min jih-pao*, September 14, 1952; *Ch'ang-chiang jih-pao*, September 9, 1952.

[24] *Chieh-fang jih-pao* (Liberation Daily), Shanghai, September 13, 1952.

[25] *Ch'ang-chiang jih-pao*, September 9, 1952.

They have treated the working people as an object of exploitation and government property as a target for attack. Many criminals, even the counterrevolutionary elements, have escaped legal punishment with the help of the underground lawyers, who are indeed the destroyers of the social order and one of the obstacles to our national construction. People's governments at all levels must, in line with the current judicial reform, be stringent in prohibiting the illegal activities of the underground lawyers."[26]

To enforce its policy of purging the "underground lawyers," the Communist regime first required all former members of the bar to register with the "people's courts" and to make their "confessions." It promised leniency to those who would "voluntarily confess, sincerely repent, and actively expose the other underground lawyers as well as the depraved elements in the courts." In the meantime it also threatened those who would dare to resist with severe punishment. After the lawyers had registered and confessed their errors, the Communists proceeded to mobilize the masses to attack them at accusation and struggle meetings, where they were punished according to the seriousness of their "crimes."[27]

There is no way for us to determine the accurate number of the lawyers purged in the Judicial Reform. But the intensity of the purge was clearly indicated by some official reports. Just within the first month of the campaign, seven hundred and eighty "underground lawyers" had registered and "confessed" in Shanghai, and eighty-six in Canton.[28]

Development of the People's Lawyer System

The constitution of the People's Republic of China, adopted in September 1954, marked the beginning of a more orderly development in the legal life of the country. China had passed the initial phase of turmoil and repression and now entered into a new stage of political stability and economic construction. The right to defense was among those democratic legal guarantees clearly defined by the Constitution and the Organic Law of the People's Courts (adopted in the same month). Article 76 of the Constitution states: "The accused has the right to defense." To elaborate

---

[26] Lin Ch'eng, *Jen-min jih-pao*, September 14, 1952.

[27] Ch'en Shu-fang, pp. 47-48. See also Chow Ching-wen, *Ten Years of Storm*, New York, 1960, p. 141.

[28] *Jen-min jih-pao*, September 14, 1952.

on this point, Article 7 of the Organic Law of the People's Courts provides: "The accused, besides personally defending his case, may designate a lawyer to defend it, or have it defended by a citizen recommended by a people's organization or approved by the people's courts, or defended by a near relative or guardian. The people's court may also, when it deems it necessary, appoint a counsel for the accused."[29]

The first indication that new lawyers were already at work in Communist China was the official announcement on November 23, 1954 of the judgment of the Military Tribunal of the Supreme People's Court on thirteen American nationals involved in two alleged espionage cases. In the announcement two professors of law of the China People's University were listed as defense attorneys for the accused.[30] At the beginning of the year 1955, thirty-three "people's courts" were reportedly experimenting with the introduction of lawyers.[31] On July 29, 1955, in a speech before the National People's Congress, Miss Shih Liang said: "We are enforcing the system of people's lawyers on trial in Peking, Shanghai, Wuhan and other major and middle cities and will gradually introduce the system as soon as we have acquired the necessary experience."[32] Early in 1956, a meeting was held in Peking to examine the experience already gained in the work of the lawyers and to discuss the drafts of the "Regulations for Lawyers" and of the "Provisional Rules for Lawyers' Fees." A spokesman for the Ministry of Justice announced at the meeting that a number of new lawyers would soon start practice in different provinces and municipalities.[33] By 1957 Shih Liang reported that there were lawyers in most cities of China to act as people's legal advisers.[34] On the basis of the evidence available, there appear to be some 3,000 lawyers and less than 1,000 Legal Advisory Offices through-

[29] Texts of the Constitution and the Organic Law are in *Chung-hua jen-min kung-ho-kuo fa-kuei hui-pien* (Compendium of Laws and Regulations of the Chinese People's Republic), Peking, Vol. I (1956), pp. 4-31; 123-132. Official English translations are in *Documents of the First Session of the First National People's Congress of the People's Republic of China,* Peking, pp. 131-163; 185-199.

[30] *Jen-min jih-pao,* November 24, 1954.

[31] *Kuang-ming jih-pao,* March 24, 1955.

[32] American Consulate General, Hong Kong, *Current Background,* No. 349, August 25, 1955.

[33] *New China News Agency,* April 6, 1956.

[34] *People's China,* No. 12, 1957, p. 16.

out the country.[35] Undoubtedly, the number of lawyers is still too small and they are mainly concentrated in large and medium-sized cities. Nevertheless, the fact that the Communist regime now permits lawyers to operate is an important change from its previous policies.

As has happened in the Soviet Union, the changed attitude of the Chinese Communists toward the bar has resulted from their efforts to regularize the judicial system. They have told the public that the various democratic systems embodied in the "people's courts," such as the system of public trial, the defense system, the assessor system, and the others, are designed to "strike decisive blows at the enemy and rationally settle conflicts among the people, so that no innocent may be wronged and no black sheep left at large."[36] They have also stressed the difference between the old and new lawyers and the desirability of having the "people's bar." One Communist writer, for example, lists five district merits of the institution of "people's lawyers."[37] First, the new system guarantees the implementation of the principle of defense in criminal proceedings as well as helps the "people's courts" to exercise correctly the judicial power of the state. Second, the existence of Legal Advisory Offices is not only convenient for the masses but also advantageous to the development of the adjudication work of the "people's courts." Third, "people's lawyers" extend aid to the broad masses, support their fight against crimes and criminals, and protect the legitimate interests of the parties concerned. Fourth, through their routine work of answering inquiries and participating in law suits, the new lawyers also perform a useful propaganda service for the policies, laws, and regulations of the state. Fifth, their participation in trials has a supervisory effect on the administration of justice, making the judicial organs more conscious of raising the quality of their work.

---

[35] There were over 2,100 full-time lawyers and 670 Legal Advisory Offices in 1956. They were expected to increase to 3,500 and 1,000 respectively by 1957. *Kuang-ming jih-pao,* January 1, 1957. Lower figures, however, are given in other sources, such as China Research Institute, *Chugoku Nenkan, 1960* (China Yearbook, 1960), Tokyo, 1960, p. 143, and Felix Greene, *Awakened China,* New York, 1961, p. 194. According to Wu Teh-feng, Chairman of the Chinese Association of Political Science and Law, there are 3,000 lawyers in China, all of whom have teaching jobs and spend only a few days a year in court. Edgar Snow, *The Other Side of the River,* New York, 1962, p. 354.

[36] *Jen-min jih-pao,* December 11, 1954.

[37] Huang Yüan, *Wo-kuo jen-min lü-shih chih-tu* (Our People's Lawyer System), Canton, 1956, pp. 2-9.

In spite of the new line, the legal profession in Communist China has remained minute in size as compared to the huge population of 750 million. The old-style lawyers have been forced out of existence, first by the Judicial Reform Movement and later by the Anti-Rightist Campaign of 1957-1958. At the same time, the new educational system is not producing a sufficient number of qualified legal practitioners. Although there are a number of university law schools as well as special legal training schools and classes in China, statistics indicate that the percentage of Chinese students engaged in the study of law is quite small. In 1957-1958 law and political science students constituted only 2.1 per cent of the total enrollment in higher education, while graduates in the same field were less than 4 per cent of the total number of graduates from colleges and universities.[38] In 1961 the enrollment figure in the law schools was estimated to be only 3,000.[39] This situation may be compensated in part by Article 7 of the Organic Law of the People's Courts, cited above, which allows a number of people, beside lawyers, to serve as defense counsel— (1) citizens recommended by people's organizations, (2) persons approved by the courts, and (3) close relatives and guardians of the accused.

Organization and Activity of People's Lawyers

The organization and activity of the "people's bar" are governed by the "Draft Regulations for Lawyers," effective since 1956. A more detailed document, the "Provisional Rules for Lawyers," was drafted in 1957 by the Ministry of Justice, but nothing has been said publicly about this document since that year.[40]

Attorneys in Communist China are organized into Lawyers' Associations, which operate in provinces, autonomous regions, and municipalities directly under the central authority. Technically, the Lawyers' Association is a voluntary organization of persons engaged in the legal profession, formed on the basis of the principle of democratic centralism. Neither a state organ nor a private group, the Association is a social body within the broad framework

---

[38] Leo A. Orleans, *Professional Manpower and Education in Communist China*, Washington, 1950, Table 4, p. 71, and Table 5, pp. 74-75.

[39] K. S. Woodsworth, "The Legal System of the Republic of China," *The Canadian Bar Journal*, August 1961, p. 307.

[40] For some descriptions of the Provisional Rules, see *Kuang-ming jih-pao*, June 17, 1957.

of China's judicial system and accepts the guidance and control of the judicial organs of the state. Its functions consist of supervising the work of Legal Advisory Offices, helping raise the standards of law practice, admitting new members, and disciplining the delinquent ones. Under the Lawyers' Associations, there are Legal Advisory Offices set up in counties and municipalities to carry on the organizational and routine work of legal practitioners.[41]

The requirements for admission to the "people's bar" are rather irregular, which reflects both the Communist concept of lawyers and the acute shortage of trained personnel in China. Nowhere is the subject of bar examinations ever mentioned. According to the regulations, a citizen who has the right to elect and be elected[42] and who meets one of the following three conditions can apply for membership to a Lawyers' Association. After the board of directors of the Association has approved his membership application, he is then assigned to a Legal Advisory Office to serve as a lawyer. The three conditions referred to are: (1) a graduate from a university law school or a secondary law school of Communist China with experience in judicial work of at least one year; (2) a person with previous experience as a judge or a procurator for at least one year in a "people's court" or a "people's procuratorate"; and (3) a person of a certain cultural standard, legal knowledge, and social experience suitable to the practice of law.

It is further provided that anyone who has received legal education in the Chinese People's Republic but who has had no practical experience in judicial work may also apply for admission to a Lawyers' Association. In this case, he will be assigned to a Legal Advisory Office to serve his apprenticeship for some length of time before the Lawyers' Association accepts him as a member. There is also a provision for part-time lawyers. Social science professors, instructors, or researchers in universities, colleges, professional schools, or research institutes, deputies of the People's Congresses who have no adminitrative duties, or officials of various people's

---

[41] Huang Yüan, p. 11; "Concerning the Question of the People's Lawyer System," *Kuang-ming jih-pao,* July 7, 1956.

[42] This may be noted together with a resolution adopted in May 1956 by the Standing Committee of the National People's Congress stating that a person who is currently deprived of political rights may not serve as defense counsel to anyone but his close kin. *Jen-min shou-ts'e, 1957,* Tientsin, 1957, p. 337.

organizations can concurrently serve as part-time lawyers if admitted to a Lawyers' Association.[43]

"People's lawyers" are public servants and not private practitioners. They all work in Legal Advisory Offices, each of which is under the supervision of a director chosen by the Lawyers' Association. To a Legal Advisory Office, citizens, state agencies, enterprises, and social groups can come for assistance of varying kinds.

Fees are paid by clients to the Legal Advisory Office rather than individual lawyers. The amount, usually small, is determined by agreement between the clients and the director of the Office in accordance with the cost of living and the type of work done. At times, free service must be rendered if the client proves too poor to pay, or is involved in pension or alimony claims, or has other justifiable reasons.[44] Lawyers receive their salaries from the Legal Advisory Offices where they practice collectively. The scale is set by the board of directors of the bar according to the ability and the amount of work of each individual.[45]

There are three major functions that the "people's lawyer" generally performs. First, he answers the inquires of the people and furnishes them with opinions on matters relating to the law and legal processes. Secondly, he prepares petitions, contracts, agreements, and other legal documents for individuals as well as groups. Thirdly, he acts as defense counsel for the accused in a criminal action or as a representative for the plaintiff, defendant, or other interested parties in a civil action.[46]

Initially, the lawyers' schedule seemed to be a busy one, as people now came to the Legal Advisory Offices for many services that were performed in the past by the people's reception offices of the courts. Just after one and a half months of operation, five Legal Advisory Offices in Shanghai were reported in 1956 to have answered 3,584 legal inquiries, drafted 879 legal papers for callers,

---

[43] Huang Yüan, pp. 10-11; *Kuang-ming jih-pao*, July 7, 1956. By way of comparison, see the description of the Soviet bar in V. Gsovski and K. Grzybowski, *Government, Law and Courts in the Soviet Union and Eastern Europe*, New York, Vol. 1, pp. 559-564.

[44] The text of the "Provisional Rules for Lawyers' fees," promulgated on July 20, 1956, is in *Chung-hua jen-min kung-ho-kuo fa-kuei hui-pien*, Vol. 4 (1957), pp. 235-238.

[45] *Kuang-ming jih-pao*, July 7, 1956.

[46] Huang Yüan, pp. 9-10. See also "Why Is the People's Lawyer System Put into Practice," *Kung-jen jih-pao* (Daily Worker), Peking, August 3, 1956.

and represented or defended clients in 281 cases.[47] A woman lawyer, at one of these Offices, in a single day managed to handle 12 cases concerning questions of marriage, debt, and housing tenancy.[48] Early in 1957, Legal Advisory Offices in some large cities and provinces began to assign lawyers to serve as regular counsellors for certain agencies, enterprises, organizations, and co-operatives.[49] Since the spring of 1958 more stress has been placed on the lawyers' work to explain questions relating to law and to publicize the socialist legal system. Like judicial officials in Communist China, "people's lawyers" have gone to factories and farms to bring their services to the masses, carry on down-to-earth investigation and examination, take part in production and labor, and conduct propaganda and education on the observance of law.[50]

Participation in lawsuits is one of the lawyer's functions that deserves special attention. In civil disputes, the first thing that the "people's lawyer" frequently does is to try to effect some form of compromise or informal settlement through his mediation and persuasion. A number of instances have been reported in which lawyers helped their clients to resolve family, marriage, debt, and property disputes without recourse to court litigation.[51] On occasions, however, the "people's lawyer" does attend the court to act for litigants in civil suits. The "General Evaluation of the Judicial Process of Civil Suits in the People's Courts at Various Levels" states that if a party is a minor, a person of vital physical defect, or a person with a mental illness who is unable to act in a litigation, he should ask an attorney or his close kin to be his agent in the suit.[52] People who have little legal knowledge or who are tied

---

[47] *Kuang-ming jih-pao,* July 6, 1956.

[48] *New China News Agency,* July 12, 1956.

[49] This development was reported in cities like Peking and Shanghai and in provinces like Shantung and Kiangsu, *Kuang-ming jih-pao,* February 18, 1957.

[50] See, for instances, reports in *Ch'ang-chou jih-pao* (Ch'angchow Daily), May 14, 1958 and *Hei-lung-chiang jih-pao* (Heilungkiang Daily), Harbin, May 7, 1958.

[51] Huang Yüan, pp. 5-6; *Ho-nan jih-pao* (Honan Daily), Chengchou, November 11, 1958; *Wen-hui pao* (Wen-hui News), Hong Kong, May 12, 1957; *An-hui jih-pao* (Anhwei Daily), Hofei, May 22, 1956.

[52] *Basic Problems in the Civil Law of the People's Republic of China,* JPRS, No. 4879, 1961, p. 94; checked with the original text, *Chung-hua jen-min kung-ho-kuo min-fa chi-pen wen-t'i* (by the Institute of Civil Law, Central Political-Judicial Cadres' School), Peking, 1958, pp. 90-91.

up by work or other matters may also have themselves represented by lawyers in civil proceedings. When a party commissions an attorney to act for him in a civil suit, he is allowed in Communist China to make the mandate (delegation of power) in either a written or an oral form. As maintained by Communist writers, the mandate must define clearly the range of authority delegated to the lawyer. They dismiss as improper and confusing the so-called plenipotentiary mandate, which confers authority with a sweeping statement such as "to take charge of all affairs."[53]

In a criminal action, the "people's lawyer" can serve as the defense counsel when entrusted by the accused or designated by the court. His task is said to consist in defending the rights and lawful interests of the accused on the one hand and helping the court in the exercise of correct judgment on the other.[54] As in the Soviet Union, the attorney for the defense is excluded from the pre-trial investigation in China. To conduct the defense, he is nevertheless permitted to take the following measures under the established procedure: studying the files and case materials, talking with the accused, questioning witnesses, experts, and the accused at the trial, summoning and questioning new witnesses, introducing new evidence, and participating in courtroom debates. If necessary, he also can, with the consent of the defendant, lodge an appeal from the judgment and present his version of the case to the court of the second instance.[55]

According to the Chinese Communists, the defense counsel is not an agent of the accused in a criminal proceeding. He is an independent party in the trial and is not bound by the will of the defendant. He must carry out his tasks within a legal framework and under no circumstances should he fabricate evidence, distort facts, or use deceptions to help his client. If the evidence presented by the prosecution is incorrect in whole or in part, the attorney should conduct the defense proceedings with a view to prove the

---

[53] *Basic Problems in the Civil Law,* p. 99; Kuo k'o-hung, "Questions Concerning the Lawyer's Authority as an Agent in Civil Suits," *Kuang-ming jih-pao,* January 15, 1957.

[54] Wang Hou-li, "An Important Democratic System—System of Defense," *ibid.,* January 14, 1955.

[55] Huang Yüan, p. 13; Chao Hsu-lun and Ma Jung-chieh, "What We Understand about the System of Defense," *Kuang-ming jih-pao,* March 24, 1955; Ma Jung-chieh, "Where There Should be a defense Council System for Court Trials," *Kung-jen jih-pao,* November 25, 1956.

innocence of the accused or to mitigate his guilt. If, on the other hand, the crime has been established beyond any doubt, then the counsel should defend the accused from the standpoint of certain extenuating circumstances, such as the motives and means of the crime, the age of the defendant, the degree of his repentance, the objective reasons for the crime, etc.[56]

To show the "democratic procedure" at work, the Chinese press has reported from time to time cases in which the accused were defended by "people's lawyers." But most of these cases were routine and non-political in nature. Only on rare occasions were there any exceptions. The presence of defense attorneys was reported at the trials of "espionage" cases in 1954 and 1960, one involving thirteen Americans and the other Bishops James Walsh and Kung P'in-mei.[57] However, no details beyond the sentences were given by the press. It is doubtful whether the lawyers in both trials did more than serve the window-dressing purpose of the regime.

In the routine, non-political cases reported by Chinese papers, defense attorneys did make more serious efforts to defend their clients. We have read, for example, a case tried in Shanghai in which an assistant manager of a store was accused of stabbing the manager with a knife. Among the reasons advanced by the counsel in support of the defendant's innocence were that the stabbing was an act of self-defense and that the defendant was arrested against the Regulations Governing Arrest and Detention of the People's Republic of China.[58] In a negligence case tried in Tsingtao, a chemist was charged with the responsibility of having caused the state a direct loss of 400,000 yuan and an indirect loss of 1,670,000. His attorney pleaded the mediocre technical level of the accused and the poor condition of the factory equipment as extenuating circumstances to mitigate the charges.[59] In a fraud case tried in Peking, a man was accused of having tried to obtain honor and position with faked papers. The defense counsel first pointed out that the defendant, in perpetrating his criminal activities, was prompted by material and personal considerations which were

---

[56] Ch'u Huai-chih and Chang Min-fu, "Toward an Understanding of the System of Defense in Criminal Proceedings in Our Country," *Hsin chien-she* (New Construction), No. 5, 1956, p. 15.

[57] *New China News Agency,* November 23, 1954 and September 17-18, 1960.

[58] *Hsin-wen jih-pao* (News Daily), Shanghai, June 4, 1957.

[59] *Ch'ing-tao jih-pao* (Tsingtao Daily), March 17, 1955.

different from political motives and counterrevolutionary activities detrimental to the political interests of the state. Then he listed a few objective factors as grounds for a plea that the defendant not be held solely responsible for the harm done to the society.[60]

Problems and Difficulties

In examining the system of "people's lawyers" of China, one must bear in mind that it is still in an experimental stage and is being tried in a new evolving Communist society. The irregularities and handicaps under which Chinese lawyers have to operate, in fact, reflect the unsettled status of the "people's bar" as well as that of the whole legal system of Communist China.

One of the problems confronting the "people's lawyer" is the existence of many gaps in Chinese law. As mentioned in preceding chapters, there is still no complete criminal code, civil code, or code of procedure in the People's Republic, and the existing statutes and regulations contain many vague and conflicting provisions. This lack of precise legislation and comprehensive codes was a subject of complaints during the "Hundred Flowers" period in the spring of 1957, when a number of prominent jurists, some of them Communist members, raised the issue of "no laws to rely on" and pleaded for the establishment of a stable and elaborate system of law.[61]

An explanation for the deficiency of China's legal system is given in Premier Chou En-lai's statement that "it is difficult to draft the civil and criminal codes before the completion in the main of the socialist transformation of the private ownership of the means of production and the full establishment of socialist ownership of the means of production."[62] Other Communist spokesmen also point out that the laws of the Chinese People's Republic are "revolutionary and changing" in nature and cannot be formulated rigidly with overdetailed provisions.[63] Be that as it may, the fact

---

60 *Jen-min jih-pao,* August 31, 1956.

61 For the complaints of the liberal jurists, consult the section on "The Reversal in 1957" in Chapter 3, and Roderick MacFarquhar, *The Hundred Flowers Campaign and the Chinese Intellectuals,* New York, 1960, pp. 114-116.

62 *New China News Agency,* June 26, 1957.

63 "Several Problems Concerning the People's Democratic Legal System of Our Country," *Cheng-fa yen-chiu,* No. 2, 1959, pp. 4-7.

remains that the practicing lawyer can find his work extremely difficult in cases where there are no definite laws and regulations to follow.

Another problem besetting the "people's lawyer" is the unfriendly attitude sometimes adopted by the judicial personnel. Since the system of legal defense is still in its infancy, there is a tendency on the part of many judges and procurators to treat legal counsellors with hostility and contempt. Some regard them as subordinates and even order them to help investigate cases. Others feel that the presence of an attorney at a trial is a "nuisance" and a "waste of time" and take such an attitude as "regardless of your argument I shall judge the case just the same." Still others consider legal defense as "loss of (revolutionary) stand" and "protection of crimes" and condemn the lawyer for "siding with questionable characters and losing the sense of right and wrong."[64]

Under the circumstances, the "people's lawyer" naturally has to perform his duties with great care. He certainly will not want to "lose his stand" by undertaking the defense of persons accused of counterrevolutionary offences. His task can be very delicate at times as the distinction between political and ordinary crimes has never been drawn too clearly in Communist China.[65]

Finally, a more serious handicap for the Chinese lawyer appears to be the position taken by the Communist government regarding his relations with the defendant and his duties to the state. It should be recalled that between 1954 and 1957 legal development in China was toward a gradual liberalization. This trend, nonetheless, was abruptly reversed in the Anti-Rightist Campaign of 1957-1958, during which many lawyers were criticized for harbouring old legal concepts and considering themselves as "men of free profession." Among other things, members of the legal

---

[64] "A Few Words in behalf of the People's Lawyer," *Kuang-ming jih-pao,* January 27, 1957. A top Communist jurist also shows concern over some of these problems, see Ma Hsi-wu, "Several Problems Concerning the Current Adjudication Work," *Hsin-hua pan-yüeh-k'an* (New China Semimonthly), Peking, No. 9, 1956, pp. 18 & 20.

[65] As mentioned in the section on "Mao's Theory of Contradictions" in Chapter 8, altogether six articles appeared in the 1958 issues of *Cheng-fa yen-chiu* (Nos. 3, 4 & 5) to discuss *inconclusively* the following questions: "Are All Criminal Offenses to be Treated as Contradictions between the Enemy and Ourselves? Are All Criminals to be Regarded as the Objects of Dictatorship?"

profession have been told to follow the mass line, submit to Party leadership, and place their activities in strict accordance with the directives of the Party committees.[66] Until and unless Peking swings back in a liberal direction, the work of defense attorneys will continue to be hampered by the Communists' new rigidity as reflected in some important essays published in Chinese legal journals.[67]

According to the thesis advanced by these essays, the "people's lawyer" should put his duty to the state above his duty to the defendant. It would be "absurd" for a lawyer to be allowed to keep professional secrets confined by the defendant. Indeed, it is the duty of the attorney to persuade the accused to confess his guilt, and, if he refuses to do so, to denounce him and reveal his secrets. The role of the defense attorney is, first of all, to "safeguard the socialist legal system and consolidate the proletarian dictatorship." In carrying out the task of defending his client, he must always proceed from the interests of the state and the people. No deviation is permitted.

Such being the current official line, one can see easily the difficult situation in which the system of legal defense finds itself in China. Not only is the lawyer's professional activity restricted in criminal procedure but his relationship with the accused is also put on a precarious basis. This, along with other factors, accounts for the latest trend to have Chinese attorneys more engaged in educational and propaganda work than in lawsuits.[68] Doubts, in fact, have been

---

[66] See, for example, the editorial of *Hei-lung-chiang jih-pao*, May 7, 1958, titled "Manifest with Thoroughness the Functions of the People's Lawyers."

[67] For some representative essays on the work of attorneys, see Ch'eng Jung-ping, "The Defense Counsel Must Work for the Socialist Legal System," *Fa-hsüeh* (Jurisprudence), No. 2, 1958, pp. 36-38; Lin Tse-chiang, "Criticize Thoroughly Bourgeois Attitudes in the Work of People's Lawyers," *ibid.*, pp. 39-43; Su I, "Should the Defense Counsel Expose the Crime or Defend It?" *Cheng-fa yen-chiu*, No. 2, 1958, pp. 76-77; Wu Lei, "Examination of the Essay on 'Study of the Role of the Defense Counsel in Criminal Procedure'," *ibid.*, pp. 78-81.

[68] Other contributing factors are the socialization of property ownership (reducing areas of civil action) and the stress on the informal settlement of minor disputes in China. According to one leading Chinese jurist, Wu Teh-feng, lawyers and judges in China do not have enough court cases now and have to perform more educational functions in the field of law. Greene, p. 194; Snow, p. 354.

expressed by some recent Japanese visitors about the future of the bar in China.[69] On the other hand, if the Soviet experience can serve as any guide, it appears quite likely that with the passage of time Communist China may abandon some of her irregular practices and give the counselor a more meaningful role to play. One basic feature of the "people's lawyer," however, will probably remain unchanged. Like his Soviet counterpart, the Chinese lawyer is not a champion of private rights but an auxiliary agent of the state.[70]

[69] The Delegation of Young Jurists Who Visited China, Horitsuka no mita Chugoku (China As Seen by Jurists), Tokyo, 1965, p. 216.

[70] See the description of the Soviet lawyer in Gsovski and Grzybowski, Vol. 1, p. 564.

Chapter 8

Administration of Justice

Theoretically, the "people's courts" in China possess the sole legal authority to administer justice. In practice, as shown in the preceding chapters, large numbers of extrajudicial organs also participate in the judicial process. The informal aspect of "people's justice" is underscored by the fact that in contrast with the Soviet Union, there is still no code of criminal procedure nor code of civil procedure in the Chinese People's Republic after sixteen years of her existence.[1]

During the mid-1950's when Communist China was developing a stable legal system patterned after the Soviet model, both the constitution of the Republic and the Organic Law of the People's Courts stipulated a number of basic principles and rules to guide the judicial organs in the administration of justice. Furthermore, in the same period the Judicial Committee of the Supreme People's Court undertook to study the civil and criminal procedures used by the "people's courts" in fourteen large and medium-sized cities. After some individual variations were adjusted, the Committee compiled two summaries of civil and criminal procedures and issued them to the lower courts on a trial basis.[2] Since 1958, however, the mass line has become the dominant feature of the legal scene. The courts have continued to experiment and revise the aforementioned tentative procedures with an emphasis on flexibility, simplicity, and "bringing justice directly to the people."[3] This chapter will examine some of the basic principles governing judicial work, Mao Tse-tung's theory on contradictions, and the actual processes of handling criminal and civil cases in China.

---

[1] Soviet Russia enacted her first code of criminal procedure in 1922 and her first code of civil procedure in 1923. Vladimir Gsovski and Kasimierz Grzybowski, *Government, Law and Courts in the Societ Union and Eastern Europe*, New York, Vol. 1, pp. 84-842.

[2] Kao Ko-lin (Vice-President of the SPC), "Work of the Supreme People's Court since 1955," *New China News Agency*, Peking, April 24, 1959.

[3] *Ibid.*; Hsieh Chüeh-tsai (President of the SPC), "Report on the Work of the Supreme People's Court," *Jen-min jih-pao* (People's Daily), Peking, January 1, 1965.

Collegiate System

Among the fundamental judicial principles and rules provided by the Constitution and the Organic Law of the Courts are public trials, equality before the law, independence of the courts, the right to defense, the right to appeal, the assessor system, the collegiate system, and the withdrawal of court officers.[4] Some of them have already been examined elsewhere in the book; a few others will be discussed in this chapter.

As under any form of dictatorship, there is always a disparity between legal niceties and political reality. This has become particularly evident in post-1957 China, where the Communist authorities frequently circumvent constitutional provisions and procedural guarantees. Nevertheless, at trials conducted for the benefit of the public or foreign visitors, the "people's courts" still maintain a façade of observing the processes of law.[5] Moreover, as long as the juridical principles that were adopted in 1954 remain in statutory books, they can provide a significant base for regenerating a trend toward liberalization and legality in the future.

Article 9 of the Organic Law of the People's Courts provides that the courts carry out the collegiate system in the administration of justice. In cases of first instance, justice is administered by a collegiate bench of a judge and "people's assessors," with the exception of simple civil cases, minor criminal cases, and cases otherwise provided by law. In cases of appeal or protest, justice is administered by a collegiate bench of judges.

Following closely the Soviet model, a collegiate bench usually consists of a judge and two "people's assessors" in the first instance and three judges in the second instance.[6] All three members of the bench in theory have equal rights and decide jointly, by a majority

---

[4] See Articles 75-78 of the Constitution and Articles 4-13 of the Organic Law. Texts of the two documents are in *Chung-hua jen-min kung-ho-kuo fa-kuei hui-pien* (Compendium of Laws and Regulations of the Chinese People's Republic), Peking, Vol. I (1956), pp. 4-31 and 123-132 respectively.

[5] For instance, see reports in Felix Greene, *Awakened China*, New York, 1961, pp. 197-209; Edgar Snow, *The Other Side of the River*, New York, 1962, pp. 570-573; The Delegation of Young Jurists Who Visited China, *Horitsuka no mita Chugoku* (China as Seen by Jurists), Tokyo, 1965, pp. 210-214.

[6] The actual size of the bench is given in Shih Liang, "The Judicial System in New China," *People's China*, Peking, No. 12, 1957, p. 17. For the Soviet system, see A. Denisov & M. Kirichenko, *Soviet State Law*, Moscow, 1960, p. 303.

vote, both questions of law and of fact. Based on the principle of "democratic centralism," the collegiate system is described as capable of "developing collective wisdom, insuring careful investigation, and improve the quality of trial work."[7]

It should be noted that the collegiate bench is subject to the direction of its chairman and the court president. If a difference of opinion exists between the court president and the bench, the matter is transferred to the judicial committee for examination and solution.[8] Often, the court adjudicates cases in an informal manner with the collegiate system providing the legal formality. The actual decision-making process of the court involves much consultation and discussion. Whenever relevant or necessary, the judge in charge seeks the views of procurators, police officers, the court president, and Party officials before a decision is reached.[9]

Public Trials

Both the Constitution (Article 76) and the Organic Law (Article 7) have the stipulation that "cases in the people's courts are heard in public unless otherwise provided by law." The holding of public (open) trials (*kung-k'ai shen-p'an*) should be distinguished from the proceeding of mass trials (*kung-shen*) used in the past. A specific device tied to the various mass movements, the latter involved the gathering of huge crowds and stimulation of mob emotion to wage a fierce struggle against the accused "landlords, counterrevolutionaries, and other class enemies." The conduct of public trials, on the other hand, is a regular court procedure applicable to all civil and criminal cases. Only in matters where state secrets, individual intimacies, and juvenile delinquency are involved, may closed trials take place. But the decisions still have to be announced publicly.[10]

According to the principle of public trials, the parties to a suit and

---

[7] Wei Wen-Po, *Tui-yü "Chung-hua jen-min kung-ho-kuo jen-min fa-yüan tsu-chi-fa" chi-pen wen-t'i ti jen-shih* (On Understanding the Basic Issues of the "Organic Law of the People's Courts of the People's Republic of China"), Shanghai, 1956, p. 12.

[8] V. Ye. Chugunov, *Criminal Court Procedures in Chinese People's Republic* (Trans. from Russian) JPRS (Joint Publication Research Service), No. 4595, 1961, pp. 43-44.

[9] For a detailed description of the informal procedures of the court, see Jerome A. Cohen, "The Criminal Process in the People's Republic of China," *Harvard Law Review*, Vol. 79, No. 3, 1966, pp. 511-515.

[10] "The Resolution of the Standing Committee of the National People's Congress on Cases Excluded from Public Trials (Adopted on May 8, 1956)," *Jen-min shou-ts'e* (People's Handbook), Peking, 1957, p. 337.

other interested persons have the right to speak and argue the case in open court. Every citizen is permitted to attend court hearings and the press may report them.[11] This procedure is officially described as having two significant effects. First, with the right to attend trials and voice criticism through newspapers and letters, the people are given an opportunity to exercise direct supervision over court work. This sharpens the sense of responsibility on the part of judicial personnel and insures the passing of fair and sound judgments. Secondly, public trials enhance the educational role of the courts. By conducting open sessions and proclaiming sentences publicly, the courts can educate the masses in the spirit of observance of the laws and vigilance against illegal acts.[12]

The constitutional principle and official pronouncements notwithstanding, the Chinese judicial organs frequently follow a nonpublic and informal process in adjudicating cases. To be sure, public trials are still held in mainland China. But they are largely for propaganda and window-dressing purposes.

In certain model cases of educational value, the "people's courts" hold open hearings on the spot, invite the masses to participate directly in the proceedings, and publicize the trials by way of the press, the radio, cartoons, and wall newspapers.[13] During the period of the ill-fated Big Leap, judicial officials throughout Communist China made full use of on-the-spot trials, integrated court hearings with mass debate, and carried out a vigorous legal propaganda campaign.[14] In 1958 courts in the urban areas of Sining, Tsinghai, reportedly handled all civil cases on the spot and conducted on-the-spot trials of over 50 percent of the criminal cases.[15] From January to October of 1959 the courts of Liaoning province alone were reported to have given 11,176 lectures on law and to have held 1,700

---

[11] Chou Fang, *Wo-kuo kuo-chia chi-kou* (State Organs of Our Country), Peking, 1955, p. 126. With permission a spectator may also address the court. See Masso Fukushima and others, *Chugoku no saiban* (Justice in China), Tokyo, 1957, p. 115.

[12] Chou Fang, p. 127; Szu Ping, "The Meaning of Holding Public Trials by the People's Courts," *Jen-min jih-pao*, February 19, 1955.

[13] *Jen-min jih-pao*, October 16, 1954; *Kuang-ming jih-pao*, (Kuang-ming Daily), Peking, September 10, 1955.

[14] *Ho-pei jih-pao* (Hopei Daily), Tientsin, October 29, 1958; *Shan-hsi jih-pao* (Shansi Daily), Taiyuan, December 8, 1958; *Jen-min jih-pao*, December 12, 1958, April 7, 1960, June 10, 1960.

[15] Yang Tzu-wei, "Work Report of the Higher People's Court in Tsinghai Province," *Ch'ing-hai jih-pao* (Tsinghai Daily), Sining, December 15, 1959.

public meetings for delivering judgments in factories, mines, streets, and villages.[16]

While the excesses of the Big Leap have gone, on-the-spot trials, nevertheless, continue to serve as an important "mass line" procedure for the "people's judiciary" to promote close ties with the broad masses.[17] Occasionally, serious counterrevolutionary cases are tried before large assemblies with an all too familiar tone of the frightening mass trials of the past. On August 19, 1962, for example, some 5,000 people attended a public trial at the Physical Culture Hall in Canton where Wu Chu, an "espionage agent of the Chiang Kai-shek gang" accused of attempting to blow up a ship, was sentenced to death and executed on the spot. Not only did the crowd greet the sentence and execution "with cheers," but Mayor Tseng Sheng of Canton took the occasion to make a speech, urging the people to continue sharpening their revolutionary vigilance and helping the government round up enemy agents in order to "safeguard the construction of socialism and the security of everyone's life and property."[18]

Two-Trial System

Under the two-trial system as stipulated in Article 11 of the Organic Law of the People's courts, a judgment or order of the court of first instance may be appealed to the court of the next higher level. An appeal may be initiated by a party to the case, or others in his behalf, or the procuracy in the form of a protest. The decision of the court of second instance is final and legally effective. This system is justified by the Chinese Communists on three grounds. 1. Because of the size of the country and the problems of communications, the limitation of court examination to two instances saves the time and money of the interested parties as well as lightens the burden of the courts. 2. The two-trial (one-appeal) system facilitates the judiciary's work in punishing criminals and protecting the people's interest. Allowing more trials and appeals would only give "cunning elements" the opportunity to delay the settlement of cases or to evade legal sanctions. 3. Fair and correct handling of cases is insured under the

[16] Liu P'eng, "Work Report of the Higher People's Court in Liaoning Province," Liao-ning jih-pao (Liaoning Daily), Mukden, December 22, 1959.

[17] Ch'en Fou, "A Tentative Discussion of Some Problems of the People's Tribunals," Cheng-fa yen-chiu (Studies of Political Science and Law), Peking, No. 3, 1964, p. 38.

[18] Yang-ch'eng wan-pao (Canton Evening Post), Canton, August 19, 1962.

system of two trials. Certain cases of a serious nature are generally reserved by laws or decrees to be given first trial in an upper court. Furthermore, if a lower court regards a case as highly important, it may also request its superior court to take over the original jurisdiction.[19]

Judging from various information available, the number of cases appealed seems to be rather small. As estimated in 1960 by Wu Teh-feng, Chairman of the Association of Political Science and Law, only about 5% of the verdicts were appealed in China.[20] Figures for some individual provinces are even lower. In Yunnan, for example, only 2.8% of all cases tried by the courts were appealed during a period of three years (1954-1956), and the trend is reported to have been toward a decrease of appeals from year to year. This is cited by a Soviet author as testifying to the correct application of laws and the improvement of trial work on the part of the "people's courts" in China.[21]

A *Cheng-fa yen-chiu* writer, on the other hand, attributes this phenomenon to the failure of judicial officers to respect the people's right of appeal and the fear of the accused to incur a heavier punishment in the second trial. In criminal cases, he notes, not a single appeal was ever attempted from the decision of some lower courts![22] Reporting before the National People's Congress in 1956, Huang Shao-hung also pointed out that a number of judges and procurators in Shanghai and Chekiang province took up a hostile attitude toward those who wished to appeal. As a result, he said, many people in these areas were afraid to use their right of appeal lest they should be branded as "obstinate counterrevolutionaries" daring to resist the will of the state.[23] This fear was further substantiated in 1958 when an official spokesman declared that in a criminal appeal the court could either reduce or increase the sentence in the interest of justice, regardless of who appealed the case.[24]

---

[19] Huang Yuan, *Jen-min fa-yüan chi-pen chi-shih chiang-hua* (Lectures on the Basic Knowledge of the People's Courts), Canton, 1956, pp. 35-36; Wei Wen-po, pp. 15-16.

[20] Snow, p. 355.

[21] Chugunov, p. 173.

[22] Hsiung Hsien-chueh, "Protect the Right of Appeal of the Accused in a Criminal Action," *Cheng-fa yen-chiu*, No. 4, 1956, pp. 37-38.

[23] *China News Analysis*, Hong Kong, No. 141, July 27, 1956, p. 3.

[24] Wang Chao-sheng, "Refute the Principle of 'Not Making the Defendant's Position Unfavorable in a Criminal Appeal'," *Hsi-pei ta-hsüeh*

There is little doubt that the fear of an increase in the sentence upon the defendant in appellate proceedings has deterred quite a few people from exercising their right of appeal. On the other hand, the courts of second instance appear to have reviewed cases with considerable vigor by setting aside a large percentage of the decisions appealed, particularly during the mid-1950's. According to a 1957 report from Szechwan province, only 44% of the civil cases on appeal had the original decisions upheld and 30.7% were sent back to the lower courts for retrial; only 26.5% of the criminal cases appealed had the original judgments upheld, 46.6% were returned for retrial, and the accused in 30% were acquitted.[25] The estimate offered by Wu Teh-feng in 1960, however, indicated that the verdicts appealed in the country as a whole fared better, as only 20% of them were reversed by the higher courts.[26]

In addition, it should be noted that a legally effective judgment in China is subject to a special form of review, judicial supervision, if some definite error in the determination of facts or application of law is found. Article 12 of the Organic Law of the People's Courts provides the following procedures of judicial supervision for such a situation. 1. The court which gave the judgment in question may refer it to the judicial committee for disposal. 2. The Supreme People's Court or an upper court may review the case themselves or direct the lower court to conduct a retrial. 3. The procuratorates may lodge a protest against the given decision in accordance with the pro-

hsüeh-pao, jen-wen k'o-hsüeh (Northwestern University Journal of Humanistic Science), No. 1, 1958, pp. 66-67. Prior to this statement, the court of second instance was not supposed to increase the original sentence if a case was appealed by the accused. For the functions and proceedings of the courts of second instance see Chugunov, Chapter 5; Ho Chan-chün, "How to Divide the Functions of the Courts of First and Second Instance," Cheng-fa yen-chiu, No. 2, 1956; Han Cheng-han, "My Opinion on How to Divide the Functions of the Courts of First and Second Instance," ibid., No. 3,1956; Chang Tzu-p'ei, "Several Questions Concerning the Functions of the Appellate Courts in Our Country," ibid., No. 4, 1956.

[25] Liu Wen-hui's report before the National People's Congress on July 5, 1957. Hsin-hua pan-yüeh-k'an (New China Semimonthly), Peking, No. 15, 1957, p. 78. In his report to the Congress Tung Pi-wu gave the following figures concerning counterrevolutionary cases in the country. Of the counterrevolutionary cases appealed or protested, over 40% were sent back to the lower courts for retrial, the sentences in 20% were reduced by the upper courts, and the accused in 3% were acquitted. Jen-min jih-pao, June 27, 1956.

[26] Snow, p. 355.

cedure established by law.[27] The implementation of this type of verdict review is linked to the mass line in judicial work, as any interested citizens, institutions, and mass organizations have the right to petition to the court or the procuratorates against a valid judgment which is improper or contrary to law.[28] Here judicial supervision, like appellate review, can also result in a harsher as well as a lighter sentence for the defendant in a criminal case.[29]

Mao Tse-tung's "Correct Handling of Contradictions"

On February 27, 1957, at the Eleventh Session of the Supreme State Conference, Mao Tse-tung delivered a four-hour speech entitled "On the Correct Handling of Contradictions Among the People."[30] In the Chinese legal circles this famous speech has since become the theoretical frame of reference for classifying cases of conflicts and methods of treating them.

In the speech Mao drew a basic distinction between two types of contradictions: "contradictions between ourselves and the enemy" (antagonistic contradictions) and "contradictions among the people" (non-antagonistic contradictions). To help "differentiate correctly" the two contradictions, Mao defined in broad terms the concepts of "the people" and "the enemy": "At this stage of building socialism, all classes, strata and social groups which approve, support and work for the cause of socialist construction belong to the category of the people, while those social forces and groups which resist the socialist revolution, and are hostile to and try to wreck socialist construction, are enemies of the people."

[27] For the purpose of comparison, see *ex officio* review of the Soviet judicial procedure in Gsovski and Grzybowski, Vol. 1, pp. 536-540.

[28] The people can exercise this right by writing letters or paying visits to the authorities. See Tung Pi-wu's speech before the National People's Congress in *Ta-kung pao* (L'Impartial), Tientsin, July 25, 1955; also Shih Liang, (cited note 6), p. 18. An illustrative case was reported in *Kuang-ming jih-pao*, January 10, 1957. An innocent woman, Chung Kui-lan, was wrongfully sentenced to jail by a court in Szechwan. Her subsequent appeal to a higher court resulted in an increase of punishment. This aroused the citizens of her county who appealed to the Party committee for intervention. As a result, the provincial higher court reviewed the case and set her free.

[29] Cohen, p. 517; Chugunov, pp. 203-204.

[30] The English text of the speech is in Supplement to *People's China*, No. 13, 1957, pp. 3-27. The Chinese text is in *Chung-hua jen-min kung-ho-kuo fa-kuei hui-pien*, Vol. 5 (1957), pp. 1-34. It should be noted that Mao had gone over the official text based on the verbatim record and made certain additions before it was released.

Since the two contradictions are of different nature, the methods of resolving them also differ. According to Mao, conflicts among the people are to be dealt with by the "method of democracy" and conflicts with the enemy by the "method of dictatorship." In settling "questions between right and wrong among the people," reliance should be placed on education and persuasion rather than compulsion. In dealing with "reactionaries, exploiters, counterrevolutionaries, landlords, bureaucrat-capitalists, robbers, swindlers, murderers, arsonists, hooligans, and other scoundrels who seriously disrupt social order," measures of dictatorship and severe sanctions must be employed.[31] Although "law-breaking elements among the people" should also be subjected to the discipline of law, stated Mao, "this is different in principle from using the dictatorship to suppress enemies of the people." Here we may note a similar statement he made in 1949 in his essay *On People's Democratic Dictatorship:* "If people break the law they will be punished, imprisoned or even sentenced to death. But these will be individual cases, differing in principle from the dictatorship imposed against the reactionaries as a class."[32]

Judging from the publicity and attention given to Mao's 1957 speech in Communist China, there seems to be little doubt that the first thing the "people's court" must do when entertaining a case is to determine whether it is a "conflict between the enemy and ourselves" or an "internal contradiction among the people." This, however, is not always an easy task as the criteria for distinguishing the two contradictions are far from precise. Mao admitted in his speech that "it is sometimes easy to confuse them. We had instances of such confusion in our past work. In the suppression of counterrevolution, good people were sometimes mistaken for bad. Such things have happened before, and still happen today."[33] Writing in 1958, Lo Jui-ching also spoke of the same problem. "In handling internal contradictions of the people," he said, "some of our public security organs and personnel often adopt compulsory orders and suppression measures, and sometimes even resort to the simple method of punishment

---

[31] This is essentially in line with Mao's earlier thesis about "democracy for the people and dictatorship for the reactionaries." In an important essay written in 1949, he advocated a policy of benevolence and persuasion toward the people but a violent and oppressive policy toward the reactionaries and counterrevolutionaries. Mao Tse-tung, *On People's Democratic Dictatorship*, Peking, 1951, pp. 16-18.

[32] *Ibid.*, p. 18.

[33] Supplement to *People's China*, No. 13, 1957, p. 8.

and detention. They fail to understand that the basic method of deal-ing with contradictions within the people is persuasion and educa-tion."[34] Reporting before the National People's Congress in 1964, Hsieh Chüeh-tsai pointed out that "because of the complex nature of the class struggle, correct differentiation of the two contradictions is indeed a matter of great importance to the work of the people's courts." In order to handle their task properly, he continued, the courts should "maintain a high degree of political alertness" and "rely upon the masses for conducting investigations."[35]

The problem of distinguishing the two different types of contradic-tions is, likewise, frequently discussed in the writings and special forums of Chinese jurists. A series of articles, for example, were pub-lished in the 1958 issues of *Cheng-fa yen-chiu* to examine the follow-ing questions: "Are all Criminal Offenses to Be Treated as Contra-dictions between the Enemy and Ourselves? Are All Criminals to be Regarded as the Objects of Dictatorship?"[36] The views expressed by the authors, most of them high judicial officials of Communist China, showed a wide range of divergence. Although the majority seemed to agree that crimes committed by "the people" should be considered mainly as internal contradictions, not subject to dictatorial treatment, there were no meeting of minds about the criteria by which to sepa-rate "the people" from "the enemy" in criminal cases.[37] In an article published in 1963 on the question of contradictions, two writers of *Cheng-fa yen-chiu* also admitted the existence of certain difficulties in drawing a sharp line between "the bad elements" on the one hand and "some law-breaking elements among the people" on the other, between "the hostile activities of the counterrevolutionaries" on the one hand and "some critical words and impulsive actions of the peo-ple" on the other. To determine the nature of contradiction in a

[34] Lo Jui-ching, "Be Ruthless toward the Enemy, Be Gentle with the Peo-ple," *Hsüeh-hsi* (Study), Peking, No. 12, 1958, p. 5.

[35] Hsieh's report on the work of the Supreme People's Court (delivered on December 26, 1964) in *Jen-min jih-pao*, January 1, 1965.

[36] There were six articles in this series. Three were in No. 3, two in No. 4, one in No. 5 of 1958 *Cheng-fa yen-chiu*.

[37] For instance, a vice-president of the Central Political-Judicial Cadres' School suggested that the chief criterion should be "whether a man commits a crime with evil intent or not." Hsieh Fei, "Are All Criminal Offenses Con-tradictions between the Enemy and Ourselves?" *Cheng-fa yen-chiu*, No. 4, 1958, p. 6. This position was disputed by two other authors, who regarded as more important criteria the nature and consequences of the crime and the background of the offender. Chu Kuo-cheng & Ouyang Chen, "We Should Never Treat All Criminal Offenses as Contradictions between the Enemy and Ourselves or as the Objects of Dictatorship," *ibid.*, No. 5, 1958, pp. 77-78.

criminal offense, they wrote, there should be a thorough and comprehensive examination of the act of offense and its consequences, the
object and motive of the offender, his social origin, personal background, class stand, political attitude, living conditions, and previous
record, as well as all other factors relevant to the case.[38]

From time to time special meetings and conferences have been
sponsored by legal societies and institutes in China to discuss Mao
Tse-tung's 1957 speech. A recent one was the forum on "The Question of How to Distinguish and Settle Correctly the Two Contradictions of Different Nature in Political and Legal Work," held in
Peking between July 30 and August 1, 1963. During the three-day
session the participants examined a number of issues, including the
criteria for differentiating the two contradictions and the possibility
for one type of conflict to be transformed into another. Various opinions were enthusiastically expressed, but the only reported consensus
was that the problem of contradictions must be "realistically analyzed"
from "a firm proletarian stand" and "a correct class viewpoint." The
forum was regarded as serving a useful purpose of prodding the legal
circles to study further Mao's theory on contradictions and to evaluate
more deeply the practical experience of political and judicial workers
in resolving the two different conflicts.[39]

All in all, it is difficult to exaggerate the significance of Mao's
1957 speech and the overriding responsibility of the "people's courts"
to separate the so-called antagonistic from non-antagonistic contradictions. Given the fluid state of Chinese law, the courts often find it
prudent to consult Party authorities before assigning cases of importance to one category or the other. As observed by a Western scholar,
the normal method of classifying any important case in China is undoubtedly for judicial officials to seek and follow the guidance of the
Party.[40]

Criminal Cases

Official statements in recent years have usually stressed the constant decrease of the number of criminal cases in China. This is evidently due partly to the fact that ordinary offenses are often disposed

[38] Hao Chin-ch'ing & Wu Chien-fan, "How to Distinguish Strictly the
Two Types of Contradictions and the Two Different Methods of Dealing with
Them in Political and Legal Work," *ibid.*, No. 2, 1963, p. 28.

[39] See the brief report on the forum in *Cheng-fa yen-chiu*, No. 3, 1963,
pp. 42. 24.

[40] Henry McAleavy, "The People's Courts in Communist China," *American Journal of Comparative Law*, Vol. 11, No. 1, 1962, p. 60.

of by administrative or informal measures. In a report to the National People's Congress in December 1964, Procurator-General Chang Ting-ch'eng said that the number of counterrevolutionary acts in 1964 was 34 percent less than in 1963, and that the number of criminal acts was 20 percent less. All told, 1964 had "the lowest figures of crimes and arrest since the founding of the People's Republic."[41] At the same Congress session, however, Premier Chou En-lai spoke of the continued class struggle in China and the illegal activities engaged in by the old and new bourgeoisie, counterrevolutionaries, and other bad elements.[42] Lately, two major political campaigns have been waged by the Communists on a nation-wide basis. One is the "socialist education" movement directed primarily against corrupt cadres in rural areas; the other is the current "proletarian cultural revolution" aimed mostly at the "anti-Party" and "anti-socialist" intellectuals and officials.[43]

Whatever the conditions in China may be, the fact remains that "people's justice" is more concerned with the suppression of crimes than with the resolution of individual disputes. Among criminal acts, greater attention is given to political crimes than ordinary ones. The fundamental objective of the "people's courts," in the words of Hsieh Chüeh-tsai, is to exercise dictatorship against the counterrevolutionaries and other criminals who resist and undermine the socialist order.[44]

This special focus on political crimes is quite evident in the criminal legislation of China. Although there is still no criminal code in the country, a number of statues and regulations, nevertheless, have been promulgated since 1949. Prominent among them are the Regulations for the Punishment of Counterrevolutionaries (1951), the Provisional Regulations on the Punishment of Undermining the State Monetary System (1951), the Provisional Regulations on Safeguarding State Secrets (1951), the Regulations for the Punishment of Corruption (1952), the Provisional Measures for the Control of

---

[41] Chang's report on the work of the Supreme People's Procuratorate (delivered on December 26, 1964) in *Jen-min jih-pao*, January 1, 1965.

[42] "Premier Chou En-lai Reports on the Work of the Government," *Peking Review*, January 1, 1965, p. 12.

[43] For the "socialist education" movement, see China News Analysis, No. 561, April 23, 1965. For the current "proletarian cultural revolution," see the entire issue of *Hung-ch'i* (Red Flag), Peking, No. 6, 1966; also Donald J. Munro, "Dissent in Communist China: The Current Anti-Intellectual Campaign in Perspective," *Current Scene*, Hong Kong, Vol. IV, No. 11, June 1, 1966.

[44] *Jen-min jih-pao*, January 1, 1965.

Counterrevolutionaries (1952), the Regulations on Reform through Labor (1954) and the Penal Regulations on Security Control (1957).[45] The strong class character of Chinese criminal law is probably best illustrated in the following passage of an official textbook:

> . . . the criminal law of our country is an important weapon of the people's democratic dictatorship. It serves the socialist construction in our country. The tasks of our criminal law are thus to struggle against all traitors, counterrevolutionaries and other criminals with penal methods in order to keep the people's democratic system and social order from being offended, to educate the citizens to observe law self-consciously, and thereby to protect and promote the successful accomplishment of the state's socialist construction and socialist transformation.

> The criminal law of our country primarily deals blows to the counterrevolutionaries, to the criminals of homicide, arson, burglary, fraud, rape, and other offenses seriously obstructing social order and socialist construction. It must be understood that the point of our criminal law is chiefly directed toward the enemies of socialism.[46]

Another noticeable feature of Chinese penal regulations is that there is plenty of "flexibility" but not enough predictability. Not only are the present laws sketchy and incomplete, but some provisions of these statutes are extremely vague, open to a wide range of interpretations. As has been indicated, there are no precise criteria for distinguishing between Mao's antagonistic and non-antagonistic contradictions. Consequently, to meet the practical need for legal standards, law enforcement officials have to consult frequently unpublished rules, instructions, reports, and handbooks.[47] By the same token, the public often has to rely upon newspaper editorials, radio commentaries, or popular rallies to supplement published legislation as guidance for behavior.

Equally important is the Chinese Communists' rejection of the

---

[45] For the original texts of various types of Chinese laws and regulations, consult the appropriate volumes of the following two collections: *Chung-yang jen-min cheng-fu fa-ling hui-pien* (Compendium of the Laws and Regulations of the Central People's Government), 1949-1954; *Chung-hua jen-min kung-ho-kuo fa-kuei hui-pien* (Compendium of the Laws and Regulations of the Chinese People's Republic), 1954 to date. English translations of some of these laws are compiled in Albert P. Blaustein (ed.), *Fundamental Legal Documents of Communist China*, South Hackensack, New Jersey, 1962.

[46] *Lectures on the General Principles of Criminal Law in the People's Republic of China*, JPRS, No. 13331, 1962, p. 18.

[47] Told by former Chinese legal officials. Cohen, p. 494.

time-honored doctrine of *nullum crimen sine lege, nulla poena sine lege*. Instead, they have adopted the principle of analogy in the field of criminal law. Article 16 of the Regulations for the Punishment of Counterrevolutionaries provides: "Persons who have committed other crimes with counterrevolutionary intent that are not specified in the law shall be punished according to analogous specified crimes in these Regulations."[48] Similarly, the textbook on General Principles of Criminal Law states: ". . . if the doer's act is socially dangerous in substance and deserves punishment, though not directly provided for by a criminal statute, our criminal law permits us to apply the most similar provisions in the existing criminal legislation to convict and punish the doer."[49] During the "Hundred Flowers" period some Chinese jurists, including the authors of the aforesaid textbook, expressed their reservations about the principle of analogy and advocated its gradual elimination from criminal law.[50] This view, however, has been attacked as unrealistic and harmful by official spokesmen, who maintain that the principle of analogy is essential in China to supplement criminal legislation which cannot possibly cover all types of crimes that may occur in the ever-changing and complicated conditions of the socialist stage.[51]

Along with analogous reasoning, retroactivity has also been incorporated into the criminal law of Communist China. Article 18, for instance, of the Regulations for the Punishment of Counterrevolu-

---

[48] These Regulations and other documents concerning the Suppression of the Counterrevolutionaries Movement are in *Chien-chüeh chen-ya fan-ke-ming ho-tung* (Resolutely Suppress Counterrevolutionary Activities), Peking, 1951. The analogy concept is also contained in Article 31 of the Penal Regulations on Security Control (October 1957), *Chung-hua jen-min kung-ho-kuo fa-kuei hui-pien*, Vol. 6 (1958), p. 254.

[49] *Lectures on the General Principles of Criminal Law*, p. 54.

[50] The book, for example, said in August 1957 (publication date) that "we hold that after several years when state socialist construction develops further ahead, our experience in struggling with crimes is further enriched, and our criminal legislation becomes more complete, we may consider to abolish the system of analogy." *Ibid.*, p. 55.

[51] See Ts'ao Kuo-ch'ing, "The Question of Whether or Not There Should be 'Reasoning by Analogy' in Our Country's Criminal Legislation," *Cheng-fa yen-chiu*, No. 3, 1957, pp. 10-12; Fan Ming, "Some Opinions on 'Lectures on the General Principles of Criminal Law in the People's Republic of China,'" *ibid.*, No. 4, 1958, p. 73. In contrast to the Chinese position, the Soviet Union has abolished the concept of punishment by analogy. Harold J. Berman, "The Dilemma of Soviet Law Reform," *Harvard Law Review*, Vol. 76, No. 5, 1963, pp. 936-937.

tionaries reads: "These Regulations are also applicable to those guilty of counterrevolutionary crimes committed before the present law came into effect." As a general rule, says the cited textbook, criminal statutes can be applied retroactively to all those offenses committed after the founding of the People's Republic that have not been tried or are pending judgment.[52] In the case of serious counterrevolutionary crimes, it states, the offenders may be punished even if their criminal acts took place before the advent of the Communist government on October 1, 1949.[53]

Turning our attention to criminal procedure, we find that informal process is the preference of the Chinese Communists. As noted before, minor offenses are generally disposed of by the police and other nonjudicial apparatus. For more serious cases where the participation of the procuracy and the courts is required, the People's Republic does not yet have a code of criminal procedure. To be sure, legal guidance over procedural matters is technically provided by the relevant stipulations in the Constitution and the organic laws of the courts and the procuracy as well as by the experimental proceedings developed in the mid-1950's by the Supreme People's Court and the Supreme People's Procuratorate.[54] Nevertheless, since the Anti-Rightist Movement the Chinese Communists have stressed the virtue of simplicity and the mass line in the judicial process. Even the few formal rules patterned after the Soviet model have not been too faithfully observed.

Broadly speaking, the "socialist" criminal procedure in China may be divided into four principal stages: (1) preliminary investigation, (2) adjudication, (3) appeal, and (4) execution of sentences. In the stage of preliminary investigation, the tasks include detention, arrest,

---

[52] *Lectures on the General Principles of Criminal Law,* p. 32.

[53] On the other hand, ordinary counterrevolutionaries who have "thoroughly confessed and pleaded guilty" will not be punished for their past. *Ibid.,* pp. 235-236. For detailed regulations, see The Standing Committee of the National People's Congress, "Decision on Lenient Disposition and Placement of Remnant Counterrevolutionary Elements in Urban Areas," (adopted on November 16, 1956) *Chung-hua jen-min kung-ho-kuo fa-kuei hui-pien,* Vol. 4 (1957), pp. 243-245.

[54] These experimental procedures have been mentioned occasionally in official reports, but their contents have not been made public. Useful information on China's criminal procedure can be found in "Concerning Trial Procedure in Criminal Cases," *Kuang-ming jih-pao,* March 11, 1955. A special study based on official source material was done by a Russian writer: Chugunov, *Criminal Court Procedures in the Chinese People's Republic* (cited note 8). Compare it with a Harvard Law professor's findings based on extensive interviews, Cohen, pp. 469-533 (cited note 9).

interrogation, search and seizure, examination of evidence, and preparation of the indictment. Most of the investigative functions are performed by the police, legally under the supervision of the procuracy, while the latter has the responsibility to decide whether or not to prosecute and to prepare the indictment.[55]

At this or any other stage of the criminal process, the use of coercion or torture to exact confessions is officially prohibited, although pressures on the accused to confess appear to be quite strong in view of the persistent official line of "leniency for those who confess and severity for those who resist."[56] There is also protection against arbitrary arrest. Article 89 of the Constitution reads: "Freedom of the person of citizens of the People's Republic of China is inviolable. No citizen may be arrested except by decision of a people's court with the sanction of a people's procuratorate." Additional safeguards are contained in the Regulations on Arrest and Detention of December 1954, which stipulates, among others, that the organ making an arrest should interrogate the prisoner within 24 hours of the arrest and should immediately set him free upon discovery of unwarranted arrest and detention.[57] More often than not, however, the procedural guarantees are either circumvented or simply ignored in China. By and large, the police and the procuracy tend to handle their work informally and to resolve their differences through interagency consultation and compromise or through a decision of the Party committee or the next higher procuracy.[58]

Technically, the procedure of adjudication in a criminal action consists of two parts: the preparatory session (preliminary hearing) and the session proper (the trial). At both sessions the court is supposed to be composed of a judge and two "people's assessors." The

---

[55] See Cohen, pp. 500-511; also Chugunov, chapter II.

[56] The prohibition of the use of torture or corporal punishment can be traced back to the Kiangsi-Yenan days. Consult Chapter 1 for relevant discussion. Speaking before the Eighth National Congress of the Chinese Communist Party in September 1956, Minister of Public Security Lo Jui-ch'ing stressed the banning of all physical or other forms of pressure to extort confessions, *New China News Agency*, September 19, 1956. In an article published in 1957, Minister of Justice Shih Liang wrote that the "people's courts" had abolished the third-degree methods so commonly used in old China. *People's China*, No. 12, 1957, p. 16.

[57] The text is in *Chung-hua jen-min kung-ho-kuo fa-kuei hui-pien*, Vol. 1 (1956), pp. 239-242. English translation is in American Consulate General, Hong Kong, *Survey of China Mainland Press*, No. 953, December 22, 1954.

[58] Cohen, p. 510.

purpose of the preparatory session is to determine whether the preliminary investigation has been conducted in accordance with the law and whether there is sufficient evidence to bind the accused over for trial. If the court decides that prosecution is in order, then it proceeds to announce the date of the trial proper, the list of people to be summoned, and the manner (an open or closed session) in which the case will be heard. The session proper of the trial is further divided into the following four stages: (1) preparation, (2) investigation, (3) debate, and (4) judgment. Following the inquisitory procedure, the court plays an active part in examining and verifying the evidence presented by both sides as well as collected on its own initiative. During the trial the accused is "assured" of his legal rights to request withdrawal, to have a defense counsel, to introduce new evidence, to make a final statement, etc. After a decision is reached, the court announces it publicly and reminds the accused that he has the right to appeal.[59]

In practice, nevertheless, the trial is often conducted quite informally. First, the case is assigned to a judge, who undertakes to question the accused, interview witnesses and experts, examine other evidence, and consult with the relevant procurators and police officers. After completing the investigation, the judge then submits a proposed judgment to his superiors and the Party secretary for approval. Finally, a public meeting is held with the presence of two "people's assessors" and a defense attorney to give the trial its "democratic" trappings and to make public the approved judgment.[60]

Throughout the entire criminal process the Communist authorities attach considerable importance to the gathering of comprehensive and reliable evidence. They frequently cite as their guiding principles Mao Tse-tung's instructions that "we must proceed from reality, depend upon the masses, conduct investigation and study, find truth from facts, rely more on evidence than statements, and verify both the evidence and statements."[61] In the 1964 issues of *Cheng-fa yen-chiu* (Nos. 1-4), a series of theoretical articles were specifically published to discuss the question of evidence in criminal proceedings.

---

[59] For the trial procedure, consult *Kuang-ming jih-pao*, March 11, 1955; Chugunov, Chapters III-IV; Wang Chi-ch'ao, "On Some Problems in Criminal and Civil Court Procedures," *Cheng-fa yen-chiu*, No. 4, 1957, pp. 42-44; Liu Ch'ing-lin, "How to Treat the Defendants in Criminal Cases," *ibid.*, No. 3, 1956, pp. 47-52.

[60] See Cohen, pp. 511-514.

[61] Hsieh Chüeh-tsai's report in *Jen-min jih-pao*, January 1, 1965.

From time to time, foreign observers have reported favorably on the criminal procedure in Communist China. Some seem to be quite impressed by the protection for individual rights offered in the Chinese system.[62] Others praise the "careful" and "objective" evaluation of evidentiary materials by Chinese officials and the active participation in the judicial process by the masses.[63]

On the other hand, it should be noted that deviations from juridical niceties are not an uncommon phenomenon in the actual administration of "people's justice." Leaving aside the complaints of non-Communist critics, even top officials like Tung Pi-wu and Lo Jui-ching have admitted the occurrences of arbitrary arrest, violation of court procedures, and maltreatment of prisoners.[64] As reported by the press, many judicial cadres had so little regard for the rights of the accused that they used coercion to induce "sincere confessions" and employed threats to dissuade the defendants from "defying the government."[65]

In addition, political considerations often take precedence over legal restraints when the Communist authorities are dealing with class enemies and other hostile elements. During the Anti-Rightist Movement, said the Soviet newspaper *Izvestia* on May 17, 1964, many hundreds of thousands of Chinese were subject to repressive measures without trial or investigation in "a gross violation of the elementary democratic rights and freedoms of citizens."[66] In one of the articles of the 1964 issues of *Cheng-fa yen-chiu*, it was emphatically stated that evidence in the cases of antagonistic contradictions must be used

---

[62] For instance, see Greene, pp. 196-197; K. C. Woodsworth, "The Legal System of the Republic of China," *The Canadian Bar Journal*, Vol. 4, August, 1961, pp. 308-309.

[63] "Chinese Justice" in *Horitsuka no mita Chugoku* (cited note 5), pp. 215-216, 217-218.

[64] Tung and Lo referred to these occurrences in their respective reports to the Eighth National Congress of the Chinese Communist Party on September 19, 1956. *New China News Agency*, September 19 & 20, 1956. During the "Hundred Flowers" period Huang Shao-hung and Liu Wen-hui (both former high Kuomintang officials) also reported the infringement on the people's rights by state and judicial organs. *Ibid.*, May 16 and 30, 1957. For complaints of other critics, see "The Reversal in 1957" in Chapter 3 of this book.

[65] *Ho-pei jih-pao* (Hopei Daily), Tientsin, April 25, 1956; *Kuang-ming jih-pao*, June 8, 1956 & November 19, 1956; *Jen-min jih-pao*, January 10, 1957.

[66] *The Current Digest of the Soviet Press*, Vol. 14, No. 21, 1964, p. 5.

primarily as a tool to wage the class struggle and exercise dictatorship against the enemy.[67]

Furthermore, the procedural rights of the defendant are obviously affected by Peking's rejection of the presumption of innocence, a principle which most countries consider as vital to a fair trial and which Post-Stalin Russia has come to accept implicitly.[68] In the "Hundred Flowers" period some Chinese jurists did urge the adoption of this principle, but the official response was to criticize it openly as a "reactionary bourgeois doctrine."[69] According to the Party line, criminal procedure in China is correctly guided by the principle that "facts are the basis; law is the criterion," and there is no place for the erroneous concept of presumption of innocence in "people's justice." To assume the accused innocent in penal prosecution would only protect the interest of the criminal and tie the hands of the judicial and procuratorial organs.[70]

In order to complete our discussion of the administration of criminal justice in the People's Republic, it is necessary here to examine

[67] Wu Yu-su, "On Evidence in Our Criminal Procedure," *Cheng-fa yen-chiu*, No. 2, 1964, pp. 40-41.

[68] The *Working Paper* of the International Congress of Jurists held in New Delhi, India, in January 1959 had this to say on the principle of presumption of innocence: "It would seem to follow from the recognition of legality that an accused person has a right to be considered innocent until his guilt has been proved. A State in which a contrary principle consistently and universally prevailed—namely, that everyone was guilty until proved innocent—would put everyone in the arbitrary power of the arresting authorities; it would indeed be a negation of the element of certainty in human relations which we have suggested is at least one element in the Rule of Law." International Commission of Jurists, *The Rule of Law in a Free Society*, Geneva, 1960, pp. 248-249. For the current Soviet position regarding this principle, see Berman, "The Dilemma of Soviet Law Reform," (cited note 51), p. 934 and Kazimierz Gryzbowski, "Soviet Criminal Law," *Problems of Communism*, Vol. XIV, No. 2, March-April 1965, p. 56. The negative aspects of Soviet Justice in the post-Stalin period are examined in Gryzbowski, pp. 56-62 and in articles by Leon Lipson and Albert Boiter in the same issue of *Problems of Communism*, pp. 72-92.

[69] A legal writer, for example, took a stand in favor of the presumption of innocence (Ch'ü Fu, "A Brief Dicussion of the Defendant's Position in Criminal Procedure," *Cheng-fa yen-chiu*, No. 3, 1957, pp. 22-27), and his position was later denounced by Party spokesmen in the same journal (Chang Hui, Li Chang-ch'un, & Chang Tzu-p'ei, "This Is Not the Basic Principle of Our Criminal Procedure," *ibid.*, No. 4, 1958, pp. 76-80).

[70] See Wu Yü-su, "Criticism of the Bourgeois Principle of 'Presumption of Innocence,'" *ibid.*, No. 2, 1958, pp. 37-41.

the Chinese position with regard to punishment. The purpose of applying penalties, in the words of an official textbook, is not only to punish and reform criminals but to educate the citizenry and to deter crimes.[71] With this proclaimed objective, the penal policy of Peking has been frequently publicized as one of "combining punishment with leniency." In concrete terms it means: "Leniency for those who confess; severity for those who resist; mitigated punishment for those who have established merits; rewards for those who have established great merits."[72] Although this policy may have contributed to certain judicial abuses mentioned before, it has been officially acclaimed as a great success. Communist leaders have cited cases to show the lenient treatment of repentant criminals, counterrevolutionary or otherwise. They have pointed with pride to the surrender to justice of a great many counterrevolutionaries and the continuing decrease of the number of crimes throughout the country.[73]

There is a wide variety of punishments in the Chinese People's Republic ranging from control and detention to life imprisonment and the death sentence.[74] The application of the death penalty is said to be limited to the few most serious crimes against the state and individuals.[75] To be sure, many people were put to death during the

---

[71] *Lectures on the General Principles of Criminal Law*, p. 149.

[72] This has been frequently stressed in the pronouncement of top officials, typical of which is Lo Jui-ch'ing, "Defend the Economic Construction of the Fatherland," *Chung-kuo ching-nien pao*, September 25, 1955. ("Merits" means the denunciation of other criminals or the offer of information to the government leading to the breakup of the cases involved.) It should be noted here that leniency toward a criminal who sincerely confesses his guilt to the authorities was also provided by law in Confucian China. Derk Bodde, "Basic Concepts of Chinese Law: The Genesis and Evolution of Legal Thought in Traditional China," *Proceedings of the American Philosophical Society*, Vol. 107, No. 5, 1963, p. 393.

[73] For reports on the lenient treatment of repentant criminals, see Lo Jui-ch'ing, *loc. cit.*, and his article, "The Struggle between Revolution and Counterrevolution over the Past Ten Years," *Jen-min jih-pao*, September 20, 1959. For reports on the achievements of the policy of "combining punishment with leniency," see Tung Pi-wu, "The Judicial Work of the People's Courts in the Past Year," *Jen-min shou-ts'e*, 1957, pp. 338-339; Lo Jui-ch'ing, "The Achievements and Future Tasks of the Struggle against Counterrevolutionaries in Our Country," *ibid.*, 1958, pp. 354-360; Chang Ting-cheng, "The Work of People's Procuratorates," *New China News Agency*, April 24, 1959; Chang Ting-ch'eng, "Reports on the Work of the Supreme People's Procuratorate," *Jen-ming jih-pao*, January 1, 1965.

[74] *Lectures on the General Principles of Criminal Law*, pp. 162-183.

[75] These include serious cases of counterrevolutionary activities, corrup-

early years of the Republic when terror and revolutionary excesses reigned. But that is the thing of the past, and the number of executions today, as far as it can be discerned, appears to be relatively small.[76] Indications are that the regime regards capital punishment as a measure of last resort and would employ it with considerable care. In his report to the Party Congress in 1956, Liu Shao-chi, for instance, urged the sparing use of the death penalty and called for its gradual abolition in China.[77] Peking's attitude is further reflected by the fact that every death sentence now requires the approval of the Supreme People's Court and that the execution of a death penalty may be suspended for two years to allow the convict a last chance to reform himself through forced labor.[78] Such procedures, of course, may become purely academic at the occasionally-held mass trials where some "flagrant criminals" are often sentenced to death and executed on the spot.[79] These exceptions are still considered at times

tion, murder, rape, etc. *Ibid.*, p. 172. For comparison with the Soviet practice, see Fu-shun Lin, "Communist China's Emerging Fundamentals of Criminal Law," *American Journal of Comparative Law*, Vol. 13, No. 1, 1964, p. 89.

[76] No official statistics are available, but Edgar Snow in *The Other Side of the River* (p. 353) estimates that executions in 1960 varied from eight to twelve a month.

[77] "The Political Report of the Central Committee of the Communist Party of China to the Eighth National Congress of the Party," *Eighth National Congress of the Communist Party of China*, Peking, 1956, Vol. I, pp. 83-84.

[78] The National People's Congress adopted a resolution in July 1957 requiring all death sentences be submitted to the Supreme Court for approval. *Jen-min jih-pao*, July 16, 1957.

The first legal provision which mentioned the stay of death sentences was Article 3 of Section II of the Regulations for Dealing with Cases of Corruption, Waste, and Bureaucracy, March 8, 1952. Earlier, however, the policy of "Suspension of the death sentence for two years" was given a full explanation in *Jen-min jih-pao*, June 1, 1951. Subsequently, many references have been made to this policy by official spokesmen (Chou En-lai, Tung Pi-wu, Lo Jui-ch'ing, and others) or in certain penalty texts (The Regulations on Reform Through Labor, 1954, Chapter 2, Section I, Article 13, for instance). It should be noted that under this policy the convict, at the end of two years, may receive a reduced sentence or may be executed depending upon his behavior during the period of labor reform.

[79] As examples, a grain thief named Tu Hung was tried and executed this way on July 7, 1961; so was an alleged Nationalist agent, Wu Chu, on August 19, 1962. *Yang-ch'eng wan-pao*, July 8, 1961 and August 19, 1962. A show trial was held on June 13, 1966 in the Peking Workers' Gymnasium where 1,300 people watched the Supreme People's Court sentence a 19-year-old epileptic named Yang kuo-ching for counterrevolutionary crimes (the

a necessary step to "frighten the enemy and support the class struggle of the masses."[80]

By far the most important and commonly used penal measure in Communist China is forced labor or the so-called reform through labor. Having its origin in the period of the Kiangsi Soviet, the program of reform through labor was given a theoretical basis by Mao Tse-tung in 1949, when he wrote that members of the reactionary classes who gave up counterrevolutionary activities would be granted the opportunity to work and to reform themselves through labor so as to become new men.[81] Corrective labor was put on an organized footing in 1954 with the enactment of the Regulations on Reform through Labor, which defined the policy objective as one of "combining punishment and control with ideological reform, productive labor activity with political education." Under these regulations, the penalty is applicable to convcited criminals in prisons or at corrective labor camps, to offenders awaiting sentences at preliminary detention centers, and to juvenile delinquents at reformatory settlements—all subject to the supervision of public security organs.[82] In 1957 the State Council adopted a far-reaching decisions on "Re-education and Rehabilitation through Labor," giving administrative agencies and social groups the right to confine practically any person in a special labor camp for an indefinite period of time. By virtue of this decision, labor re-education may be imposed on "idlers," "rascals," "noncooperators," "reactionaries," "violators of discipline," and other undesirable elements without going through regular judicial proceedings.[83]

It is difficult to tell with certainty how many forced laborers are in China and under what conditons they work.[84] There can be no doubt,

---

stabbing of two foreign visitors). The people shouted their approval of the Court's verdict and chanted slogans as Yang was led off to face a firing squad. *The Washington Post*, June 28, 1966 (with pictures).

[80] Hsieh Chüeh-tsai's report on the work of the Supreme People's Court in *Jen-min jih-pao*, January 1, 1965.

[81] *On People's Democratic Dictatorship*, p. 18.

[82] The text of these Regulations is in *Chung-yan jen-min cheng-fu fa-ling hui-pien*, 1954, pp. 33-43.

[83] The text of this decision (August 3, 1957) is in *Chung-hua jen-min kung-ho-kuo fa-kuei hui-pien*, Vol. 6 (1957), pp. 243-244. For a detailed analysis of this decision, see "Powers and Functions of the Police" in Chapter 6.

[84] Much has been written and many views have been expressed on forced labor in China. A highly critical work, based on official documents and in-

nevertheless, that vast numbers of Chinese, including "rightist" intellectuals and "anti-Party" persons, have been sent to labor camps throughout the country to undergo various kinds of pressure and exploitation. Equally true is the fact that however repressive and appalling, the system of reform through labor performs useful functions for the government by converting the "dangerous" elements of society into a source of economic and political strength. As in the Soviet Union, forced labor in China has much to contribute to the development of the national economy. Reports show that corrective laborers have participated actively in the construction of industrial projects, irrigation systems, highways and railroads, and other public works in the mainland.[85] Moreover, reform through labor serves as a very effective instrument for political education and ideological indoctrination. An undisputed master of the most skillful techniques of thought control, the Peking regime would rather purge an opponent's "reactionary thinking" than liquidate him physically. Through the constant pressure of hard work and the incessant process of "brainwashing," the system of reform through labor can break the resistance of hostile individuals and "remold" their values and attitudes to suit the needs of the socialist revolution.[86]

Civil Cases

If there is a constant decrease of the number of criminal cases in China as officially claimed, it must be even truer in the case of civil suits. From the Communist Chinese point of view, civil disputes are mainly "internal contradictions among the people" but sometimes may

terviews with some refugees, is Commission International Contre le Régime Concentrationaire, *White Book on Forced Labor in the People's Republic of China*, Paris, 1956, 2 Vols. More sympathetic reports are found in Snow, Chaps. 47-48, and Greene, Chap. 20.

[85] *Jen-min jih-pao*, September 27, 1964, reported: "83 per cent of all criminals have participated in agricultural industrial production, or have been organized into various engineering corps for the felling of timber, construction of buildings, restoration and construction of conservation works, and building of railroads and highways." For other official reports, see *White Book*, Vol. II, pp. 96-97.

[86] Among many published works on thought control in China, note particularly: Theodore H. E. Chen, *Thought Reform of the Chinese Intellectuals*, Hong Kong, 1960; Edward Hunter, *Brain-Washing in Red China*, New York, 1953; Robert J. Lifton, *Thought Reform and the Psychology of Totalism*, New York, 1963; Allyn and Adele Rickett, *Prisoners of Liberation*, New York, 1957.

also include "contradictions between the enemy and ourselves."[87] In the early days of the People's Republic, for example, both the Marriage Law (1950) and the Agrarian Reform Law (1950) were enforced in the form of class struggle and played significant parts in revolutionizing the social structure of China.[88] Subsequently, Peking has moved to communize the entire economic life of the country by enacting statutes and regulations on cooperatives, communes, and other socialist measures.[89] This has greatly narrowed the area of private property relationships, an important source of civil disputes in the Western countries.

To be sure, the system of private ownership is not wholly eliminated in China, and there are still disputes over property rights, contracts and inheritance.[90] Contractual disputes, in fact, are gaining new importance as the communes and other economic units have come to use increasingly the institution of contracts.[91] All told, however, marriage cases have always made up the bulk of the civil cases handled

[87] *Basic Problems in the Civil Law of the People's Republic of China,* JPRS, No. 4879, 1961, pp. 12-15; checked with the original text, *Chung-hua jen-min kung-ho-kuo min-fa chi-pen wen-t'i* (by the Institute of Civil Law, Central Political-Judicial Cadres' School), Peking, 1958, pp. 6-9.

[88] Official English texts for the two Laws were published in 1950 by the Foreign Languages Press of Peking. For the implementation of these Laws, see C. K. Yang, *The Chinese Family in Communist Revolution,* Cambridge, 1959, and Chao Kuo-chun, *Agrarian Policy of the Chinese Communist Party 1921-1959,* Bombay, 1960, Chapter III.

[89] There have been many individual statutes and regulations concerning the various phases of Peking's socialization program. Consult *Szu-ying Kung-shang-yeh ti she-hui chu-i kai-tsao cheng-ts'e fa-ling hsüan-pien, 1949-1952* (Selections of Policies, Laws, and Regulations Concerning the Socialist Transformation of privately-owned Industry and Commerce, 1949-1952), Peking 1957, Vols. 1-2, and *Chung-hua jen-min kung-ho-kuo fa-kuei hui-pien,* Vols. 1-12.

[90] *Basic Problems in the Civil Law* (cited note 119); Yeh Ku-lin, "Develop Fully the Role of People's Conciliation Work in the Construction of Socialism," *Cheng-fa yen-chiu,* No. 4, 1964, pp. 13, 14. Also consult M. H. van der Valk, "The Law of Inheritance in the People's Republic of China," *Law in Eastern Europe,* Leyden, No. 5, 1961, pp. 297-364, and M. H. Van der Valk, "Security Rights in Communist China," *Osteuropa-Recht,* September 1963, pp. 210-236.

[91] For the official view on contracts, see *Basic Problems in the Civil Law,* Chapters XIII-XX; Hsieh Ming, "On the Contract System," *Cheng-fa yen-chiu,* No. 2, 1959, pp. 41-43; "The Problems of the Contract System after the Institution of People's Communes," *ibid.,* No. 4, 1959, pp. 32-36. For the views of researchers in the West, see Gene T. Hsiao, "The Role of Economic Contracts in Communist China," *California Law Review,* Vol. 53, No. 4, 1965, pp. 1029-1060, and Richard M. Pfeffer, "The Institution of

in Communist China. The following reports serve to illustrate this point. From January to May 1951 the "people's courts" in the Central-South Region had 32,881 matrimonial suits, which constituted over 60 percent of all civil suits received.[92] In the first part of 1955 the "people's court" of the county of Yench'ing, Hopei province, handled 106 civil cases, of which 78 were matrimonial cases. During the corresponding period of 1956 the same court received only 57 civil cases, of which 40 were matrimonial suits.[93] This trend appears to have persisted throughout the country, though little statistical data is currently available. From all other evidence, one can feel safe to say that while civil cases in general and property disputes in particular have shown a steady decrease in China, marital discord has remained to be the single most important cause of "internal conflicts" among the Chinese people.[94]

As has been mentioned before, the Chinese Communists are by and large not so much concerned with the resolution of individual disputes as with the suppression of crimes. This attitude is actually in accord with the traditional Chinese view that law was primarily an instrument to protect the political and social order rather than a guardian of private rights and interests. There are cases in Communist China where negligence in civil litigations on the part of the judicial organs have been reported. In one instance, the Special Office of Yengchow in Fukien province granted divorces to twenty-one couples without having given a hearing to the other party's story.[95] In another instance, the court of Feihsiang county in Hopei province

Contracts in the Chinese People's Republic," *The China Quarterly*, No. 14, April-June 1963, pp. 153-177, and No. 15, July-September 1963, pp. 115-139.

[92] *Jen-min jih-pao*, September 29, 1951. For other reports on matrimonial suits in the early 1950's, see S. K. Yang, p. 70.

[93] Li Yang-ch'i and T'ien Yeh, "Investigation of Civil Disputes in Rural Areas of Hopei Province," *Cheng-fa yen-chiu*, No. 4, 1957, p. 31.

[94] For reports on the steady decrease of civil suits, see Liu P'eng, "Work Report of the Higher People's Court in Liaoning Province," *Liao-ning jih-pao*. December 22, 1959; Greene, p. 194; Snow, pp. 355-356; Woodsworth, p. 309. For the relations of marriage disputes to "internal contradictions of the people," consult Yang Ta-wen and Liu Su-p'ing, "On the Tasks and Functions of the Marriage Law of Our Country," *Cheng-fa yen-chiu*, No. 2, 1963, pp. 41-42. According to the report of a group of Japanese jurists, the majority of civil disputes in Communist China have always been divorce cases, and the principal causes for divorce have been personal incompatibility, conflicts of interests, and differences of ideological background. *Horitsuka no mita Chugoku*, 1965, pp. 212-213.

[95] C. K. Yang, p. 77.

granted a local official's wish for divorce on the basis of a "confidential letter" from him alone, notwithstanding the strong protest of his wife against the decision.[96] On still another occasion, a vice-president of the Provincial Higher Court of Hunan admitted that there were 4,410 unsettled civil cases in his province which kept over 8,000 people in "cruel suspense."[97]

Inasmuch as no code of civil procedure has been promulgated in Communist China, legal proceedings in civil matters are apparently governed by experimental rules, unpublished regulations and the relevant provisions in the Constitution and the Organic Law of the People's Courts. As a rule, there is no preliminary hearing in a civil suit; otherwise, court activities and procedural guarantees are quite similar to those described in criminal procedure.[98] A civil action is instituted through the filing of a written petition with the court by the plaintiff or his representative. The plaintiff my be an individual, institution, enterprise, or organization.[99] Moreover, the Procuracy may initiate or intervene in any civil suit at any stage of the proceedings if it considers the case to be of great political or economic significance.[100]

One exceedingly important feature of Communist China's civil procedure is the emphasis on conciliation, a practice distinctly consistent with the traditional preference of the Chinese for the informal and amicable settlement of disputes. Besides the police, Party cadres, mass organizations, local groups, and other extrajudicial agencies which help solve many disputes, there are in the People's Republic numerous semi-official conciliaton committees specifically charged with the responsibility for the conciliatory resolution of civil and petty criminal cases. While conciliation is not a compulsory procedure prior

---

[96] "A Strange Letter Found in a File," *Kuang-ming jih-pao*, August 17, 1956.

[97] *Hsin hu-non pao* (New Hunan Journal), Changsha, May 14, 1957.

[98] Wang Chi-ch'ao, "On Some Problems in Criminal and Civil Court Procedures," *Cheng-fa yen-chiu*, No. 4, 1957, pp. 39-44; Tu Li-hua, "The Basic Rights and Duties of the Plaintiff and Defendant in Judicial Proceedings," *Hsi-chang jih-pao* (Tibetan Daily), Lhasa, April 6, 1957.

[99] "The Procedure of Instituting a Civil Action," *Hei-lung-chiang jih-pao* (Heilungkiang Daily), Harbin, February 4, 1957.

[100] Some detailed discussion of the Procuracy's role in civil suits is in Kao Hsin-tien, "The Chief Procurator's Participation in Civil Actions," *Fa-hsüeh* (Jurisprudence), Shanghai, No. 4, 1957, pp. 55-59. By way of comparison, see discussions of the Soviet practice in Harold J. Berman, *Justice in the U.S.S.R.*, New York, 1963, pp. 308-309; Gsovski and Grzybowski, Vol. 1, pp. 892-893.

to litigation, parties in a civil dispute usually appeal to the committee for help before bringing their case to the court.[101]

In handling civil suits, the practice is for the "people's court" or "people's tribunal" to work closely with the masses, rely upon the methods of persuasion and education, and use legal judgment sparingly as a last resort. The overriding objective is to settle internal contradictions by conciliation, uphold law and discipline, facilitate production work, strengthen the unity of the people, and promote the development of socialist virtues.[102] Efforts to mediate disputes are made by the court not only at the first trial but even in the appeal.[103] The court hearings are generally conducted in an informal atmosphere, with the participation of the relatives, friends, neighbors, and co-workers of the litigants in a joint endeavor to resolve the disputes. If matters of major importance are involved in a civil action, then a large-scale "democratic debate meeting" is held so that more people can take part in the discussion to help clarify the issues and reconcile the parties to the suit.[104] It goes without saying that in the process the court conducts propaganda and education among both the litigants and the public at large concerning the obedience to the laws and policies of the state.

The prevalent use of conciliation in Chinese civil procedure may be seen from the statistics and individual accounts cited below. In a report from Honan province, during 1959 some 85.2 per cent of the civil cases before the courts were settled by conciliation and only 14.8 per cent by decisions rendered.[105] According to statistical data from Liaoning province, between January and October of 1959 the litigants in 75.9 per cent of the civil cases handled by the courts were per-

---

[101] For the organization and work of the conciliation committees, see Chapter 4 and Yeh Ku-lin, *Cheng-fa yen-chiu*, No. 4, 1964, pp. 12-17.

[102] Kao Ko-lin's report in *New China News Agency*, April 24, 1959 and Hsieh Chüeh-tsai's report in *Jen-min jih-pao*, January 1, 1965.

[103] See, for instance, Lu Ch'un-ch'ing, "My Understanding of the Conciliation Work in Civil Suits in the Court of Second Instance," *Cheng-fa yen-chiu*, No. 3, 1959, pp. 31-33. At the second trial of a divorce case witnessed by visiting Japanese lawyers in 1965, the appellate court tried to effect a reconciliation without success. *Horitsuka no mita chugoku*, p. 211.

[104] Chiang Szu-min and others, "Correctly Handle the Internal Contradictions of the People," *Cheng-fa Yen-chiu*, No. 4, 1959, pp. 29-30; Jeno Benedek, *The Chinese System of Administering Justice* (Trans. from Hungarian) JPRS, No. 3121, 1960, pp. 12-13.

[105] Wang Kuang-li, "Work Report of the Higher People's Court in Honan Province," *Ho-nan jih-pao* (Honan Daily), Chengchou, March 1, 1960.

suaded into reaching reconcilment and withdrawing their suits.[106] As reported by the *People's Daily* on September 19, 1961, a woman assessor in Chaoyang *ch'ü*, Peking municipality, had assisted the "people's court" on many occasions to mediate successfully intra-family disputes, the most notable one being a divorce case in which after two visits with the couple she was able to convince them to drop the suit and reunite to form a "new democratic and harmonious family."[107] In Felix Greene's account of the divorce trial he witnessed in Shanghai in 1960, the judge also managed to effect a reconcilia-tion between the two parties on the condition that the husband would improve his future behavior without fail.[108]

Finally, what should not be overlooked in our discussion is the fact that the Chinese Communists have insisted that the class line, too, must be maintained in handling civil disputes. From their stand-point, different classes and strata still exist in the economic life of Chinese society. There is a distinction between the proletariat and the peasantry. There are also differences among poor peasants, lower-middle peasants, and rich middle peasants. Consequently, internal conflicts among the people often reflect contradictions between the road of socialism and the road of capitalism, and must be handled in the interest of socialism and the unity of all the people.[109] Such being the official line, the judges have thus been told to use a clear and firm class viewpoint to analyze the problems when dealing with civil dis-putes. [110] So have the conciliation committees in performing their functions.[111] The class stand is even applied to the treatment of letters from the people. For example, the Party committee and the "people's council" of T'aihu county in Anhwei province instructed in 1964 their respective subordinate offices to implement the class line by handling on a priority basis letters and calls from poor and lower-middle peasants.[112]

[106] Liu P'eng, *Liao-ning Jih-pao*, December 22, 1959.

[107] Sun Shih-k'ai, "Wang Lan-ying, A People's Assessor," *Jen-min jih-pao*, September 19, 1961.

[108] Greene, pp. 199-209.

[109] *Basic Problems in the Civil Law*, pp. 15-16; "In Handling the Internal Contradictions of the People, Is It Necessary to Use the Method of Class Analysis?" *Chung-kuo ch'ing-nien pao*, September 6, 1962; also three articles on the correct handling of internal contradictions in *Hsüeh-hsi*, No. 12, 1958, pp. 28-32.

[110] See Hsieh Chüeh-tsai's report in *Jen-min jih-pao*, January 1, 1965.

[111] Yeh Ku-lin, *Cheng-fa yen-chiu*, No. 4, 1964, p. 14.

[112] "Handling on a Priority Basis Letters and Calls from Poor and Lower-Middle Peasants," *Jen-min jih-pao*, November 14, 1964.

Conclusion

A single, integrated judicial system exists now in the Chinese People's Republic, even though the entire legal order of China still looks highly fluid. As shown in the preceding chapters, the current pattern of "people's justice" is a product of many years of experiment and adaption that go back to the early days of the Kiangsi regime. During the course of developing "people's courts" and laws in response to the "objective" conditions of the revolution, the Chinese Communists have drawn extensively upon the rules and institutions of the Soviet system. At the same time, they have assimilated, intentionally or not, certain concepts and practices of traditional China. From this gradual process of blending Russian and indigenous experiences, there has been emerging in mainland China what may be called the Chinese variety of socialist legality. Some of its basic features are clearly discernible, and this is particularly true in the judicial field.

Closely patterned after the Soviet model, the judiciary in Communist China has followed as guiding principles the Marxist-Leninist concepts of class justice and the indivisibility of law and politics. Its first and foremost function is to enforce revolutionary changes and to suppress elements hostile to the socialist order. Toward class enemies and counterrevolutionaries, "people's justice" in the forms of revolutionary tribunals and struggle meetings has often been swift and brutal. Mao Tse-tung once said: "Such state apparatus as the army, the police and the courts are instruments with which one class oppresses another. As far as the hostile classes are concerned these are instruments of oppression. They are violent and certainly not 'benevolent' things."[1]

It would be a mistake to note only the terror aspect of the system of "people's justice" and overlook its more subtle and less violent methods of social control. As in the case of the Soviet Union, the judicial organs in China are conceived as a means of educating the population at large in the spirit of socialist legality and the Party Line. To this end the Chinese Communists have successfully developed in judicial administration some remarkable techniques of mass persuasion and "brainwashing." They have

---

[1] Mao Tse-tung, *On People's Democratic Dictatorship*, Peking, 1951, p. 17.

utilized to full advantage the method of "reform through labor" to convert unreliable elements of society into useful forces for the new order. They have employed such mass line devices as circuit courts and on-the-spot trials to encourage mass participation in the judicial process and bring official influence directly to bear upon the public. The tendency on the part of the Communists to stress reform and education and to adopt a direct, common-sense approach to justice is, however, not entirely divorced from the Chinese past. Even more closely related to the old pattern is the special role that conciliation has in Communist China's mechanism of dispute resolution. Distinctly in line with the traditional preference of the Chinese for the informal settlement of disputes, the Communists have consistently urged the use of the extrajudicial means of conciliation and reconcilement to resolve "internal contradictions" and promote the unity of the people.

Informality, indeed, must be considered a prominent feature of the entire legal system of the Chinese People's Republic. To be sure, the Chinese Communists apparently are not insensitive to the need for formal institutions and rules as the foundation of their monolithic state. There are in China, for example, highly centralized structures of courts and procuratorates, elaborate constitutional provisions for individual rights and judicial independence, and several basic statutes and numerous provisional regulations and directives. All this reflects strong Soviet influence. On the other hand, the Chinese tradition of holding law in low esteem is also evident in Communist China. Unlike the Soviet Union, the Chinese People's Republic still does not have comprehensive civil, criminal, and procedural codes. Since the abrupt reversal of the trend toward liberalization in 1957, the Peking regime has shown little effort to channel the Chinese legal development in the direction of codification and stability. Instead, the official line insists that flexibility rather than "rigidity" should be the approach to the question of law in the rapidly changing conditions of China. It also rejects the concepts of presumption of innocence and *nullum crimen sine lege* as unsuitable to "people's justice," although these "bourgeois" principles have won new respectability in post-Stalin Russia. A large number of disputes and offenses in China are now handled by the police and other extrajudicial organs, whereas more important cases are adjudicated by the courts often according to informal procedures.

Moreover, to the extent that the Communists are preoccupied with China's internal transformation and external challenges, the concern for legal niceties is overshadowed by the policy of letting "politics take command." Thus, procedural guarantees are necessarily conditioned by the overriding imperatives of national security. Judicial activities must be subject to the absolute leadership of the Communists. Article 78 of the Constitution notwithstanding,[2] Party committees can, in practice, interfere with the trial work of the courts even in individual cases.

There is little doubt that the existing system of "people's justice" reflects to a large degree the mood of a country in transition. As the revolution becomes settled down, and as a mature socialist society emerges, one can expect a more stable legal order and a greater respect for juridical procedures and restraints to develop in the Chinese People's Republic. On the other hand, given the unique background and nature of Chinese Communism, it is quite likely that conciliation and other mass line techniques will continue to play important parts in the judicial process of mainland China. What is more, the judiciary will continue to be not so much a protector of individual rights as an instrumentality of the People's Democratic Dictatorship.

---

[2] The Article reads: "In administering justice the people's courts are independent, subject only to the law." *Chung-hua jen-min kung-ho-kuo fa-kuei hui-pien* (Compendium of the Laws and Regulations of the Chinese People's Republic), Peking, Vol. 1 (1956), p. 26.

Selected Bibliography

Selected Bibliography

BOOKS AND DOCUMENTS

Barnett, A. Doak. *Communist China: The Early Years, 1949-1955*. New York: Praeger, 1964.

Berman, Harold J. *Justice in the USSR*. New York: Vintage Books, 1963.

Blaustein, A. P. (ed.). *Fundamental Legal Documents of Communist China*. South Hackensack, N. J.: Rothman, 1962.

Bonnichon, André. *Law in Communist China*. The Hague: International Commission of Jurists, 1956.

Chao, Kuo-chun. *Agrarian Policy of the Chinese Communist Party 1921-1959*. Bombay: Asia Publishing House, 1960.

Chen, Chi-yu. *Hsin-chung-kuo chien-cha chih-tu kai-lun* (A sketch of New China's Procuracy). Peking: Jen-min ch'u-pan-she, 1950.

Chen, Shu-fang. *Chung-kung ti szu-fa kai-ko* (The Judicial Reform of the Chinese Communists). Hong Kong: Yu-lien ch'u-pan-she, 1953.

Chen, Theodore H. E. *Thought Reform of the Chinese Intellectuals*. Hong Kong: Hong Kong University Press, 1960.

Cheng, J. Chester (ed.). *The Politics of the Chinese Red Army*. Stanford: Hoover Institution, 1966.

Chiang ko-ming chin-hsing tao-ti (Carry out the Revolution to the Successful End). Shanghai: Hsin-hua shu-tien, 1949.

Chien-chüeh chen-ya fan-ke-ming huo-tung (Resolutely Suppress Counterrevolutionary Activities). Peking: Jen-min ch'u-pan-she, 1951.

Chih-fei fan-tung wen-chien hui-pien (A Collection of Red Bandit Reactionary Documents). Compiled under General Ch'en Ch'eng, June 1935. Reprinted in Taipeh, 1960. 6 vols.

Chinese Academy of Sciences. *Shan-Kan-Ning pien-ch'ü ts'an-i-hui wen-hsien hui-chi* (Compendium of Documents of the People's Political Council of the Shensi-Kansu-Ninghsia Border Region). Peking: Arthur, 1958.

Chou, Fang. *Wo-kuo kuo-chia chi-kou* (State Organs of Our Country). Peking: Chung-kuo ch'ing-nien ch'u-pan-she, 1955.

Chow, Ching-wen. *Ten Years of Storm*. New York: Holt, Rinehart & Winston, 1960.

Chu, Pu-fu. *Chung-kung jen-min ching-cha tou-shih* (Perspective on the "People's Police" in Communist China). Hong Kong: Freedom Press, 1955.

Chü, Tung-tsu. *Law and Society in Traditional China.* Paris: Mouton, 1961.

Chugunov, V. Ye. *Criminal Court Proceedings in the Chinese People's Republic.* Moscow, 1959. Translated by Joint Publications Research Service (No. 4595), 1961.

Chukyo seiken no genjo bunseki (Analysis of the Current Situation of the Chinese Communist Regime). Tokyo: Nihon gaisei gakkai, 1961.

Chung-hua jen-min kung-ho-kuo fa-kuei hui-pien. (Compendium of Laws and Regulations of the Chinese People's Republic). Peking: Fa-lü ch'u-pan-she, 1954–1964. 13 vols.

Chung-hua jen-min kung-ho-kuo yu-kuan kung-an kung-tso fa-kuei hui-pien (Compendium of Laws and Regulations of the Chinese People's Republic Concerning Public Security Work). Peking: Ch'ün-chung ch'u-pan-she, 1957.

Chung, I-mou. *Hai-lu-feng nung-min yün-tung* (the Peasant Movement in Hai-lu-feng). Canton: Jen-min ch'u-pan-she, 1957.

Chung-yang jen-min chang-fu fa-ling hui-pien (Compendium of the Laws and Regulations of the Central People's Government). Peking: Jen-min ch'u-pan-she, 1952–1955. 5 vols.

Cohen, Jerome A. *Preliminary Materials on the Laws of Communist China.* Unpublished Classroom Manual, University of California at Berkeley, 1961.

––––––. *The Criminal Process in the People's Republic of China, 1949–1963: An Introduction.* Cambridge, Mass.: Harvard University Press, to be published in December 1967.

Communist China 1955–1959. Cambridge, Mass.: Harvard University Press, 1962.

Delegation of Young Jurists who Visited China. *Horitsuka no mita Chugoku* (China as Seen by Jurists). Tokyo: Nihon hyoron sha, 1965.

Documents of the First Session of the First National People's Congress of the People's Republic of China. Peking: Foreign Language Press, 1955.

Eighth National Congress of the Communist Party of China. Peking: Foreign Language Press, 1956. 3 vols.

Escarra, Jean. *Le Droit Chinois.* Peking: Editions H. Vetch, 1936.

First Five-Year Plan for Development of the National Economy of China in 1953–1957. Peking: Foreign Language Press, 1956.

Fukushima, Masao, Naokichi Ubukata, and Ryoichi Hasegawa. *Chugoku no saiban* (Justice of China). Tokyo: Toyo keizai shimposha, 1957.

Gelder, George Stuart (ed.). *The Chinese Communists.* London: V. Gollancz, 1946.

Greene, Felix. *Awakened China.* New York: Doubleday, 1961.

Gsovski, V. and K. Grzybowski. *Government, Law and Courts in the Soviet Union and Eastern Europe.* New York: Praeger, 1959. 2 vols.

Gudoshnikov, L. M. *Legal Organs of the People's Republic of China.* Moscow, 1957. Translated by JPRS (No. 1698–N), 1959.

Harper, Francis (ed.). *Out of China: A Collection of Interviews with Refugees from China.* Hong Kong: Dragonfly Books, 1964.

Hatano, Kenichi (ed.). *Chugoku kyosanto shi* (History of the Chinese Communist Party). Tokyo: Jiji Press, 1961. 7 vols.

Hazard, John N. *Law and Social Change in the U.S.S.R.* London: Stevens, 1953.

Hsia, Tao-tai. *Guide to Selected Legal Sources of Mainland China.* Washington, D.C.: Library of Congress, to be published in June 1967.

Hsien-fa wen-ti ts'an-k'ao wen-chien (Reference materials on Problems relating to the Constitution) Peking: Jen-min ch'u-pan-she, 1954.

Hua-pei jen-min cheng-fu fa-ling hui-pien (Compendium of Laws of the North China People's Government). Peking: Secretariat of the North China People's Government, 1949.

Huang, Yüan. *Jen-min fa-yüan chi-pen chi-shih chiang-hua* (Lectures on the Basic Knowledge of the People's Courts). Canton: Jen-min ch'u-pan-she, 1956.

————. *Wo-kuo jen-min lü-shih chih-tu* (Our People's Lawyer System). Canton: Jen-min ch'u-pan-she, 1956.

Hudson, Geoffrey, A. V. Sherman, and A. Fanherman. *The Chinese Communes.* London: Soviet Survey, 1959.

Hunter, Edward. *Brain-Washing in Red China.* New York: Vanguard Press, 1953.

Hutheesing, Raja. *The Great Peace.* New York: Harper, 1953.

Institute of Civil Law, Central Political-Judicial Cadres' School. *Chung-hua jen-min kung-ho-kuo min-fa chi-pen wen-t'i* (Basic Problems in the Civil Law of the People's Republic of China). Peking: Fa-lü ch'u-pan-she, 1958.

International Commission of Jurists. *The Rule of Law in a Free Society.* Geneva: Arthur, 1960.

Jan, George P. (ed.). *Government of Communist China.* San Francisco: Chandler, 1966.

Japanese Association of International Jurists (ed.). *Chugoku no ho to shakai* (Law and Society in China). Tokyo: Shin dokushosha, 1960.

Labor Laws and Regulations of the People's Republic of China. Peking: Foreign Language Press, 1956.

Laws of the Republic of China. Taipei: Law Revision Planning Group, 1961.

Lectures on the General Principles of Criminal Law on the People's Republic of China. By the Institute of Criminal Law Research, Central Political-Judicial Cadres' School, Peking, 1957. Translated by JPRS (No. 13331), 1962.

Lee, Luke T. "Toward an Understanding of Law in Communist China," in E. F. Szczepanik (ed.). *Symposium on Economic Social Problems of the Far East.* Hong Kong: Hong Kong University Press, 1962.

Leng, Shao-chuan, "Chinese Law" in Arthur Larson (ed.), *Sovereignty within the Law*. Dobbs Ferry, N. Y.: Oceana, 1965.

Lewis, John Wilson (ed.) *Leadership in Communist China*. Ithaca: Cornell University Press, 1963.

Li, Kuang-ts'an. *Lun kung-fan* (On Joint Offense). Peking: Fa-lü ch'u-pan-she, 1957.

————. *Wo-kuo kung-min ti chi-pen chüan-li ho i-wu* (The Fundamental Rights and Duties of the Citizens of Our Country). Peking: Jen-min ch'u-pan-she, 1956.

Li, Ta. *Chung-hua jen-min kuo-ho-kuo hsien-fa chiang-hua* (Lectures on the Constitution of the Chinese People's Republic). Peking: Jen-min ch'u-pan-she, 1956.

Lifton, Robert J. *Thought Reform and the Psychology of Totalism*. New York: Norton, 1963.

Lin, Fu-shun. *Chinese Law Past and Present: A Bibliography of Enactments and Commentaries in English Text*. New York: East Asian Institute, Columbia University, 1966.

Loh, Robert. *Escape from Red China*. New York: Coward-McCann, 1962.

Lung, Chien-fu. *Chung-kung szu-fa pou-shih* (An Analysis of the Chinese Communist Judiciary System). Hong Kong: Freedom Press, 1957.

Mac Farquhar, Roderick. *The Hundred Flowers Campaign and the Chinese Intellectuals*. New York: Praeger, 1960.

Mao Tse-tung. *Mao Tse-tung hsüan-chi* (Selected Works of Mao Tse-tung). Peking: Jen-min ch'u-pan-she, 1951–1960. 4 vols. English version published in 4 volumes by Foreign Language Press, Peking, 1961–1966.

————. *On People's Democratic Dictatorship*. Peking: Foreign Language Press, 1951.

————. *On the Correct Handling of Contradiction Among the People*. Peking: Foreign Language Press, 1957.

Ministry of Judicial Administration. *Kung-fei szu-fa hsien-kuang* (Current Situation in the Judicial System of the Communist Bandits). Taipei: State Security Bureau, 1960.

Ministry of National Defense (ed.). *Fan-kung yu-chi-tui t'u-chi Fu-chien Lien-chiang lu-huo fei-fang wen-chien hui-pien* (Collection of Bandit Documents Seized at Lien-chiang, Fukien, by Anti-Communist Commandos). Taipei, 1964.

Mu, Fu-sheng. *The Wilting of the Hundred Flowers*. New York: Praeger, 1963.

Myrdal, Jan. *Report from a Chinese Village*. London: Heinemann, 1965.

Orleans, Leo A. *Professional Manpower and Education in Communist China*. Washington: U. S. Government Printing Office, 1960.

Pei, Yu-ming. *O lai-tzu tung-pei nu-kung ying* (I Came from the Slave Labor Camps in the Northeast). Hong Kong: Asia Press, 1954.

Rickett, W. Allyn (ed.). *Legal Thought and Institutions of the People's*

Republic of China: Selected Documents. Unpublished classroom manual, University of Pennsylvania, 1964.

Rickett, Allyn and Adele. *Prisoners of Liberation.* New York: Cameron Associates, 1957.

Schurmann, Franz. *Ideology and Organization in Communist China.* Berkeley: University of California, Press, 1966.

Secretariat of the Peking People's Court. *Jen-min szu-fa kung-tso chü-yü* (Illustrative Examples of People's Judicial Work). Peking: Hsin-hua shu-tien, 1949.

Shang-hai chieh-fang i-nien (One Year after Shanghai's Liberation). Shanghai: Liberation Daily Company, 1950.

Shansi-Chahar-Hopei Border Region Administrative Committee. *Hsien-hsing fa-ling hui-chi* (Compendium of Current Laws and Directives). 1945.

Shensi-Kansu-Ninghsia Border Region Government. *Shan-kan-ning pien-chü cheng-tse t'iao-li hui-chi* (Compendium of Policies and Regulations of the SKN Border Region). Yenan: Arthur, 1944.

Shih-sou Collection (General Chen Cheng's private collection of Chinese Communist documents relative to the Kiangsi Soviet period). Microfilm available at Harvard, Stanford, and other centers.

Snow, Edgar. *The Other Side of the River.* New York: Random House, 1962.

Strong, Anna Louise. *The Rise of the Chinese People's Communes.* Peking: The New World Press, 1964.

Szu-ying kung-shang-yeh ti she-hui chu-i kai-tsao cheng-tse fa-ling hsüan-pien (Selections of Policies, Laws, Regulations, Concerning the Socialist Transformation of private-owned Industry and Commerce). Peking: Ts'ai-cheng ching-chi ch'u-pan-she, 1957. Vol. 1 (1949–1952).

Tang, Peter S. H. *Communist China Today.* Washington: Research Institute on the Sino-Soviet Bloc, 1961.

Teng, Hsiao-ping. *Report on the Rectification Campaign.* Peking: Foreign Language Press, 1957.

Tennien, Mark. *No Secret Is Safe.* New York: Farrar, Straus & Young, 1952.

Ti-i-tzu kuo-nei ko-ming chan-cheng shih-chi ti nung-min yün-tung (The Peasant Movement in the Period of the First Revolutionary Civil War). Peking: Jen-min ch'u-pan'she, 1953.

Union Research Institute. *Communist China, 1949–1959.* Hong Kong: Union Research Institute, 1961.

Van der Valk, M. H. *The Law of Inheritance in Eastern Europe and in the People's Republic of China.* (No. 5 of the series on Law in Eastern Europe.) Leyden: University of Leyden, 1961.

Van der Sprenkel, Sybille. *Legal Institutions in Manchu China.* London: The Athlone Press, 1962.

Vyshinsky, Andrei Y. *The Law of the Soviet State* (trans. Hugh W. Babb). New York: Macmillan, 1948.

Wang, Chien-min. *Chung-kuo kung-ch'an-tang shih-kao* (History of the Chinese Communist Party). Taipei: Arthur, 1965. 3 vols.

Wei, Henry. *Courts and Police in Communist China to 1952.* Lackland Air Force Base, Texas 1955.

Wei, Wen-Po. *Tui-yü "Chung-hua jen-min kung-ho-kuo jen-min fa-yüan tsu-chi-fa" chi-pen wen-ti ti jen-shih* (On Understanding the Basic Issues of the "Organic Law of the People's Courts of the People's Republic of China"). Shanghai: Jen-min ch'u-pan-she, 1956.

White Book on Forced Labour and Concentration Camp in the People's Republic of China. Paris: Commission Internationale Contre Le Régime Concentrationnaire, 1957. 2 vols.

Yakhontoff, Victor A. *The Chinese Soviets.* New York: Coward-McCann, 1934.

Yang, C. K. *Chinese Communist Society,* Cambridge, Mass: MIT Press, 1965.

Yu, Frederick T. C. *Mass Persuasion in Communist China.* New York: Praeger, 1964.

Newspapers and Periodicals

(Because of limitations of space, individual articles cited in the notes are not listed below.)

American Journal of Comparative Law, Ann Arbor, Michigan.

American Political Science Review, Washington, D. C.

Annals of the American Academy of Political and Social Science, Philadelphia.

An-hui jih-pao (Anhwei Daily), Hofei, Anhwei.

Asian Survey, Berkeley, California.

California Law Review, Berkeley, California.

Chang-chiang jih-pao (Yantze Daily), Hankow.

Cheng-fa yen-chui (Studies in Political Science and Law), Peking.

Chieh-fang-chun pao (Liberation Army News), Peking.

Chieh-fang jih-pao (Liberation Daily), Shanghai.

China News Analysis, Hong Kong.

The China Quarterly, London.

China Weekly Review, Shanghai.

Ching-hai jih-pao (Tsinghai Daily), Sining, Tsinghai.

Ching-tao jih pao (Tsingtao Daily), Tsingtao, Shantung.

Chugoku nenkan (China Yearbook), Tokyo. (Now called *Shin Chugoku nenkan.*)

Chung-ching jih-pao (Chungking Daily), Chungking.

Chung-kuo ching-nien (Chinese Youth), Peking.

Current Background, Hong Kong, American Consulate General.

Current Digest of the Soviet Press, Ann Arbor, Michigan.

Fa-hsüeh (Jurisprudence), Shanghai.

Fu-chien jih-pao (Fukien Daily), Foochow, Fukien.
Harvard Law Review, Cambridge, Massachusetts.
Hei-lung-chiang jih-pao (Heilungkiang Daily), Harbin, Heilunkiang.
Ho-nan jih-pao (Honan Daily). Chengchou, Honan.
Ho-pei jih-pao (Hopei Daily), Tientsin.
Hsi-chang jih-pao (Tibetan Daily), Lhasa.
Hsin chien-she (New Construction), Peking.
Hsin hu-nan pao (New Hunan Journal). Changsha, Hunan.
Hsin-hua jih-pao (New China Daily), Chungking.
Hsin-hua pan-yüeh-k'an (New China Semi-monthly), Peking.
Hsin-hua yüeh-pao (New China Monthly), Peking.
Hsin-wen jih-pao (News Daily), Shanghai.
Hsüeh-hsi (Study), Peking.
Hung-chi (Red Flag), Peking.
International and Comparative Law Quarterly, London.
Jen-min jih-pao (People's Daily), Peking.
Jen-min shou-ts'e (People's Handbook), Peking.
Journal of Asian Studies, Ann Arbor, Michigan.
Journal of the International Commission of Jurists, Geneva.
JPRS Reports, Washington, D. C., U. S. Joint Publications Research Service.
Kuang-chou jih-pao (Canton Daily), Canton.
Kuang-hsi jih-pao (Kwangsi Daily). Nanning, Kwangsi.
Kuang-ming jih-pao (Kuang-ming Daily), Peking.
Kung-jen jih-pao (Daily Worker), Peking.
Kuei-chou jih-pao (Kweichow Daily), Kweiyang, Kweichow.
Liao-ning jih-pao (Liaoning Daily), Mukden, Liaoning.
Nan-fang jih-pao (Southern Daily), Canton.
The New York Times, New York.
Osteuropa-Recht, Köln-Sülz.
Peking Review, Peking.
People's China, Peking.
Problems of Communism, Washington, D. C.
Shan-hsi jih-pao (Shansi Daily), Taiyuan, Shansi.
Shen-yang jih-pao (Mukden Daily), Mukden, Liaoning.
Shih-shih shou-ts'e (Current Affairs Handbook), Peking.
Survey of the China Mainland Press, Hong Kong, American Consulate General.
Szu-chuan jih-pao (Szechwan Daily), Chengtu, Szechwan.
Ta-kung pao (L'Impartial), Tientsin and Peking.
Wen-hui pao (Cultural Exchange News), Shanghai and Hong Kong.
Yang-cheng wan-pao (Canton Evening News), Canton.
Yün-nan jih-pao (Yünnan Daily), Kunming, Yünnan.

Index

Index